REVIEW
AND
PROGRESS
IN
GERMAN

W. P. Lehmann

Helmut Rehder

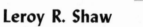

Leroy R. Shaw

S. N. Werbow

THE UNIVERSITY OF TEXAS

REVIEW
AND
PROGRESS

IN
GERMAN

HOLT, RINEHART AND WINSTON, INC. NEW YORK

Preface

Review and Progress in German is intended for students entering intermediate language courses.

In their elementary work most students have learned to make simple statements, questions, and requests, and they have acquired a basic vocabulary and an elementary control over grammar; but they can read few narrative or expository texts that have not previously been simplified with respect to grammar and vocabulary. *Review and Progress in German* is designed to increase the student's control of the essential patterns of German and to equip him with the techniques for analyzing the lexical and grammatical features of more complicated texts.

Each chapter of the book reviews a specific and fundamental aspect of the German language. New patterns and vocabulary are introduced in the short texts at the beginning of each lesson. These patterns are then varied in multiple form in the exercises, and through this intensive practice in variation the student becomes familiar with specific points of grammar. These in turn are applied to different contexts in the concluding narrative of the lesson.

In the brief time allotted American students for language work, they are usually given a carefully selected vocabulary and well-edited glossaries; ultimately, they are trained to use dictionaries. No similar procedure has been developed for grammar. Students accordingly waste considerable time repeating grammatical material without moving past elementary matters. In *Review and Progress in German* the authors have attempted to increase the student's competence in the language by training him to use a grammar for reference, just as he uses a dictionary. One section of each lesson is devoted primarily to a discussion of grammatical material. For review, and for a relatively complete treatment of any facet of grammar, the student is referred to the pertinent sections of the Appendix.

The use of grammar as a reference, and the constant application of basic sentence patterns in new contexts, will introduce the student to the structure of the German language rather than to an abstract grammatical system. After completing *Review and Progress in German* he will have learned to think of grammar as a useful tool for analyzing new texts and will have consequently become able to deal independently with more complicated reading material in the area of his specialty.

To the teacher

In using *Review and Progress in German*, students should be introduced to the initial texts of each lesson through intensive choral work. Frequent repetition or even memorization of these short texts is recommended. As a second step, the grammatical content of the lesson should be discussed, with examples drawn from the texts. Students thereupon are ready to practice by using the exercises. Most of these should be done orally in class or at the board before the student is asked to write them out as homework. Oral work at home and in class is, indeed, essential for proper mastery of the basic, introductory German text and of the variation drills. Finally, the terminal reading passage should be introduced in class by choral work and assigned as home reading. For the sake of varying vocabulary and style, additional reading may be assigned from other texts as time permits or as the instructor desires. The questions which follow the terminal reading passage are intended to provide an opportunity for speaking, and may serve to begin oral discussion of the narrative itself. In general, the authors are convinced that ability in speaking German is fundamental to whatever ultimate use the individual student desires to make of his knowledge. Oral facility is an aid in the learning of vocabulary, of sentence patterns and of connected discourse. The objective of this book, whether the student is interested primarily in reading or in speaking German, is to have him learn living language material in useful patterns rather than through grammatical rules and their mechanical application.

Review and Progress in German is arranged so that the verb forms are treated as a sequential unit in the first nine lessons. In this way, students are given a longer time in which to practice the use of forms which are usually presented so briefly in introductory courses that proper assimilation is impossible.

Word-formation, too, is an important part of the work of intermediate courses; accordingly, the formation of verbs, adjectives and nouns is stressed in this book. A large proportion of the vocabulary comprises compound words so that students may become familiar with the analysis of the more complex forms they will encounter in technical and literary German.

The end vocabulary contains words needed for recognition only as well as those which make up the active vocabulary. Words that have been glossed in the text are not considered as part of the active vocabulary, nor are words marked with a question mark (?), for the latter are either cognate or compound words at whose meaning students are encouraged to guess. The English-to-German word-list contains only those words that are required in the English-to-German exercises.

To the student

The best means of expanding your mastery of German grammar and vocabulary is by repetition and variation of frequently used sentence patterns. In this book these patterns are given to you in the short texts at the beginning of each lesson. It is not essential to memorize these texts so that you can recite them in order, but you should be able to reproduce their basic patterns. When you can do this, analyze them for their grammar and their new vocabulary.

In order to learn the grammar, work through the variation drills. These concentrate on the grammatical point under study. If you can do the drills, you have mastered the grammar. Then, to consolidate your mastery, study the analysis in the lesson, and in the corresponding section of the Appendix. Remember, however, that the grammar sections merely describe the basic patterns of German for you; the texts and drills actually teach you how to use the language.

After you know the grammar, read the narrative at the end of the lesson. In it you will find the grammar and vocabulary applied once more. Try, to as great a degree as possible, to determine the meanings of new words from the context before using the end vocabulary. Intelligent guessing of word meanings is one of the keys to rapid reading of texts.

There are three steps to the mastery of a language:

1. learning the patterns
2. using variants of them
3. applying them freely.

In order to make progress you should always work with a sentence, not with a single word or a mere set of forms. Learning sentences orally is a simple method and by far the most economical one; furthermore, recording devices are easily available to help you. If you know patterns, you will be able to speak and to derive the words and grammar you need—from the patterns.

Repetition and memorization play larger roles in the study

of foreign language than does analysis. The resultant mastery of a new language will improve your understanding of your own language and consequently your ability to communicate. It will also enable you to see more distinctly those traits of culture which are conditioned by our language—cf. the relatively simple problems caused by the lack of exact German correspondences for the verbs 'like' and 'walk'—and will bring you a broader understanding of other nations and their culture.

Foreign language study in college will also instruct you in an increasingly important skill in the compact world of today: the method of acquiring the elements of a new language in a short time. Greater demands for world travel will require college graduates of the future to use languages even though they will have little chance for extensive study. By using the techniques of this book—

> learning frequent patterns under the direction of competent speakers;
>
> varying these patterns;
>
> using them freely in everyday speech—

you will not face a blank wall when you meet people of other language backgrounds.

January, 1959.   W. P. L.
                                            H. R.
                                            L. S.
                                            S. N. W.

Contents

· Verbal prefixes · Use of **gern haben, gefallen, lieben**
Entschlüsse

REVIEW
AND
PROGRESS
IN
GERMAN

Lesson 1

PRESENT TENSE

IMPERATIVE FORMS

USE OF "WIE"

Ein Gespräch im Jahre 2075

„Guten Morgen, Frau Ley! Was tun Sie hier so früh auf dem Flughafen?"

„Ich warte auf meinen Mann. Er kommt in einer Stunde vom Mond zurück."

„Bleibt er nun etwas länger zu Hause?"

„Nein, leider nicht. Er fliegt heute abend schon wieder nach dem Mars ab."

„Wie lange fährt er schon eine Rakete?"

„Seit einem halben Jahr."

„Sagen Sie mir, was ißt so ein Raketenführer eigentlich?"

„Ja, denken Sie nur! Da funkt er mir vor zwei Stunden: ‚Lege zweihundert Pillen ins Handköfferchen. Und vergiß nicht den Mikrofilm!' "

„Mikrofilm? Wozu braucht er den?"

„Ja, er liest gerne Weltliteratur, wenn er durch den Weltraum segelt."

Best results will be obtained by repeating the Basic Text of each lesson orally ten times, or until it has been mastered.

I

　　　*brauchen　need
　der Flughafen　airport
　　　funken　radio (transmit by radio)
*das Gespräch　conversation
　das Handköfferchen　overnight bag
*der Mond　moon
　die Rakete　rocket
　der Raketenführer　rocket pilot
　　　segeln　sail
　der Weltraum　outer space

EXERCISES

A. Repeat the following sentences, changing only the words in heavy type.　Make complete sentences.

1. Was **ißt der Polizist** eigentlich?　(does the pilot find, is he doing, is she reading, does he say, does the driver see)
2. **Fährst** du jeden Tag um sechs?　(come, eat, sing, wait)
3. Der Raketenführer **liest** immer **gerne.**　(likes to write, likes to drive, likes to fly)
4. **Ich warte** auf unsere Freunde.　(we are waiting, she is waiting, he is waiting, you are waiting)
5. Was **tun Sie** hier so früh?　(does she find, is he looking for, are they doing, do we want)
6. Wozu **braucht man** das?　(is he using, are we buying, do we study, does he read, am I asking)
7. **Bleibt er** bei Ihnen oder in der Stadt?　(are they living, do they eat, is he sleeping)
8. **Warten Sie** nur noch **eine Stunde!**　(work . . . a day, read . . . a moment, stay . . . a week)
9. **Setze** es bitte auf den Tisch!　(put, place)

* Words marked with an asterisk belong to the basic vocabulary of the lesson and are therefore included in the vocabulary list at the end of the lesson.

10. **Vergiß den Mikrofilm** nicht! (don't take ... the car, don't beat ... the child, don't lose ... the pills, don't close ... the window, don't read ... it)

B. Repeat the following sentences, changing only the words in heavy type.

1. **Er sieht** es heute Abend zum erstenmal. (I shall do, he's going to eat, we're bringing, they'll hear)
2. **Sie geht** jedes Wochenende nach Hause. (he flies, we are going to drive, they will go)
3. Wie lange **fährt er** schon **die Rakete?** (has she been reading ... the book, have we been calling ... the doctor, has he been flying ... the machine, has he had ... that sickness)
4. Da **funkt** man mir **vor zwei Stunden** ... (wrote ... a month ago, told ... a week ago, telegraphed [telegraphieren] ... two days ago ...)
5. **Es regnet** schon seit drei Stunden. (he's been sleeping, we've been talking, they've been running, she's been playing)

C. Following the patterns, give German equivalents for the English sentences. Word order will be exactly the same as in the pattern sentences.

1. **Ich warte auf meinen Mann.**
   A. She's waiting for the new year.
   B. We shall wait for the pilot of the rocket.
   C. They're going to wait for me.

2. **Bleibt er nun zu Hause?**
   A. Is he living in the city now?
   B. Are they staying at your place now?
   C. Does she study at home now?

3. **Die Rakete fährt er schon seit einem halben Jahr.**
   A. He's been driving the car for a month already.
   B. We've been studying German for a year now.
   C. I've been asking **(stellen)** this question for six months (already).

4. **Er liest doch auch gerne.**
   A. She does like to swim, after all.
   B. After all, we also like to dance.
   C. But he likes to play too.

5. **Vergiß den Mikrofilm nicht!**
   A. Don't lose the pills!
   B. Don't eat this bread!
   C. Don't buy the car!

6. **Er kommt in einer Stunde zurück.**
   A. They're coming back in a day.
   B. She'll return in a moment.
   C. He will return in half an hour.

7. **Warum bleibst du hier ganz allein zu Hause?**
   A. Why does she sit here all alone at home?
   B. Why are they living all alone in the country?

8. **Dann hört er, wie die Sirene hinter ihm heult.**
   A. Then he sees the rocket sailing through outer space.
   B. Then she hears her husband returning from the moon.

GRAMMAR

1 Review the forms of the **present tense** and the **imperative.** [*See Appendix 6.*] Some irregular forms and the uses of forms are reviewed briefly below.

1.1 Some strong verbs undergo a change of stem vowel in the **du** and **er** forms of the present tense.

In most strong verbs with the stem vowel **e,** the change is
to **i** or **ie** :

ich spreche	du sprichst	er spricht
ich sehe	du siehst	er sieht

This change does not take place in:

gehen	du gehst	er geht
stehen	du stehst	er steht

In strong verbs with the stem vowel **a,** the change is to **ä** :

ich falle	du fällst	er fällt
ich fahre	du fährst	er fährt
ich laufe	du läufst	er läuft

1.2 Verbs whose stem ends in an **s** sound **(s, ss, ß, tz)** generally add only **t,** rather than **st,** in the **du** form :

ich esse	du ißt	er ißt
ich lese	du liest	er liest
ich sitze	du sitzt	er sitzt

1.3 Verbs whose stem ends in **d, t,** or in a consonant (other
than **r** or **l**) plus **m** or **n** add **-est, -et** in the **du** and **er** forms :

ich warte	du wartest	er wartet
ich begegne	du begegnest	er begegnet
but: ich warne	du warnst	er warnt

1.4 German has only one present tense form.   This corresponds
to the English simple form as well as to the progressive [is
. . . ing] and the emphatic [do . . .] form:

Ich warte. I am waiting.
Wozu braucht er den? What does he need that for?

1.5 The present tense is used for future time when the future
is clearly indicated by the context or by an adverbial expression:

Bleibt er nun etwas länger zu Hause?
Is he staying (will he stay, is he going to stay) at home somewhat
longer this time?

1.6 The present tense is used for a past action which is still going on.   This use is always accompanied by a time expression, such as an adverb or a prepositional phrase introduced by **seit.** The expression is sometimes heightened by **schon** :

Er fährt sie schon seit drei Jahren.
He has been driving it now for three years.

1.7 Colloquially, especially in narrative, the present tense is used for action completed in the past; when so used, the tense is called the historical present.   The time is made clear by the context or by an adverbial expression:

Da funkt er mir vor zwei Stunden.
Then he radioed [*coll.* radios] me two hours ago.

1.8 German has three **imperative forms,** one used to people addressed as **du,** one to people addressed as **ihr,** and one to people addressed as **Sie** :

Sprich!	Sprecht!	Sprechen Sie!
Fahre!	Fahrt!	Fahren Sie!
Setze dich!	Setzt euch!	Setzen Sie sich!

As illustrated here, the verbs that change the vowel **e** to **i** or **ie** in the present tense undergo the same change in the **du** form of the imperative.   These verbs do not usually have the ending **-e,** *e.g.*, **gib, nimm,** but **siehe.**   The imperative of **sein** is irregular:

Sei so gut!   Seid so gut!   Seien Sie so gut!

1.9 The word **wie** is used after verbs like **hören, sehen,** and **wissen** to introduce dependent clauses, *e.g.*, **Er weiß nicht, wie er es machen soll.**   In English we would use "how" with an infinitive after "to know": 'He doesn't know how he is to do it.' *or* 'He does not know how to do it.'
After **hören** and **sehen,** English uses an infinitive or gerund:

Er sah, wie ihr Wagen . . . vorbeiglitt.
He saw her car glide by . . .
Denn schon hört er, wie die Sirene heult.
For he already hears the siren blaring.

NARRATIVE*
Die Schnecke

Gerald Hunter war, wie alle jungen Leute seines Alters, ein leidenschaftlicher [passionate] Autofahrer [?]. Wenn er über Land fuhr, vereinigte [united] er Schnelligkeit mit Wagemut [daring]. Er beschäftigte sich vor allem mit dem Problem, die Geschwindigkeit seines alten und klappernden 5 [rattling] Wagens zu steigern [increase]. Immer gab es etwas zu verändern, was sein Fahrzeug [vehicle] verschönern [?] und vervollkommnen [make perfect] sollte. Gewöhnlich raste er, als ob es irgendwo brennte und er allein das Feuer löschen müßte. Seine Freunde neckten [teased] ihn daher und nannten ihn 10 „die Schnecke" [snail]. —

„Jerry," sagten sie zu ihm, „warum verbesserst du nicht den Zylinderdruck [compression] deines Wagens? Dann schlägst du noch den Geschwindigkeitsrekord [?] von Liechtenstein."

Doch Gerald ließ sich durch solche Reden nicht beeinflussen. 15 Er fuhr und fuhr—und verringerte [decreased] seine Geschwindigkeit nur, wenn Hunde und Frauen mit kleinen Kindern über die Straße liefen.

So fuhr er lange unbehindert [?], bis an einem schönen Frühlingstage das Schicksal ihn einholte. Es war in der Gestalt 20 einer jungen und schönen Dame, die mit lächelndem Munde an ihm vorüberfuhr. Gerald sah, wie ihr Wagen an dem seinen vorbeiglitt [glided by], auf der Landstraße vor ihm immer kleiner wurde und schließlich um eine Kurve verschwand.

„Was will die von dir?" dachte Gerald und setzte ihr nach 25 [set out after]. In wenigen Minuten hatte er sie eingeholt. Er lächelte höflich, als er sie überholte und nicht nur sie, sondern auch einen andern Wagen, dem sie geduldig folgte.

Und das war sein Untergang [downfall]. Denn schon hört er, wie die Sirene des Polizeiwagens hinter ihm heult; und 30 schon steht er vor dem Polizeibeamten [police-official] und

* Words with meanings in brackets need not be memorized; queried words should be guessed at. These words are in the main vocabulary, but *not* in the lesson vocabulary.

versucht sich zu verteidigen [defend]. „Entschuldigen Sie,
bitte," stammelt [stammers] er. „Junger Mann," sagt der
Polizist, „wissen Sie nicht, daß dies keine Rennbahn [race
35 track] ist? Achtzig Meilen! Wie leicht können Sie einen Unfall
verursachen. Und dann noch mit solch einem alten Wagen!
Nein, da gibt's einen Strafzettel [ticket]." Gerald will etwas
zu seiner Rechtfertigung [justification] sagen. Aber da fährt
das Schicksal mit lächelndem Munde an ihnen vorüber, und
40 er sagt nichts und starrt auf den Boden. —

Während er langsam nach Hause fuhr, flüsterte ihm eine
Stimme ins Ohr. Und die klang, als ob sie sagte: „Du
Schnecke, mich kannst du doch nicht einholen."

Questions

Answer the questions in each lesson in German, using complete sentences.

1. Was tut Gerald Hunter leidenschaftlich gern?
2. Woher wissen wir, daß sein Wagen alt ist?
3. Warum versucht er dies Fahrzeug zu verändern?
4. Warum nennen seine Freunde ihn „die Schnecke"?
5. Wann fährt er etwas langsamer?
6. Was geschieht an einem schönen Frühlingstag?
7. Was tut die junge Dame, als sie an ihm vorbeifährt?
8. Woher wissen wir, daß das Auto dieser Dame einen guten Motor hat?
9. Warum fährt sie langsam hinter einem anderen Wagen her?
10. Woher weiß Gerald, daß er einen Polizeiwagen überholt hat?
11. Warum gibt der Polizeibeamte ihm einen Strafzettel?
12. Was glaubt er zu hören, als er nach Hause fährt?

Vocabulary*

das Alter, –   age
beeinflussen   influence

* This list contains only "active vocabulary" items. For other words, consult the end vocabulary.

sich **beschäftigen** be busy
der **Boden, ∹** ground, floor
 brauchen need
 daher therefore
 ein-holen catch up with
 entschuldigen excuse; **sich** . . . be sorry
 flüstern whisper
der **Führer, –** driver, leader
 geduldig patient
die **Geschwindigkeit** speed
das **Gespräch, -e** conversation
die **Gestalt, -en** form, shape
 heulen howl, scream
 höflich polite
 irgendwo somewhere
 klingen (a, u) sound
 lächeln smile
die **Landstraße, -n** highway
der **Mond, -e** moon
der **Mund, -e** mouth
das **Ohr, -en** ear
die **Polizei** police
 reden speak, talk
das **Schicksal** fate
 schließlich finally
die **Schnelligkeit** speed
 starren stare
 überholen overtake, pass
der **Unfall, ∹e** accident
 verändern alter, change
 verbessern improve
 verursachen cause
 wenig few

Idioms

 immer kleiner smaller and smaller
 vor allem above all

Lesson 2

PAST TENSE

COMPOUND NOUNS

USE OF "FRAGEN" AND "BITTEN"

Das Porto

Ein kleines Mädchen trat an den Schalter in der Post und bat den Beamten: „Würden Sie so gut sein und dies Paket für mich einwickeln?" Der Beamte lächelte, nickte und wickelte es ein. „Und würden Sie nun auch bitte die Adresse darauf schreiben?" — „Gerne," sagte der Beamte. „Was ist denn die Anschrift?" — „O, die ist auf einem Zettel im Paket."

Der Beamte sah das kleine Mädchen etwas zweifelnd an, band das Paket wieder auf, nahm das Zettelchen heraus, verpackte die Sache wieder und schrieb die Adresse darauf. „Das kostet eine Mark Porto," sagte er, als er den letzten Knoten gemacht hatte.

„O," sagte das Mädchen. „Haben Sie das Geld nicht gefunden? Mama hat es ins Paket gelegt."

die Anschrift address
auf-binden untie
*__der Beamte__ official

> **ein-wickeln**   wrap
> der **Knoten**   knot
> **nicken**   nod
> *das **Paket**   package
> das **Porto**   postage
> die **Post**   post office, mail
> *die **Sache**   thing
> der **Schalter**   window
> **verpacken**   pack
> der **Zettel**   slip of paper
> **zweifelnd**   doubtingly

EXERCISES

A. Follow the directions given below.

1. The past tense (3d person sing.) of **fragen** is **er fragte.**
   A. What are the corresponding forms for:

flüstern	segeln	verbessern
starren	verändern	überholen

   B. Use these verbs to say:

we were whispering	she sailed	I improved
you were staring	he changed	they overtook

2. The past tense (2d person sing.) of **antworten** is **du antwortetest.**
   A. What are the corresponding forms for:

warten	dichten	reden
berichten	arbeiten	begegnen

   B. Use these verbs to say:

he waited	you were writing poetry	I spoke
she was reporting	he worked	they met

3. The past tense (3d person sing.) of **bleiben** is **er blieb.**
   A. What are the corresponding forms for:

schreiben	leihen	verzeihen
steigen	schweigen	

B. Use these verbs to say:

I wrote   you lent   we forgave
they were climbing   he was silent

4. The past tense (3d person sing.) of **schneiden** is **er schnitt.**

A. What are the corresponding forms for:

gleiten   reiten
greifen   reißen

B. Use these verbs to say:

we were gliding   they rode
he grasped   I did tear

5. The past tense (3d person pl.) of **helfen** is **sie halfen.**

A. What are the corresponding forms for:

werfen   verderben
sprechen   sterben

B. Use these verbs to say:

they threw   it was spoiling
she was speaking   he died

6. The past tense (3d person sing.) of **fahren** is **es fuhr.**

A. What are the corresponding forms for:

schlagen   laden   graben
tragen   waschen

B. Use these verbs to say:

he hit   you loaded   we were digging
I was carrying   he washed

7. The past tense (3d person sing.) of **wenden** is **er wandte,** of **kennen** is **er kannte.**

A. What is the corresponding form for:

senden   nennen
brennen   rennen

B. Use these verbs to say:

I sent   they called
it was burning   we ran

B. Replace the words in heavy type with the words in parentheses.

1. Ein kleines Mädchen **trat** an den Schalter. (ran, went)
2. Er **verpackte** die Sache. (sold, sent, brought, knew, burned)
3. Dann **erkannte** er den Beamten und **erzählte** ihm etwas. (saw . . . sold, hear . . . answered)
4. **Sie weinte,** als der Polizist sie einholte. (he was smiling, they stammered, I laughed)
5. Er **verschwand** um eine Ecke. (went, was driving, rushed)
6. Seine Freunde **liebten** ihn. (were calling, beat, were looking for, influenced)
7. Danach **versicherte** er sein Fahrzeug. (sold, changed, fetched)
8. **Er fuhr** mit der Geschwindigkeit einer Schnecke. (they went, we disappeared, I walked)

C. Translate the following paragraph, then rewrite it in the past tense.

Gerald Hunter fährt eines Tages die Landstraße entlang. Plötzlich braust ein hübsches Mädchen an seinem Wagen vorbei. Zuerst sieht er ihr erstaunt nach, denn seine eigene Geschwindigkeit ist auch recht groß. Dann setzt er ihr nach und holt sie schließlich ein. Der Polizist aber, an dem er auch vorbeirast, hat keinen Humor. Er gibt ihm einen Strafzettel.

D. Following the patterns, give German equivalents for the English sentences. Word order will be exactly the same as in the pattern sentences.

1. **Die Mutter legte das Geld ins Paket.**
   A. The official took the slip out of the package.

B. They found the money inside the package.

C. She wrote the address on the package.

2. **Das Mädchen lächelte freundlich.**
   A. The official nodded politely.
   B. The policeman drove slowly.
   C. The fire burned brightly.

3. **Was verlangte er dann?**
   A. What did he think of it?
   B. Why was he running away?
   C. What was he doing there?

4. **Er nickte geduldig, als er es einwickelte.**
   A. They stared angrily when they saw him.
   B. When she caught up with him, she smiled prettily.
   C. The siren was howling before the policeman overtook him.

5. **Der Beamte bat das Mädchen um das nötige Porto.**
   A. Gerald was asking the man for a new job.
   B. I asked him for a piece of paper.
   C. The policeman asked the driver for his license [Führerschein].

6. **Ich fragte, wo sie jetzt wohnt.**
   A. He asks why they are driving so fast.
   B. The man is asking where we are going tomorrow.
   C. The official is inquiring where the money is now.

E. Analyze the following compound nouns according to their elements. Notice how the meaning can be derived from the meanings of the component parts.

1. Holzindustrie
2. Baumstamm
3. Wochenende
4. Tannenwald
5. Berghang
6. Windrichtung
7. Frühlingstag
8. Straßengraben
9. Handköfferchen
10. Schauspielerin

11. Lastkraftwagen	18. Hochgebirge
12. Weltraum	19. Abendsonnenschein
13. Werkzeug	20. Lebenszeit
14. Straßenbahnwagen	21. Flachland
15. Lebensraum	22. Scheinwerfer
16. Sommerschule	23. Innenstadt
17. Landarbeit	24. Schulgeld

F. Combine a noun in column A with a noun in column B to make a German equivalent for the English words.

	A	B
1. sawmill	Werk-	-werk
2. foreman	Groß-	-träger
3. postman	Fahr-	-schule
4. railway ticket	Grund-	-messer
5. metropolis	Säge-	-führer
6. hospital	Knaben-	-ton
7. conversational tone	Auto-	-stoff
8. desk	Schreib-	-bahn
9. speedometer	Kranken-	-schein
10. super highway	Brief-	-tisch
11. basic element	Gesprächs-	-stadt
12. boys' school	Geschwindigkeits-	-haus

GRAMMAR

2 Review the forms of the **past tense** and their uses. [*See Appendix 6.*]

2.1 Most verbs in German are weak, just as most verbs are regular in English. It is often possible to recognize from its infinitive whether a verb is weak. Verbs with the stem vowels **ä, ö, ü, u, eu,** and **au** are, with few exceptions, weak; *e.g.*, **hören, heulen, suchen.** Moreover, verbs having certain suffixes are weak: **-igen, -ieren, -eln, -ern;** *e.g.*, **beschäftigen, reparieren, wickeln, verändern.**

On the other hand, the strong verbs, like the irregular verbs in English, refer to everyday activities (**bleiben, sprechen, essen,** and so on) and occur very commonly. You must memorize strong verbs, for you will have to know the infinitive in order to look them up in the dictionary. Review the principal parts of the strong verbs given in the Appendix.

2.1,1 Weak verbs with stems ending in **-t, -d,** or in a consonant (other than **r, l**) plus **m** or **n** add **-e-** before the **-te** of the past: **wartete, endete, widmete, öffnete** (*but* **warnte**).

2.1,2 Strong verbs with stems ending in **s, ß,** or **sch** add **-est** in the **du-**form of the past: **du lasest** 'you read,' **aßest** 'ate,' **wuschest** 'washed.'

2.1,3 The past tense is not used as widely in German as it is in English. In written German it is restricted to narration, as in *Das Porto*, and to uses in which the speaker wishes to indicate a drawn-out action, *e.g.:*
Er wartete zwei Stunden. 'He waited for two hours.'
In conversation it is rarely heard, even in these uses; in the last paragraph of *Das Porto*, for example, the present perfect is used when conversation is introduced.

2.2 Compound nouns. German technical and literary materials often seem difficult because of the length of such words as **Geschwindigkeitsrekord.** Much of this difficulty is visual. In English we use compound expressions, too, but we usually do not run the components together; we say "world literature" where German makes one word, **Weltliteratur.** It is therefore important to separate unfamiliar long words into their components and determine the English equivalent of each part.

2.2,1 The commonest type of noun compounding in German is the joining of two (or more) nouns.   The compound takes the gender of the last element.   The stress is on the first member. Some compounds have an **s** or an **n** between the elements; disregard the **s** or **n** when looking up the elements in the dictionary:

> die Geschwindigkeit + s + [der] Rekord =
> der Geschwindigkeitsrekord
> die Woche + n + [das] Ende = das Wochenende

2.2,2 After determining the elements of compounds, one must choose the proper English equivalent for the entire term.

The German compound may correspond to a simple English word, *e.g.*, **die Arbeitsstellung** 'the job'; **der Lastkraft-wagen** 'the truck.'

A different synonym may be used in either of the two English components or in both, *e.g.*, **der Waldbrand** 'the forest fire'; **das Sägewerk** 'the sawmill.'

The elements of the German compound and the English term or phrase may be roughly the same and may be given either in the same order, as in **das Wochenende** 'the week-end,' or in different order, as in **die Windrichtung** 'the direction of the wind.'

2.3 The use of **fragen** and **bitten:** Some difficulties in language study are caused by the complexity of meaning of apparently simple words.   In English, for example, *ask* is used for 'to question' and for 'to request.'   Different words are used to convey these meanings in German: for 'to ask = to question' one must use **fragen,** *e.g.*, **Frage ihn, ob er kommt.** 'Ask him whether he's coming'; for 'to ask = to request' one must use **bitten,** *e.g.*, **Bitte ihn um das Geld.** 'Ask him for the money.'

NARRATIVE

Gerald sucht Arbeit

Als die Zeit der Ferien herankam, machte Gerald alle
möglichen Vorbereitungen, sich eine Arbeitsstellung zu verschaffen [get], in der er schnell und sicher viel Geld verdienen
könnte. Obgleich er gar nicht gieriger [greedier] war als
5 andere Menschen, hielt er doch das Geld für eine nützliche
[useful] und angenehme Sache, die einem eine gewisse Freiheit
und Unabhängigkeit [independence] gibt. „Wer nichts versucht, gewinnt nichts," sagte er, „und ich habe nichts zu
verlieren."

10 Er fragte herum und wartete, und schließlich entschloß er
sich, nach Kalifornien zu fahren. Er hatte so viel von dem
grünen und goldenen Staate gehört, in dem es nie regnet. Da
gab es Schiffe [?] und Autos und schöne Schauspielerinnen
[actresses], Wasser und Sonnenschein [?]; und einer seiner
15 Freunde hatte dort einen herrlichen Sommer verbracht.

Drei Wochen später war Gerald in den dunklen und dichten
[?] Wäldern im nördlichen [?] Kalifornien so gut wie verschwunden. Er teilte niemandem mit, wo er sich aufhielt;
schon die Arbeit [the work itself] erlaubte es ihm nicht, lange
20 Briefe zu schreiben. Zwar fällte er keine Bäume wie Paul
Bunyan — die waren doch etwas größer, als er es sich vorgestellt
hatte. Auch fuhr er keinen jener großen Lastkraftwagen
[trucks], die die Landstraße entlang rasten und ihn bei seiner
Ankunft im Westen beinahe in den Straßengraben [ditch]
25 abgedrängt [forced off] hatten.

„Haben Sie schon einmal einen Dieselmotor bedient [run,
take care of]?" hatte der Mann mit dem rötlichen [?] Haar im
Sägewerk [sawmill] ihn gefragt, bei dem er um Arbeit nach-
gefragt hatte. Und als Gerald dies höflich verneinte, steckte
30 man ihn in eine Gruppe von jungen Arbeitern, welche die
Lastwagen mit Baumstämmen [?] beladen [load] sollten.

Das war schwere Arbeit, aber sie überstieg [exceed] nicht seine Kraft, auch wenn sie ihn gründlich erschöpfte [exhausted]. Morgens wachte er in der gleichen Stellung auf, in der er abends eingeschlafen war. Es taten ihm alle fünfhundertunddreiund- 35 siebzig Muskeln in seinem Körper weh. Aber wenn das Wochenende kam und er seine Bezahlung [pay] empfing, so vergaß er das alles und sagte: ,,Es freut mich doch, daß ich nach Kalifornien gekommen bin.''

Im August geschah etwas, was jeden Sommer so oft geschieht 40 und immer die gleichen Klagen [complaints] über die Nach-lässigkeit [negligence] oder Hilflosigkeit [?] der Menschen verursacht; es brach ein Waldbrand aus [?], der sich in kurzer Zeit über mehrere Berghänge [slopes] ausbreitete [spread] und die schönsten Wälder vernichtete [?]. Niemand wußte, wie 45 das Feuer entstanden war. Den ganzen Tag standen die Männer in Hitze und Rauch und versuchten, die Ausbreitung der Flammen zu verhindern [?].

Gerald half bei dieser Arbeit fleißig mit. Es war seine Aufgabe, für die durstigen Männer Wasser zu holen und so 50 fuhr er in seinem alten Wagen unermüdlich [indefatigably] hin und her, bergauf und bergab, durch Flammen und Rauch und Hitze. Bei dieser Gelegenheit entdeckte er gegen Abend, daß sich die Windrichtung [direction] verändert hatte und daß es in einer kleinen Schlucht [gorge] hinter den Männern zu brennen 55 anfing. Atemlos [breathless] rannte er zu den Leuten zurück und es gelang ihm, sie zu seinem Wagen zurückzuführen und in Sicherheit [?] zu bringen.

Gegen Morgen brannte das Feuer sich aus. Als Gerald ins Sägewerk kam, faßte der Mann mit dem rötlichen Haar seine 60 Hand und schlug ihm freundlich auf die Schulter [?]: ,,Alle Achtung [Well done!], junger Mann!'' sagte er. ,,Sie haben sechs Leuten das Leben gerettet.''

Questions

1. Was wollte Gerald in den Ferien tun?
2. Warum wünschte er viel Geld zu verdienen?
3. Was hatte er von Kalifornien gehört?
4. Warum konnte er keine langen Briefe schreiben?
5. Welche Arbeit tat er in Kalifornien nicht?
6. Was war beinahe geschehen, als er in Kalifornien ankam?
7. Wo fragte er um Arbeit nach?
8. Welche Arbeit gab man ihm?
9. Warum freute es ihn, nach Kalifornien gekommen zu sein?
10. Was geschah im August?
11. Wie war der Waldbrand entstanden?
12. Was sollte Gerald bei diesem Waldbrand tun?
13. Welche Entdeckung machte er am Abend?
14. Wie rettete er sechs Leute?
15. Was geschah am nächsten Morgen?

Vocabulary

die **Ankunft, ⸚e** arrival
die **Arbeitsstellung, -en** job
sich **auf-halten (ie, a, ä)** stay, spend time
der **Beamte, -n** official
beinahe almost
die **Beschäftigung, -en** occupation
besonders special
durstig thirsty
empfangen (i, a, ä) receive
entdecken discover
sich **entschließen (o, o)** decide
entstehen (-stand, ist -standen) arise
erlauben [*dat.*] permit
die **Freiheit** freedom

führen lead
die Gelegenheit, -en opportunity
gründlich thoroughly
das Holz wood
der Körper, – body
die Kraft, ⸚e strength, force
die Muskel, -n muscle
obgleich although
das Paket, -e package
der Rauch smoke
die Sache, -n thing
sonst otherwise
verbringen (-brachte, -bracht) spend (time)
verlieren (o, o) lose
verneinen deny, say no
die Vorbereitung, -en preparation
der Wald, ⸚er forest, woods
zwar to be sure, indeed
auch wenn even if

Idioms

Es tut ihm weh It hurts him
Er hielt es für nützlich He considered it useful
Er fuhr die Landstraße entlang He drove along the highway

PRESENT PERFECT TENSE

PAST PERFECT TENSE

VERBAL PREFIXES

USE   OF   "GERN   HABEN,"   "GEFALLEN,"   "LIEBEN"

Nebel

„Wie gefällt Ihnen dieses Wetter?   Haben Sie jemals einen dickeren Nebel gesehen?"

„Ja, wirkliche Erbsensuppe.   Aber das ist nichts gegen das, was mir einmal in Los Angeles passiert ist.   Ich war morgens in die Stadt gefahren, hatte mir einen Parkplatz gesucht und war dann gleich ins Büro gegangen.

„Wie ich aus dem Geschäft komme, hat ein dicker Nebel die ganze Gegend bedeckt.   Da bin ich ganz langsam gefahren, immer hinter dem roten Stopplicht her, das vor mir war.   Auf einmal dreht der Mann vor mir sein Licht aus und hält an. ‚Hören Sie mal,' schreie ich, ‚wissen Sie nicht, daß Sie hier im Verkehr nicht halten dürfen?' ‚Das tut mir leid', sagt der Mann und steigt aus.   ‚Dies ist meine Garage.' "

> **auf einmal**   suddenly
> **aus-drehen**   turn off
> ***aus-steigen**   get out

22

*bedecken cover
*das Büro office
*dick thick
die Erbsensuppe pea soup
*jemals ever
*der Nebel fog
das Stopplicht tail light
*der Verkehr traffic

EXERCISES

A. Replace the words in heavy type with the words in parentheses.

1. Am Morgen **hat** er drei Stunden **geruht.** (worked, drove, slept)
2. Er **hat** die Freiheit **verloren.** (loved, did win)
3. Wann **sind sie verschwunden?** (did it break out, did it arise, did he inquire)
4. Wie **war** das Feuer **ausgebrochen?** (had arisen)
5. Schließlich **hatte** er uns **erlaubt,** mit ihm zu fahren. (had invited, had asked)
6. **Hat er** sich lange **aufgehalten?** (did he keep busy, were they conversing)
7. Haben Sie je so **einen Nebel gesehen?** (did you drive . . . a car, have you known . . . a teacher, did you break . . . a speed record, have you lost . . . a job)
8. **Wir sind** bis zu dem Berghang **gekommen.** (they had climbed, she drove, he has walked)
9. **Sie haben** die Schwierigkeiten nicht **erklärt.** (they had not understood, we haven't forgotten, they hadn't caused)
10. **Hat er** die Arbeitsstellung **bekommen?** (had she lost, did they refuse [ablehnen], have we accepted)

B. Following the pattern, give German equivalents for the English sentences. Word order will be exactly the same as in the pattern sentences.

1. **Ist dir das auch passiert?**
   A. Did that happen to them also?
   B. Had it occurred [einfallen] to the student too?
   C. Did he succeed (in) that too?

2. **Der Nebel hatte die ganze Gegend bedeckt.**
   A. Gerald lost his whole family.
   B. The smoke covered the entire forest.
   C. He had discovered a new friend.

3. **Haben Sie je so einen Nebel gesehen?**
   A. Did he ever cause such an accident?
   B. Have I ever had an opportunity like that?
   C. Had he ever run such a motor?

4. **Wie hat Ihnen dieses Wetter gefallen?**
   A. How did Gerald answer her?
   B. Why did this accident happen to me?
   C. What did the voice say to him?

5. **Später ist er nach Kalifornien gefahren.**
   A. A fire once broke out in this area.
   B. He disappeared later in the smoke.
   C. Afterwards he lived at home.

6. **Hat der Mann laut geschrieen?**
   A. Did the car stop suddenly?
   B. Did he return later?

C. Replace the words in heavy type with the words in parentheses.

1. Er **hat** moderne Musik **meistens** gern. (always liked, has never liked)
2. **Mir gefällt** dieses Wetter gut. (she ... liked, they ... will like, he ... did like)
3. Gerald **arbeitet** gern **im Walde.** (likes to drive ... on the highway, likes to see ... pretty girls, likes to write ... letters, likes to stay ... in bed)

D. Prefixes.

1. Prefix **be-** to the following words and guess at the meaning of the new verbs you have formed.

decken	Frage
steigen	Frucht
setzen	Glück
arbeiten	Ton
denken	Rede
dienen	Grund (*verb with umlaut*)

2. Prefix **ent-** to the following words and guess at the meaning of the new verbs.

leer	Haupt
fern	kommen
schuldig	stehen
Flamme	führen
Fett	wickeln
Decke	falten

3. Prefix **ver-** to the following words and guess at the meaning of the new verbs.

alt	danken	kaufen
schöner	teilen	Ursache
besser	dienen	Ehre
einig	brennen	graben
mehr	bluten	Pflicht
sicher	brauchen	
wirklich	führen	

4. Rewrite the following sentences, using the prefix **be-** to make new verbs from the words printed in heavy type. Omit the words in brackets.

    Example: Er hat [auf] meine Frage nicht **geantwortet.**
                 Er hat meine Frage nicht beantwortet.

  A. Sie **sprechen** gerade [über] das Problem.
  B. Die Truppen **siegen** [über] den Feind.

    c. Das hat ihn **ruhig** [gemacht].

    D. Er **trat** [auf] die Bühne.

    E. Die feindliche Artillerie **schießt** [auf] die Stadt.

GRAMMAR

3 Review the forms of the **present perfect** and the **past perfect** and their uses. [*See Appendix 6.*]

3.1 The German present perfect and past perfect are formed, as in English, with an auxiliary and a past participle:

    Haben Sie jemals einen dickeren Nebel gesehen?

        Have you ever seen a thicker fog?

The past perfect is limited in both languages to basically one use:

    Ich hatte mir einen Parkplatz gesucht.

        I had looked for a parking place.

The present perfect is much more frequently used in German than in English. Especially in conversation it is used where the simple past is used in English:

    Da bin ich ganz langsam gefahren.

        Then I drove quite slowly.

See also the uses of the present-perfect and past-tense forms in *Das Porto*. The past is used in the expository sections, *e.g.,* **Der Beamte lächelte, nickte und wickelte es ein.** 'The official smiled, nodded, and wrapped it up.' The present perfect is used in the conversational sections, *e.g.,* **Haben Sie das Geld nicht gefunden? Mama hat es ins Paket gelegt.** 'Didn't you find the money? Mama put it in the package.'

3.2 The verbs **haben** and **sein** are used as auxiliaries in the perfect tenses: **haben** is used as perfect auxiliary for all transitive verbs, **sein** only for those intransitives which indicate a change of condition or location, *e.g.,* **entstehen** 'arise,' **erscheinen** 'appear,' **fahren** 'travel,' **folgen** 'follow,' **gehen** 'go, travel,' **verschwinden** 'disappear.'

Simple verbs and compounds formed from them do not necessarily have the same auxiliary. Simple intransitives may require **haben : Er hat lange geschlafen.** 'He slept for a long while,' whereas compound intransitives made from the same verb may require **sein : Er ist schnell eingeschlafen.** 'He went to sleep quickly.' Another such pair is **stehen** 'stand' and **entstehen** 'arise'

On the other hand, the simple verb **kommen** requires **sein,** the compound verb **bekommen** requires **haben.** Another such pair is **treten** and **betreten.**

The auxiliary for any verb, whether simple or compound, is determined by its meaning. Occasionally, in imaginative writing, the auxiliary **haben** or **sein** is omitted in subordinate clauses for stylistic reasons:

Nachdem die meisten Arbeiter bereits schlafen gegangen, . . .

After most of the workers had already gone to bed, . . .

. . . die Gerald neulich aus dem Feuer geführt.

whom Gerald had recently led out of the fire.

3.3 Verbal prefixes, *e.g.,* **ver-, be-,** and **ent-,** are like English prefixes in that each has a meaning which is difficult to define precisely but is nonetheless constant: compare *forget* with *get, forgive* with *give;* in these, *for* has the meaning 'away.' In German many more compounds are used than in English, and new ones may be formed to convey new concepts. By learning the meanings of new prefixes and some compounds in which they occur, one can determine the meaning of new compounds in context without looking them up in dictionaries.

3.3,1 ver- is used to form transitive verbs, many of which indicate a change or development:

besser	better	**verbessern**	to improve
gleichen	resemble	**vergleichen**	to compare
nein	no	**verneinen**	deny, say no
Ursache	cause	**verursachen**	cause

3.3,2 be- is used to form transitive verbs, often from intransitives:

decken	cover	**bedecken**	cover [*trans.*]
Einfluß	influence	**beeinflussen**	influence

3.3,3 ent- has the basic meaning of separation, and corresponds to English prefixes like *un-* or adverbs like *away*:

fern	distant	**entfernen**	to remove, take away
Last	load	**entlasten**	to unburden
laufen	run	**entlaufen**	to run away
stehen	stand	**entstehen**	to originate, arise

3.4 The use of **gern haben, gefallen,** and **lieben.** The English verb **like** corresponds to various expressions in German. Its translation generally requires a complete reworking of the English sentence.

English **like** plus an infinitive, *e.g.*, 'He likes to drive a car,' corresponds to a German finite verb plus **gerne : Er fährt gerne einen Wagen.**

English **like** with a noun object, *e.g.*, 'He likes this car,' corresponds to German **gern haben,** *e.g.*, **Er hat diesen Wagen gern,** or to **gefallen** 'please' (the English object is the German subject), *e.g.*, **Dieser Wagen gefällt ihm.**

English **like** in the sense of **love** corresponds to German **lieben :**

'Reynolds didn't seem to like his children especially.'
Reynolds schien seine Kinder nicht besonders zu lieben.

NARRATIVE

Entschlüsse

Abends saßen die Männer in dem großen Eßsaal, den die Gesellschaft für ihre Angestellten gebaut hatte. Es war schon etwas stiller im Raume geworden. Nachdem die meisten Arbeiter bereits schlafen gegangen, saßen einige noch plaudernd

vor dem Feuer im großen Kamin [fireplace], sprachen von der ₅
Arbeit, von den Ereignissen des Tages, von Politik und den
schlechten Lebensumständen. Aus der Küche klang das
Klappern [clatter] des Geschirrs [dishes] und das Geschwätz
[chatter] der Mädchen.

Gerald hatte sich neben Hildebrand gesetzt, einen älteren ₁₀
Mann mit breiten [broad] Schultern und großen, schweren
Händen. Er war unter den Leuten gewesen, die Gerald neulich
aus dem Feuer geführt. Hildebrand sprach nie viel und lachte
selten. Gewöhnlich saß er allein und hörte zu, was die andern
zu sagen hatten. ₁₅

„Übers Wochenende gehe ich angeln [fishing]," sagte
Reynolds, ein jüngerer Mann mit dünnem Hals [neck] und
langen Fingern. „Darauf habe ich mich schon lange gefreut.
Meine Frau will freilich, daß ich einmal nach Hause komme,
weil ich sie und die Kinder schon seit einem halben Jahr nicht ₂₀
gesehen habe. Aber was für ein Vergnügen ist das schon, die
Rasselbande [noisy gang] schreien zu hören, wenn man die
ganze Zeit gearbeitet hat und einmal seine Ruhe haben möchte?"

Er blickte um sich, aber keiner gab ihm eine Antwort. Smith
und Caramelli, zu seiner Linken [left], sprachen von den letzten ₂₅
Baseball-Resultaten, und Bates und Latour, rechts neben ihm,
unterhielten sich mit Witzen [?] über eine schöne Schauspielerin,
die sich schon zum vierten Mal hatte scheiden lassen [get a
divorce], und über eine andere, ebenso schöne, die zum vierten
Mal das Joch [?] des Ehestandes [marriage] auf sich nehmen ₃₀
wollte. — „Ich glaube, ich gehe in die Klappe [hit the hay],"
sagte Reynolds, gähnte [yawned] und verschwand. — Hildebrand saß mit gefalteten [folded] Händen und blickte in die
letzten Flammen im Kamin. Und Gerald träumte. Er
träumte von Sportwagen, von der Veränderung, die er am ₃₅
kommenden Wochenende an seinem alten, klappernden Wagen
vornehmen [undertake] wollte, und von dem ungewissen Wohlgefühl [?] eines drängenden Triebes [driving urge] nach
vorwärts.

Latour hatte sich zu Bates gewandt, der inzwischen an- ₄₀

gefangen hatte, von seinen eigenen Schicksalen zu erzählen.
Er war aus dem Krieg in Korea gesund zurückgekommen und
hatte gehofft, eine Jugendfreundin [?] zu heiraten. Aber die
hatte sich anders entschlossen und hatte einen anderen genom-
45 men, einen eleganten und gewandten [sophisticated] Bankierssohn, über dessen Vogelgesicht [?] und braunen Sportrock
'Bates sich früher schon immer geärgert hatte. „Da hab ich
noch einmal einen Brief an sie geschrieben und ihr viel Glück
gewünscht," sagte Bates, „und was glauben Sie, daß sie geant-
50 wortet hat? Sie hat sich· gewissermaßen [to a certain extent]
entschuldigt und geschrieben: ‚Meine Mutter hat's gewollt.'
Da hab ich mir gesagt: Mensch, du hast doch nicht viel verloren,
und bin nach dem Westen gegangen." — „Ich nehme an, das
muß ein schwerer Entschluß gewesen sein," lachte Latour, zog
55 seine Lederjacke zu [zipped up] und ging nach dem Ausgang
[?].   Bates folgte ihm bald mit schwerfälligen [heavy] Schritten.

Questions

1. Was hatte die Gesellschaft für ihre Angestellten gebaut?
2. Was taten einige Arbeiter im Eßsaal?
3. Wo hatte Gerald schon früher Hildebrand getroffen?
4. Warum wollte Reynolds nicht nach Hause fahren?
5. Worüber sprachen Bates und Latour?
6. Von was für einem Wagen träumte Gerald?
7. Was war geschehen, als Bates aus Korea zurückkam?
8. Warum war Bates schließlich ‚nach dem Westen'
   gegangen?
9. Wie sahen Hildebrand, Reynolds und Latour aus?
10. Wie sah der Sohn des Bankiers aus?

Vocabulary

der Angestellte, -n employee
ärgern annoy; **sich ärgern (über)** be annoyed (at)

aus-steigen (ie, ist ie)   get out
bedecken   cover
bereits   already
das Büro, -s   office
dick   thick
dünn   thin
ebenso   just as, equally
der Entschluß, -schlüsse   decision
das Ereignis, -se   event
der Eßsaal, -säle   dining hall
freilich   of course, to be sure
inzwischen   meanwhile
jemals   ever
die Kellnerin, -nen   waitress
der Krieg, -e   war
der Lebensumstand, ⁻e   situation
der Nebel, –   fog
neulich   recently
passieren (ist)   happen
plaudern   chat
die Ruhe   quiet, rest
schlecht   bad
der Schritt, -e   step
ungewiß   uncertain
sich unterhalten (ie, a, ä)   entertain oneself, converse
die Veränderung, -en   change
die Vergangenheit   past
der Verkehr   traffic
vorwärts   forward; **nach vorwärts**   ahead
sich wenden (wandte, gewandt)   turn
zu-hören   listen

Idioms

Er freut sich auf das Wochenende.
He's looking forward to the week-end.
Von was für einem Wagen träumte er?
What kind of a car was he dreaming about?

FUTURE TENSE

FUTURE PERFECT TENSE

VERBAL PREFIXES

SUFFIX -IEREN

USE OF "KOMMEN"

Die Zukunft

Viele Menschen wundern sich über die Zukunft, und nur wenige können sich recht vorstellen, wie alles kommen wird. Der eine fragt: Wie werde ich schnell reich? und der andere fragt: Wie werde ich wieder schlank? Kein Mensch kann wissen, was aus uns in einem Jahr geworden sein wird. Und später kann man immer sagen: Nun, wir werden uns wohl geirrt haben.

Zum großen Doktor Einstein kam einmal ein Journalist: „Sie werden meine Frage entschuldigen. Aber können Sie mir sagen, welche Waffen man im Dritten Weltkrieg gebrauchen wird?" — Doktor Einstein versank in Schweigen und schüttelte den Kopf: „Nein, aber ich kann Ihnen sagen, womit man im Vierten Weltkrieg kämpfen wird — mit Knüppeln und Steinen."

*gebrauchen use
*sich irren be mistaken
*kämpfen fight

der **Knüppel** stick
*der **Kopf** head
*reich rich
schlank slender
*schütteln shake
*versinken sink
*sinken sink
die **Waffe** weapon
*wenige few

EXERCISES

A. Replace the words in heavy type with the words in parentheses.

1. Wie wird das **kommen?** (be, happen, cease)
2. Inzwischen werde ich es **erklären.** (change, repeat, sell, use)
3. Womit **wird man** denn **kämpfen?** (will they . . . travel, am I going . . . to write, will he . . . begin)
4. Was **wird man** nachher **gebrauchen?** (are they going . . . to buy, will he . . . be, will he . . . know, am I going . . . to do)
5. Er wird bald **schlafen** gehen. (fishing, dancing, to eat)
6. In drei Stunden **werden wir marschieren.** (they are going . . . to fight, he will . . . come, she'll . . . play, it will . . . disappear)
7. **Sie wird** es wohl **wissen.** (he's . . . reading, you must be . . . using, he must be . . . looking for)
8. Wie **finde ich es?** (explain . . . the discovery, get . . . the money, report . . . the accident)
9. Du wirst es wohl **entdeckt** haben. (known, understood, used, found)

B. Rewrite the following sentences, making the appropriate changes in tense. (Remember that compound tenses involve changes in the word order of the sentence.)

1. **Welche Waffen gebraucht man?**
   A. are we using
   B. did he use
   C. will one use
   D. are they probably using

2. **Der große Doktor schüttelte den Kopf.**
   A. will shake
   B. is probably shaking
   C. had shaken
   D. must have shaken

3. **Was wird aus uns?**
   A. became
   B. has become
   C. will have become
   D. had become

4. **Viele Menschen wundern sich über dieses Wetter.**
   A. are angry
   B. were happy
   C. will be surprised
   D. must have been angry

5. **Vielleicht irren wir uns.**
   A. they have made a mistake
   B. he's making a mistake
   C. I was mistaken
   D. she had made a mistake

C. Following the patterns, give German equivalents for the English sentences. Word order will be exactly the same as in the pattern sentences.

1. **Wo werde ich sie noch einmal treffen?**
   A. When is the doctor going to see them again?
   B. How will Gerald beat the speed record now?
   C. What shall I tell her afterwards?

2. **Am Wochenende werde ich in meinem Garten arbeiten.**
   A. His friends are going to the park this morning.
   B. Saturday they'll drive into town.
   C. I am going to fly to Dallas tomorrow.

3. **Du wirst wohl das Buch verstehen.**
   A. He must be reading the newspaper.
   B. The workers are probably telling jokes.
   C. The fog must cover the entire city.

4. **Nächstes Jahr sucht er eine neue Stellung.**
   A. She's going to visit her relatives next week.
   B. He'll make those changes soon.

5. **Wir werden uns wohl geirrt haben.**
   A. The man must have decided.
   B. He was probably surprised.
   C. I suppose [= probably] you got angry.

D. Prefixes and suffixes.

1. Guess at the meaning of the following verbs formed with the suffix **-ieren :**

exterminieren	subtrahieren
isolieren	marinieren
terminieren	merkurieren
multiplizieren	ionisieren
kritisieren	absorbieren

2. Guess at the meaning of the verbs formed with the prefixes **er-** and **zer-** in these sentences:
   A. Die Arbeit hat ihn gründlich erschöpft.
   B. Ein dünner Mann kann die Kälte nicht ertragen.
   C. Wer hat eine neue Methode erfunden?
   D. So was habe ich noch nie erlebt.
   E. Und dann hatte sie sich erkältet.
   F. Der Biologe zerlegte den Fisch.
   G. Ein Krieg wird alles zerstören.
   H. Also hat er eines der großen Fenster zerbrochen.

GRAMMAR

4 Review the forms of the **future** and **future perfect tenses** and their uses. Review also the rules on the position of infinitives and participles. [*See Appendix 6*]

4.1 The future and future perfect tenses correspond in form and in basic uses to these same tenses in English:

Ich kann Ihnen sagen, womit man kämpfen wird.

I can tell you what people will fight with.

Er wird es bis Montag getan haben.

He will have done it by Monday.

4.1,1 In German the future tense is used less commonly than in English. The present tense is generally used if the sentence contains an adverb of time:

Er kommt in einer Stunde vom Mond zurück.

He is coming back from the moon in an hour.

As in this translation, English commonly uses the present progressive with future meaning.

4.1,2 The future and future perfect are used to indicate probability in present and past time:

Sie werden den Namen Einstein wohl kennen.

You probably know the name Einstein.

Wir werden uns wohl geirrt haben.

We were probably mistaken.

(We must have made a mistake.)

The adverb **wohl** emphasizes the idea of probability, but it is not required.

4.1,3 In addition to its use as auxiliary for the future, **werden** is the auxiliary for the passive [*See 5.1*]. It is also an independent verb with the meaning 'to become, to get'; when so used, it is followed by a noun in the nominative case or by an uninflected adjective:

Wie werde ich Rennfahrer? How do I become a racing driver?

Wie werde ich reich? How do I get rich?

4.2 The **verbal prefixes** include **er-** and **zer-**, in addition to those already discussed [*See 3.3-3.3,3*].

4.2,1 er- carries the basic sense of completion.

Used with adjectives, **er-** forms verbs meaning 'to make . . .':

klar	clear	**erklären**	to clarify
warm	warm	**erwärmen**	to make warm

Used with verbs, **er-** adds the meaning of successful or final completion:

füllen	to fill	**erfüllen**	to fulfill
kennen	to know	**erkennen**	to recognize

4.2,2 zer- has the basic meaning 'to pieces' (*cf. dis-*):

brechen	to break	**zerbrechen**	to break to pieces
teilen	to part	**zerteilen**	to separate, distribute

4.3 The suffix -ieren. A common suffix, especially in technical writing, is **-ieren.** Some verbs with **-ieren** have English equivalents ending in *-ize:*

    hypnotisieren   oxydieren   entalkoholisieren

Other verbs have English equivalents ending in *-ate:*

    dehydrieren   eliminieren   extrapolieren

The English equivalents of many verbs have no suffixes, but the meanings are easy to guess from the stems:

    dividieren   reparieren   telephonieren

Only rarely will it be difficult to derive the English meaning:

    passieren   happen

All verbs ending in **-ieren** are weak and have no **ge-** in the past participle.

4.4 The use of kommen. The German verb **kommen** has a greater range of meaning than its English cognate. It must often be translated by 'get':

Haben Sie denn nie versucht, mit Ihrer Familie in Verbindung zu kommen?

Haven't you ever tried to get in touch with your family?

    Wie kommst du hierher?   How did you get here?

In the following sentence the translation 'turn out, come out, come about' is required:

    Kein Mensch kann wissen, wie alles kommen wird.

    No one can know how things will turn out.

NARRATIVE

Geister

Es war Gerald aufgefallen, daß Hildebrand ihn schon eine
Weile von der Seite beobachtet hatte. Jetzt wandte sich der
alte Mann an ihn und fragte zögernd: „Darf ich fragen, ob Ihre
Mutter mit Ihnen aus Deutschland gekommen ist?" Gerald
5 war verwundert [?] und schüttelte den Kopf. „Nein, meine
Eltern sind beide hierzulande geboren. Warum?" — „O,
ich meine nur. Ihr Gesicht erinnert mich an einen jungen
Menschen, den ich im letzten Weltkrieg drüben gesehen habe."
  Nach einer Weile des Schweigens rückte [moved] Hildebrand
10 etwas näher. „Sie wundern sich vielleicht über meine Frage."
Gerald nickte und sah ihn neugierig [inquisitively] an. Jedoch
Hildebrand faltete seine Hände, sank in sein Schweigen zurück
und starrte in die glühende Asche. Dann aber kam wieder
Leben in ihn und er fuhr fort, als wenn er zu sich selber spräche.
15 „Ja, sehen Sie, ich bin nämlich in Deutschland geboren und
habe drüben eine Familie gehabt." „Und was ist aus ihr
geworden?" fragte Gerald, obgleich er wußte, daß dies nicht
die richtige Frage war. — „Das weiß ich eben nicht. Ich habe
sie vor über dreißig Jahren verlassen."
20   Gerald konnte sich nicht recht vorstellen, wie so etwas
möglich war, und der alte Mann fing langsam an zu erklären.
„Sie haben wohl von der Inflation gehört, die 1923 in Deutschland geherrscht hat. Damals war ich noch ein junger Mann,
etwas unerfahren [inexperienced] und etwas sentimental, wie
25 die meisten. Wie alle jungen Leute hab' ich ein leichtes Leben
geführt. Man konnte Millionen verdienen; aber am Ende fand
man heraus, daß sie nicht das Papier wert [worth] waren, worauf
sie gedruckt [printed] waren. Es ist kein Vergnügen, in solchen
Zeiten zu leben, wenn man morgen verlieren wird, was man
30 heute gewonnen hat, und wenn man sieht, wieviele Versprechungen nicht erfüllt werden. Da wurde eines Tages ein

politischer Führer erschossen. Den Täter [culprit] hat man
nie gefunden, nie gefangen. In der gleichen Zeit bin ich aus
Deutschland verschwunden — und habe Frau und Kinder sitzen
lassen.“   35
   „Haben Sie denn nie versucht, mit Ihrer Familie wieder in
Verbindung zu kommen?“ fragte Gerald gutherzig [?]. „Doch,
aber erst nach mehr als zwanzig Jahren. Da war ich längst
amerikanischer Bürger, trug amerikanische Uniform und gehörte
zu der Armee, die wieder Freiheit nach Deutschland bringen 40
sollte. Im Winter standen wir in den Ardennen, bereit zum
letzten Angriff auf Deutschland. Plötzlich waren wir auf allen
Seiten umgeben von der deutschen Artillerie, die Zufuhr
[supplies] war abgeschnitten und wir hatten schwere Verluste.
Aber trotzdem ergaben wir uns nicht. ‚In wenigen Tagen‘, 45
hieß es, ‚werden wir aus dieser Hölle [hell] herauskommen.‘
Also graben [dig] wir uns ein und hoffen, daß morgen Hilfe
kommen wird. Bei dieser Gelegenheit hab’ ich meinen Sohn
wiedergesehen.“
   Gerald hörte etwas zweifelnd zu. Er wußte nicht, ob er dem 50
Manne glauben sollte oder nicht. Aber der sprach weiter, als
ob er keine Zuhörer hätte. „An einem kalten Morgen waren
drei von uns auf Vorposten [outpost duty]. Wir waren vor
Sonnenaufgang in ein kleines Dorf geschlichen [sneaked], das
die Deutschen während der Nacht verlassen zu haben schienen. 55
Wie wir um eine Ecke kommen, da stehen auf einmal drei
Deutsche vor uns. ‚Ergebt Euch!‘ schreie ich, und zwei von
ihnen werfen ihren Karabiner [?] weg und rennen wie besessen
[as if possessed] hinters nächste Haus. Aber der dritte lacht
höhnisch [scornfully]. ‚Wo hast du denn Deutsch gelernt?‘ 60
Und will schießen. Doch sein Gewehr geht nicht. Da will
er wegspringen und noch im letzten Augenblick eine Handgranate werfen. Aber da hat er es auch schon weg [but he had
already had it], fällt zusammen [?] und liegt im Schnee. Und
wie ich genauer hinsehe, da ist es der Dieter, mein eigener 65
Sohn.“
   „Sie werden sich wohl geirrt haben,“ sagte Caramelli, der

die Geschichte mit angehört hatte.   „Geirrt?" sagte Hildebrand
fast feindselig [hostile].   „Mit dem Gesicht und der Erkennungs-
70 marke [dog tag] und allem konnte es keinen Zweifel mehr
geben."

Smith und Caramelli waren aufgestanden.   „Komm, Jerry,"
sagten sie, „es ist Zeit zum Schlafen und Hilly sieht wieder
einmal Geister."   Aber Hildebrand hörte sie nicht.   Als sie
75 aus der Tür gingen, sah Gerald, wie der Alte noch weiter in
den dunklen Kamin starrte.

Questions

  1. An wen erinnert Gerald den alten Hildebrand?
  2. Wen mußte Hildebrand in Deutschland verlassen?
  3. Was herrschte 1923 in Deutschland?
  4. Wie lebten die jungen Leute damals in Deutschland?
  5. Weiß man, wer den politischen Führer erschossen hat?
  6. Was tat Hildebrand, als er aus Deutschland verschwand?
  7. Wann kam Hildebrand wieder nach Deutschland?
  8. Wo stand die amerikanische Armee im Winter?
  9. Von wem waren die Soldaten umgeben?
10. Worauf hofften sie noch?
11. Woran erkannte Hildebrand seinen Sohn?
12. Wer bezweifelte die Wahrheit seiner Erzählung?

Vocabulary

der Angriff, -e attack
beobachten observe
drüben over there
sich ergeben (a, e, i) surrender
erinnern an [*acc.*] remind
erschießen (o, o) kill
gebrauchen use

der **Geist, -er** spirit, ghost
das **Gewehr, -e** gun, rifle
    glühen glow
    heraus-finden (a, u) find out
    hierzulande in this country
sich **irren** be mistaken
    jedoch however
    kämpfen fight
der **Kopf, ⁼e** head
    längst for a long time
    nicken nod
    reich rich
    schütteln shake
das **Schweigen** silence
der **Sonnenaufgang, ⁼e** sunrise
    umgeben (a, e, i) surround
die **Verbindung, -en** contact
der **Verlust, -e** loss
    versinken (a, ist u) sink
die **Versprechung, -en** promise
die **Weile** while
    wenige few
der **Zuhörer, –** listener
der **Weltkrieg, -e** world war
    zögern hesitate
der **Zweifel, –** doubt
    zusammen-brechen
        (brach, ist -brochen) collapse

Idioms

Es hieß They said, it was reported
Es fällt mir auf I notice

THE PASSIVE

AGENT NOUN SUFFIXES

USE OF "BRINGEN" AND "NEHMEN"

Der hohe Offizier

Im letzten Weltkrieg flog ein hoher Offizier über den Himalaya. Plötzlich wurde sein Flugzeug durch geheimnisvolle Kräfte angehalten und zum Landen gezwungen. Er wurde von unzähligen kleinen Menschen gefangen genommen und in einen Berg gebracht.

In einem großen Saal saß ein alter Mann, von vielen Apparaten umgeben. Der Raum war hell erleuchtet. Überall wurde atemlos gearbeitet und doch war kein Laut zu hören. Man nahm seine Papiere, legte sie in rötliches Wasser und gab sie ihm wieder zurück. Dann wurde er wieder entlassen.

Als er landete, waren zwanzig Jahre vorüber und der Krieg längst vorbei. Die Leute schüttelten den Kopf. Auf seinen Papieren war nichts zu lesen als: „Werde der du bist!"

> **atemlos** breathlessly
> ***entlassen** dismiss
> **erleuchtet** illuminated

*das **Flugzeug**   airplane
   gefangen nehmen   take prisoner
   geheimnisvoll   mysterious
der **Laut**   sound
   *schütteln**   shake
   *überall**   everywhere
   unzählig   countless
   *zwingen**   force

EXERCISES

A. Change the verbs in heavy type according to the tense indicated in parentheses.   (Watch the word order.)

1. Gerald **wurde** eine Weile von der Seite beobachtet.   (had been, will be, is being)
2. Der Tisch **wird** von dem Mädchen gewaschen.   (was, had been, has been)
3. Viele Fragen **sind** an den Alten gestellt **worden.**   (had been, will be, are being)
4. Wieviele Versprechungen **werden nie** erfüllt!   (were, have been, will be)
5. Von allen Seiten **wird** die Armee von der Artillerie beschossen.   (had been, has been, was)
6. **Ist** über seinen Sohn etwas gesagt **worden**?   (will be . . . written, is being . . . reported)
7. Was **wird** dabei **verloren**?   (will be . . . gained, was . . . earned, had been . . . learned)
8. Es **wurde** ein leichtes Leben geführt.   (has been, will be)
9. Dann **wurde** lustig getanzt.   (will be, has been)
10. Bei solchem Artilleriefeuer **war** nichts anderes zu machen.   (is, will be)

B. The use of the passive voice in German is often avoided in favor of the active voice with **man** as the subject.

Example: **Was ist er schon gefragt worden?**
   Was hat man ihn schon gefragt?

Follow this example in making changes in the sentences below. Be sure to keep the same tense.

1. Was wird versucht?
2. Was ist schon gewonnen worden?
3. Was wurde am Abend getan?
4. Der Hund ist nie gefunden worden.
5. Sein Sohn wurde an einer Erkennungsmarke erkannt.
6. Die Karabiner werden weggeworfen.
7. Morgen wird wieder verloren, was heute gewonnen wird.

C. Following the patterns, give German equivalents for the English sentences. Word order will be exactly the same as in the pattern sentences.

1. **Der Flieger ist in einen Berg gebracht worden.**
   A. During the night the city was abandoned.
   B. The soldier has been sent to Europe.
   C. The child hasn't been found yet.

2. **Sein Flugzeug wurde durch geheimnisvolle Kräfte angehalten.**
   A. Their artillery was cut off by the new attack.
   B. The conditions of his life were changed by this accident.
   C. Millions were lost through the German inflation.

3. **Seine Papiere werden in rötliches Wasser gelegt.**
   A. The army is being surrounded on all sides.
   B. Money is being lost every day.
   C. Stories are being told about his experiences.

4. **Man hat ihn wieder entlassen.**
   A. They reminded me of it.
   B. The culprit [Täter] was never found.
   C. People left the old man alone.

5. **Überall wurde atemlos gearbeitet.**
   A. There is a lot of talk about it.
   B. People always laugh at it.
   C. Now we'll drive fast!

6. **Darauf war nichts zu lesen.**
   A. Nothing could be done with it.
   B. Not a sound was to be heard there.
   C. Nothing was to be expected from her.

D. Noun formation.

1. Form masculine agent nouns from the following verbs by adding **-er** to the stem. Form their feminine counterparts by adding **-in** to the masculine form.

   A. zuhören   F. kennen
   B. führen   G. backen (*noun with umlaut*)
   C. lesen   H. malen
   D. dichten   I. rauchen
   E. fliegen   J. zuschauen

2. Give the designation for each of the individuals indicated.
   A. The man who works in the following fields (*e.g.*, die Mathematik, der Mathematiker):

      1. die Phonetik   4. die Ästhetik
      2. die Physik   5. die Dogmatik
      3. die Poetik   6. die Ethik

   B. A person who subscribes to the following doctrines (*e.g.*, der Realismus, der Realist):

      1. der Materialismus   4. der Darwinismus
      2. der Kommunismus   5. der Existentialismus
      3. der Idealismus   6. der Sozialismus

3. Identify the following:
   A. If der Berliner is a person from Berlin, what is
      1. der Münchener   4. die Pariserin
      2. der Prager   5. die Kopenhagenerin
      3. der Philadelphier
   B. If der Däne is a person from Denmark, what is
      1. der Franzose   4. die Schwedin
      2. der Portugiese   5. die Chinesin
      3. der Tscheche

GRAMMAR

5 The passive. Review the forms of **werden,** the forms of
the passive, and the present and the past of **sein.** [*See
Appendix 6.5*]

5.1 The passive is formed with the past participle of the verb
plus the proper form of the auxiliary **werden.** Compare the
following synopsis of the passive with the synopsis of **werden**
in the meaning 'to become':

Er wird dorthin gebracht. .	Er wird alt.
Er wurde dorthin gebracht.	Er wurde alt.
Er ist dorthin gebracht **worden.**	Er ist alt **geworden.**
Er war dorthin gebracht **worden.**	Er war alt **geworden.**
Er wird dorthin gebracht werden.	Er wird alt werden.
Er wird dorthin gebracht **worden** sein.	Er wird alt **geworden** sein.

The past participle of **werden** is **worden** in passive constructions.

5.2 In translating passives, use 'is,' 'is being,' or 'is getting'
as the auxiliaries:

Er wird zum Landen gezwungen. He is forced to land.
Er wird dorthin gebracht. He is being taken there.
Er wird gerade untersucht. He is just getting examined.

5.3 A phrase with the preposition **von** (to indicate agency) or
durch (to indicate means) is used to state by whom or by what
the action is being done:

Der hohe Offizier wurde **von** den kleinen Menschen in den
    Berg gebracht.
Sein Flugzeug wurde **durch** geheimnisvolle Kräfte angehalten.

5.4 Passives are often used in German without a subject
(impersonal passives). This usage is not found in English;
instead, we use impersonal subjects, *e.g.*, 'people,' 'one,' 'you,'

'they,' or we convert the verb into a noun, as in the third example below.

Überall wurde atemlos gearbeitet.
People were working furiously everywhere.
Jetzt wird einmal tüchtig gegessen!
And now you're really going to eat!
Im Krankenhaus wurde gerade operiert.
There was an operation in progress at the hospital.

5.5 On the other hand, the passive is avoided by many German stylists. One substitute for it is a verb in the active voice with **man** as subject:

Man nahm seine Papiere.
His papers were taken. (They took his papers.)
Forms of **sein** plus **zu** and the infinitive correspond to English passive constructions with 'is/are to be . . .' or 'can be . . .':

Doch war kein Laut zu hören.
But not a sound was to be (could be) heard.
Auf seinen Papieren war nichts zu sehen.
There was nothing to be seen in his papers.

5.6 The use of past participles with forms of **sein** differs in no way from that of other adjectives:

Der Raum war leer.	The room was empty.
Der Raum war verlassen.	The room was abandoned.

5.7 Among the **agent noun suffixes** are **-er, -aner, -e, -ist, -ling,** and **-ler.**

5.7,1 In German as in English, **-er** is the usual suffix used to indicate someone performing an action; *cf. work:* arbeiten, *worker:* Arbeiter.

After **-er** and other suffixes, **-in** is added to indicate that the agent of an action is a woman:

besitzen	possess	**der Besitzer**	the possessor	**die Besitzerin**
lehren	teach	**der Lehrer**	the teacher	**die Lehrerin**

-er is also used as a suffix to indicate specialists:

die Botanik botany   **der Botaniker** the botanist
                                                die Botanikerin
die Chemie chemistry   **der Chemiker** the chemist
                                                die Chemikerin

-er is also used to designate natives of cities and of some countries:

München Munich   **der Münchner**   **die Münchnerin**
Italien Italy   **der Italiener**   **die Italienerin**
Spanien Spain   **der Spanier**   **die Spanierin**

-aner is used for natives of some states and countries:

Amerika America   **der Amerikaner die Amerikanerin**

5.7,2 -e is used for natives of some countries:

Griechenland Greece   **der Grieche   die Griechin**
die Türkei   Turkey   **der Türke   die Türkin**

5.7,3 -ist is used with certain foreign stems, especially those ending in **-ismus** :

Realismus   realism   **der Realist   die Realistin**
komponieren compose **der Komponist die Komponistin**

5.7,4 -ling generally is used only for words of masculine gender:

jung   young   **der Jüngling** youth
lehren teach   **der Lehrling** apprentice

5.7,5 -ler is used like **-er** :

die Kunst art **der Künstler** artist **die Künstlerin**
die Wissenschaft science **der Wissenschaftler** scientist
                                                die Wissenschaftlerin

5.8 The use of **bringen** and **nehmen.** The German verbs **bringen** and **nehmen** are often used for 'bring' and 'take,' respectively. However, **bringen** is sometimes used where we say 'take' in English in the sense of 'convey':

Er wurde in einen Berg gebracht.
He was taken into a mountain.
Sie mußte ihre Tochter zum Arzt bringen.
She had to take her daughter to the doctor.

NARRATIVE

Unfall im Walde

Am 15. August geschah ein Unfall bei der Arbeit im Wald. Eine der Stahltrossen [steel cable], womit die Baumstämme auf dem Lastwagen festgebunden werden, riß, schnellte zurück [snapped back] und traf Gerald an Kopf und Schulter. Er brach zusammen, wurde blutend [bleeding] ins Krankenhaus 5 gebracht, lag dort einige Tage schwach und bewußtlos [unconscious], kam aber doch bald wieder zu sich und wartete schon auf die Stunde, in der er aus dem Krankenhaus entlassen werden konnte.

Gerald war ruhelos. Warum hielt man ihn hier fest, wenn 10 es noch so viel zu tun gab? Da war noch der Zylinderdruck zu verbessern, ein neuer Vergaser [carburetor] mußte gekauft werden und noch viele andere Dinge mußten repariert werden. Aber danach wurde er hier einfach nicht gefragt. Hier behandelte man ihn automatisch — wie eine teure Maschine: 15 „Ist Nummer 21 schon gewaschen worden?" sagte man, oder „Hat Nummer 21 schon neue Wäsche bekommen?" oder „Wann wird Nummer 21 wieder gemessen werden?" [have his temperature taken]. — Nein, Gerald wollte nicht wie ein Kranker gepflegt werden! Er wollte so schnell wie möglich wieder aus 20 diesem Haus herauskommen, wo Chloroform in jedem Zimmer zu riechen war.

Zum ersten Mal in seinem Leben war Gerald wirklich allein. Wie eintönig [monotonous] das war, mit seinen eigenen Gedanken allein zu sein! Vor vierzehn Tagen war er zwanzig 25 Jahre alt geworden, und doch wußte er noch nicht, was er werden wollte. Er wollte vorwärts kommen, aber niemand zeigte ihm ein Ziel. — Er richtete sich in seinem Bett auf. Sein rechter Arm tat ihm noch etwas weh, aber er war leicht zu bewegen: also war er doch nicht gebrochen! Auch der 30 Kopf schmerzte ihm noch, und Gerald erschrak, als er im

Spiegel sah, wie er vom Arzt verbunden worden war. Sein
Gesicht war kaum wiederzuerkennen. Er tastete seinen Kopf
ab [felt or ran his fingers over], und als er dies tat, schien eine
35 Stimme aus tiefer Vergangenheit ihm zuzuflüstern: „Heile,
heile, Segen! Drei Tage Regen! Drei Tage Sonnenschein:
wird alles wieder heil sein!" Mit diesen Worten hatte seine
Mutter ihre Hand ihm auf den Kopf gelegt, wenn er — als
kleines Kind — irgendwo Schmerzen hatte. . .
40 Als es im Zimmer dunkel wurde, wachte Gerald plötzlich
wieder auf. Bates war dagewesen und hatte Blackie mitgebracht. Blackie war ein kleiner schwarzer Hund, den Gerald
eines Tages gefunden und zu sich genommen hatte. Vielleicht
war er von seinem Herrn vergessen worden; auf jeden Fall
45 hatte er allein im Regen gesessen und geheult, und Gerald
hatte ihn auf sein Zimmer gebracht und ihn gefüttert [?] und
gepflegt, bis er wieder warm und gesund wurde. Gerald
wunderte sich, daß Bates mit dem Hund unter seiner Lederjacke überhaupt ins Krankenhaus hereingelassen worden war.
50 Denn er mußte wissen, daß Hunde in einem Krankenhaus
verboten sind. Aber dann hatten sie Blackie unter der Decke
versteckt, und niemand hatte ihn gesehen.
Eine Krankenpflegerin trat ins Zimmer und drehte das Licht
an. „Nun, was macht denn unser Patient auf Nummer 21?"
55 Gerald richtete sich langsam auf und tastete die Decke ab.
„Was ist denn los?" lachte das Mädchen, „haben Sie etwas
verloren?" — „Ich muß wohl geträumt haben," lächelte Gerald.
Da wurde von einer Helferin [?] ein mageres [skimpy] Abendessen hereingetragen, und die Schwester fuhr mit eifriger
60 Herzlichkeit [with eager, exaggerated cordiality] fort: „Jetzt wird
einmal tüchtig gegessen!" Dann legte sie ihm die Hand auf
den Kopf und sagte zweifelnd: „Ich glaube nicht, daß Sie in
drei Tagen schon wieder entlassen werden können."

Questions

1. Was für ein Unfall geschah bei der Arbeit im Walde?
2. Warum wurde Gerald ins Krankenhaus gebracht?
3. Warum war Gerald ruhelos?
4. Wie wurde er im Krankenhaus behandelt?
5. Warum wollte er das Krankenhaus so schnell wie möglich verlassen?
6. Woher wußte Gerald, daß sein Arm nicht gebrochen war?
7. Warum konnte er sein Gesicht kaum wiedererkennen?
8. Was hatte seine Mutter getan, wenn er Schmerzen hatte?
9. Was hatte Gerald eines Tages im Regen gefunden?
10. Was hatte Gerald von Bates geträumt?
11. Was suchte Gerald unter der Decke?
12. Warum drehte die Krankenpflegerin das Licht an?

Vocabulary

das **Abendessen**   supper, dinner
an-drehen   turn on
der **Arzt, ⸚e**   physician
sich **auf-richten**   sit up
atemlos   breathless
behandeln   treat, handle
bewegen   move
einfach   simple
entlassen (ie, a, ä)   dismiss
erkennen (-kannte, -kannt)   recognize
fest-halten (ie, a, ä)   keep
das **Flugzeug, -e**   airplane
heil   well, whole
der **Kranke, -n**   sick man, patient
das **Krankenhaus, ⸚er**   hospital
die **Krankenpflegerin, -nen**   nurse

das **Mal, -e**   time, instance
pflegen   take care of, nurse
reißen (riß, -rissen)   tear
riechen (o, o)   smell
ruhelos   restless
der **Schmerz, -en**   pain
schwach   weak
der **Segen, –**   blessing
der **Spiegel, –**   mirror
tief   deep
überall   everywhere
überhaupt   at all, in general
verbinden (a, u)   bandage
waschen (u, a, ä)   wash
zwingen (a, u)   force
das **Ziel, -e**   goal

Idiom

Was ist denn los?   What's the matter anyway?

MODAL AUXILIARIES

NOUN SUFFIXES

USE OF "WISSEN," "KENNEN," "KÖNNEN"

Das Haus an der Kurve

„Guten Morgen, Frau Schlager! Das ist aber schön! Wie kommt das Auto in Ihr Wohnzimmer?"

„Ja, das kann ich auch nicht recht verstehen. Der Fahrer muß zu schnell gefahren sein, sonst hätte er den Wagen wohl noch anhalten können."

„So einen Unfall habe ich schon längst kommen sehen. Wenn man an einer solchen Kurve wohnt, darf man kaum etwas anderes erwarten. Ihr Mann hätte eine Mauer bauen lassen sollen!"

„Ja, ich weiß. Das hat er aber nicht gewollt. Die Leute sollen langsamer fahren!"

„Warum will er das nicht? Es läßt sich eben nichts anderes machen."

„Nein, wir müssen doch sehen, was auf der Straße geschieht, und wir wollen auch von der Straße gesehen werden!"

> *die Kurve curve
> *die Mauer wall
> *läßt sich machen can be done

53

EXERCISES

A. Replace the words in heavy type with the words in parentheses.

1. Man **wollte** einen neuen Vergaser kaufen. (had to, intended to, ought to, would like to)
2. Wann **kann** er das Krankenhaus verlassen? (is he supposed to, does he have to, does he want to)
3. Wir **haben** viele andere Dinge reparieren **müssen.** (were supposed to, wanted to, have been able to)
4. Da wird man ihn wie eine Maschine behandeln **wollen.** (have to, be able to, be allowed to)
5. **Hörst** du ihn den Hund **rufen?** (see ... hiding, help [*with dative*] ... take care of)
6. Gerald **wollte** nicht wie ein Kranker gepflegt werden. (should, could, would like, had to)
7. Er **mag** aber nicht weg. (wants to, is able to, is permitted to, would like to)
8. Das **hätten** wir nicht tun **müssen.** (could have, should have)

B. Change the verbs in heavy type to the tenses indicated by the material in parentheses. Watch the word order.

1. Das **kann** ich auch nicht recht verstehen. (could, have been able to, will be able to)
2. Man **darf** kaum etwas anderes erwarten. (should, can, could, could have)
3. Das **hat** er aber nicht **gewollt.** (did have to, was allowed to, wanted)
4. Wir **müssen** doch sehen, was geschieht. (shall want to, are able to, shall have to)
5. Wir **wollen** auch von der Straße gesehen werden. (can, could, were supposed to)
6. So einen Unfall **hat er** schon längst kommen **sehen.** (they ... saw, we ... had seen)

C. Following the patterns, give German equivalents for the English sentences. Word order will be exactly the same as in the pattern sentences.

1. **Das kann ich auch nicht verstehen.**
   A. He wasn't able to do that either.
   B. We mustn't [**dürfen**] forget him either.
   C. I wouldn't like to try that either.

2. **Er mußte zum Landen gezwungen werden.**
   A. The sick man ought to be taken to the hospital.
   B. His jacket has to be washed on Monday.
   C. The car is supposed to be repaired every month.

3. **Er hätte den Wagen anhalten können.**
   A. He should have hidden the dog.
   B. They could have caused an accident.
   C. Gerald would have had to earn the money.

4. **Ich habe einen solchen Unfall längst kommen sehen.**
   A. He saw a car like that race by yesterday.
   B. Last week he helped repair the car.

5. **Warum will er das?**
   A. When is he supposed to (do) it?
   B. How did he intend to (do) it?
   C. Why does he have to?

6. **Es läßt sich doch nichts machen.**
   A. Something can be done after all.
   B. Nevertheless it can't be changed.

D. Noun formation.

1. Give the field with which each of the following persons would be associated.

> *Example:* der Physiologe: die Physiologie.
>
> A. der Pharmakologe   F. der Dramaturg
> B. der Philologe   G. der Chirurg
> C. der Pathologe   H. der Philosoph
> D. der Biologe   I. der Theosoph
> E. der Demokrat   J. der Anatom

2. A. Form nouns from the following verbs, using **-nis.**

Example: (sich) ereignen: das Ereignis.

1. verderben	4. (sich) ergeben
2. hindern	5. erleben
3. ersparen	6. erzeugen

B. Form nouns from the following words, using **-tum.**

Example: deutsch: das Deutschtum.

1. heilig	4. Jude (+ n)
2. der König	5. (sich) irren (der)
3. der Heide (+ n)	6. reich (der)

GRAMMAR

6.1 Modal auxiliaries indicate an attitude toward the activity that is expressed by the dependent infinitive. Their meanings vary widely and are best learned from context. (*The following are most common; for further examples, and for the forms of modal auxiliaries, see Appendix 6.4.*)

dürfen :

Indicating permission :

> **Er durfte dann weiterfahren.**
> He was allowed to go on then.

Indicating denial of permission or restriction :

> **Das dürfen wir nicht.** We mustn't do that.

können :

Indicating ability :

> **Sonst hätte der Fahrer anhalten können.**
> Otherwise the driver could have stopped.

mögen :

Indicating possibility :

> **Das mag sein.** That may be.

Indicating wish, liking :

> **Ich mag Erbsensuppe nicht.** I don't like pea soup.

müssen :
 Indicating compulsion:
 Wir müssen einfach weg. We simply must leave.
sollen :
 Indicating obligation:
  Die Leute sollten langsamer fahren.
   People should drive more slowly.
 Indicating reported information:
  Der Junge soll sehr krank sein.
   The boy is said (supposed) to be very sick.
wollen :
 Indicating desire:
  Das hat der Arzt aber nicht gewollt.
   But the doctor did not want (to do) that.
 Indicating intention:
  Der Patient will morgen abfahren.
   The patient intends to leave tomorrow.
 Indicating a claim:
  Er will ein reicher Bankier sein.
   He claims to be a wealthy banker.

6.1,1 The past subjunctive II of modal auxiliaries is used with a
dependent infinitive to express the English 'could have,' etc. plus
a past participle :
  hätte . . . können   could have . . .
  hätte . . . sollen   should have . . .
  hätte . . . müssen   would have had to . . .
Das hätten Sie hören sollen. You should have heard that.

6.1,2 Modal auxiliaries can be used without dependent infinitives when a) an adverb expresses motion, as in the example
under *müssen;* or   b) when a noun or pronoun is the object
of the modal, as in the first example under *wollen.*

6.2 When the perfect tenses of modals are used with infinitives,
the participle has the form of the infinitive, as in the example
under *können* **(double infinitive).**

The double infinitive construction is also used with **helfen, hören, lassen, lehren, lernen** and **sehen.**

Einen solchen Unfall habe ich längst kommen sehen.
[Not **ge**sehen]
I've seen an accident like that coming for a long while.
Ihr Mann hat eine hohe Mauer bauen lassen.
[Not **ge**lassen]
Her husband had a high wall built.

6.2,1 In subordinate word order, forms of **haben** and **werden** stand before the double infinitive:

Ich weiß, daß er den Wagen nicht hat reparieren lassen.
(wird reparieren lassen)
I know that he didn't have the car fixed.
(. . . that he won't . . .)

6.3 As in English, the passive infinitive (participle plus infinitive of **werden**) is used with modal auxiliaries:

Das kann nicht mehr geändert werden.
That can't be changed any more.

sich lassen plus the active infinitive corresponds to **können** plus the passive infinitive:

Das läßt sich nicht mehr ändern.
That can't be changed any more.

sein plus **zu** and the active infinitive is similar to this in meaning [*See 5.5*]:

Das ist nicht mehr zu ändern.
That can't be changed any more.

6.4 Noun suffixes.

6.4,1 -ung is used to make nouns indicating an activity or the result of an activity; in this, it is similar to English *-tion* and *-ery*:

beobachten	observe	**Beobachtung**	observation
entdecken	discover	**Entdeckung**	discovery
stellen	place	**Stellung**	position

6.4,2 -schaft is used to make collectives in the same way as the English *-ship*, *-y*, and *-ion*:

Freund	friend	**Freundschaft**	friendship
Geselle	companion	**Gesellschaft**	society, company
leiden	suffer	**Leidenschaft**	passion

6.4,3 -heit and **-keit** are used to make abstract nouns; compare English *-ness* and *-ty*:

dunkel	dark	**Dunkelheit**	darkness
krank	sick	**Krankheit**	sickness
eitel	vain	**Eitelkeit**	vanity

When a stem ends in **-ig** or **-lich, -keit** is used rather than **-heit :**

schwierig	difficult	**Schwierigkeit**	difficulty
wirklich	actual	**Wirklichkeit**	actuality

6.4,4 Certain other feminine abstract nouns have suffixes of Latin or Greek origin which are similar to English suffixes:
-ie is used for certain branches of scholarship and science:
die Anthropologie anthropology   **die Chemie** chemistry
-ik is also used for branches of scholarship and science:
  die Ethik ethics   **die Mathematik** mathematics
-tät is used to indicate an abstract noun :
  die Aktualität actuality   **die Realität** reality
-tion is used to indicate an abstract noun :
  die Nation nation   **die Zivilisation** civilization
Compounds of German elements with **-kunde** or **-kunst** may also be used for branches of scholarship and science:

     die Völkerkunde = die Anthropologie
     die Seelenheilkunde = die Psychiatrie
     die Dichtkunst = die Poesie
     die Tonkunst = die Musik

6.4,5 -nis, -nisse (*cf.* English *-ness*) is also used to form abstract nouns. Most nouns ending in **-nis** are feminine; some are neuter.

    die Finsternis darkness   **das Ereignis** event

6.4,6 -tum (*cf.* English *-dom*) forms abstract nouns, most of which are neuter:

das Christentum Christendom   **das Eigentum** property
Only **der Irrtum** 'error' and **der Reichtum** 'riches' are masculine.

6.4,7 -ismus (*cf.* English *-ism*) forms nouns indicating doctrines. The nouns are masculine:

   der Idealismus idealism   **der Realismus** realism

6.5 The use of **wissen, kennen,** and **können.** Both **wissen** and **kennen** mean 'to know,' but they must be carefully distinguished. **Wissen** means to know something as a fact and can be used without an object:

  Wissen Sie, daß er morgen kommt? Ja, ich weiß.
    Do you know he's coming tomorrow? Yes, I know.
    Kennen Sie dieses Buch? Ja, ich kenne es.
    Do you know this book? Yes, I know it.

können is sometimes translated 'to know,' but here a mastery of a subject or a skill is implied:

    Er kann aber gut Deutsch.
    But he certainly knows German well.

NARRATIVE

Nummer 21 verabschiedet sich

  Endlich kam der Tag heran, an dem Gerald aus dem Krankenhaus entlassen werden sollte. Der Arzt war seit zwei Tagen nicht mehr da gewesen, und als er am dritten Tag schließlich auf kurze Zeit erschien, sagte er scherzend: „Was? Sie sind
5 noch hier? Sie mögen wohl nicht von hier weg?"
  Gerald fühlte den Spott. Der Doktor mochte recht haben. Er war hier wirklich in den letzten zwei Wochen so herrlich behandelt worden, wie noch nie in seinem Leben. Kein

Wunder, daß er sich bald an dieses Dasein [existence] ohne
Sorgen gewöhnt hatte. Hier durfte er den ganzen Tag schlafen, 10
ohne fürchten zu müssen, durch einen Wecker [alarm clock]
aus dem Schlaf aufgeschreckt zu werden. Wenn er aufwachte,
stand ein hübsches Mädchen an seinem Bett, fühlte seinen Puls
oder reichte ihm eine Mahlzeit, ein Glas Orangensaft [?] oder
ein paar Pillen. Wenn er den Fernsehapparat wollte, schob 15
man ihn in sein Zimmer, und wenn er müde wurde, schob
man ihn wieder hinaus. Nein, dieses Leben konnte nicht so
weiter gehen; es war viel besser, als er es sich jemals im Traum
vorgestellt hatte.

Aber Gerald ließ sich nicht täuschen. Er hörte, wie das 20
Leben draußen wieder nach ihm rief, sah die Arbeit, die getan
werden sollte, fühlte den ungewissen Drang, der ihn vorwärts
trieb.

In seinem besten Anzug und mit einer kleinen Handtasche,
die man ihm ins Krankenhaus gebracht hatte, stand er unten 25
im Büro und wollte sich verabschieden. „Gerald Hunter, von
Nummer 21?" sagte eine ältere Dame, die hinter einem Glasfenster saß und ihn streng ansah. „Es tut mir leid, aber wir
können Sie nicht gehen lassen. Erst muß die Rechnung
bezahlt werden, fünfhundertsiebzig Dollar. Wollen Sie in bar 30
[cash] bezahlen oder per Scheck?"

Gerald hätte in den Boden sinken können. Dies hatte er
nicht kommen sehen. Es war ihm, als ob er wieder zu dem
kleinen Jungen würde, der mit seiner Mutter zu der Nachbarin
gehen sollte, um für die Fensterscheibe [window pane] zu 35
bezahlen, die beim Fußballspiel [?] zerbrochen worden war.
Er fühlte, wie er rot wurde, und dachte nach. ,Was ich verdient
habe, soll mir hier nicht genommen werden; und an meine
Eltern mag ich mich wirklich nicht wenden — wegen jeder
Kleinigkeit.' 40

„Warum rufen Sie nicht im Sägewerk an?" sagte er ruhig.
„Die werden wohl schon für mich bezahlen."

„Ach so? Sie haben also Versicherung? Dann ist die
Sache ja leicht zu erledigen."

45 Gerald mußte eine halbe Stunde warten, während eifrig hin-
und her-telefoniert wurde: jemand wird ihn abholen. Und
der wird dann auch einen Scheck mitbringen und wird die
Rechnung bezahlen. „Also schön, alles in Ordnung. Auf
Wiederhören."

50 Der Wagen fuhr vor. Eine junge Dame trat rasch ans Glasfenster und erledigte die Sache mit wenigen Worten. Dann
drehte sie sich um und fragte lächelnd: „Herr Hunter? Ich
soll Sie abholen."

Gerald war aufgesprungen und lächelte ebenfalls. Auch sein
55 Herz lächelte: in diesem Augenblick erkannte er, daß sie vor
mehreren Monaten aneinander vorbeigefahren waren.

Die Frau hinterm Glasfenster sah ihnen lange nach [?].
Dann wurde sie aus ihren Gedanken aufgeschreckt. Eben
wurde durch die Hintertür [?] ein neuer Fall ins Krankenhaus
60 geschoben.

Questions

1. Woher wissen wir, daß die Worte des Arztes Spott waren?

2. Warum konnte Gerald sich so leicht ans Leben im
   Krankenhaus gewöhnen?

3. Warum durfte dieses Leben nicht so weitergehen?

4. Warum bekam Gerald einen Schreck, als er das Krankenhaus verlassen sollte?

5. Warum war die Rechnung im Krankenhaus so leicht zu
   bezahlen?

6. Wer bezahlte diese Rechnung?

7. Warum lächelte Gerald, als er aus dem Krankenhaus
   abgeholt wurde?

8. Wodurch wurde die Frau hinterm Glasfenster aufgeschreckt?

Vocabulary

der **Anzug, ⸚e** suit
auf-schrecken startle
bezahlen pay
der **Drang** urge, drive
ebenfalls likewise, also
erledigen take care of
erscheinen (ie, ist ie) appear
der **Fernsehapparat, -e** television set
sich **fürchten** fear, be afraid
heran-kommen (a, ist o) approach
hübsch pretty
der **Junge, -n** boy
die **Kurve, -n** curve
die **Mahlzeit, -en** meal
die **Mauer, -n** wall
die **Ordnung, -en** order
rasch quick
reichen pass, hand
die **Rechnung, -en** bill
scherzen joke
schieben (o, o) shove
der **Spott** sarcasm
streng severe
täuschen deceive
treiben (ie, ie) drive
sich **verabschieden** leave
die **Versicherung, -en** insurance
vor-fahren (u, ist a, ä) drive up in front of
das **Wohnzimmer, –** living room

Idiom

Es läßt sich nichts machen Nothing can be done

INSEPARABLE AND SEPARABLE VERB COMPOUNDS

ADJECTIVE SUFFIXES

USE OF "ZEIT," "UHR," "MAL"

Der Konnaisseur

„Habe ich Ihnen schon erzählt, was uns einmal in Arizona begegnet ist? — Wir waren am ‚versteinerten Wald‘ vorbeigefahren, hielten den Wagen an und stiegen aus, um uns die Gegend anzusehen. Da kommt ein alter Klapperkasten die Straße entlang, hustet zweimal und bleibt stehen. Zwei Indianer springen heraus und kommen zu uns herüber."

„Um Gotteswillen, man hat Sie doch nicht überfallen?" „Keineswegs. ‚Entschuldigen Sie, bitte,‘ sagt der eine. ‚Haben Sie vielleicht etwas Brennstoff?‘ — Nun hatte ich einen Syphon mitgebracht. Der Indianer steckt den Syphon in den Tank und fängt an zu saugen. Da bekommt er den Mund voll Benzin. Aber er verliert nicht die Ruhe. Er wischte sich die Lippen ab und sagte lächelnd: ‚Ethyl, nicht wahr?‘ "

ab-wischen wipe off
begegnen (ist) happen
das Benzin gasoline

*der **Brennstoff** fuel
husten cough
*keineswegs** by no means
die **Ruhe** composure
saugen suck
*stehen-bleiben (ist)** stop
überfallen attack
um Gotteswillen for heaven's sake
versteinert petrified

EXERCISES

A. Change the verbs in heavy type in accordance with the pattern indicated in parentheses. (Watch the word order.)

1. Ich **erzähle** es ihm später.   (told, did tell, shall tell, must tell, hope to tell)
Use the corresponding forms of **entdecken.**
2. Aber er **verliert** die Ruhe nicht. (lost, did lose, will lose.)
Use the corresponding forms of **verdienen.**
3. Da **bekommt** er den Mund voll Benzin. (got, has got, is going to get, can get, deserves to get)
4. Wir **fahren** am ‚versteinerten Wald' **vorbei.** (were driving, have driven, shall drive, want to drive, hope to drive)
Use the corresponding forms of **vorbeirasen.**
5. Da **halte** ich den Wagen **an.** (stopped, did stop, shall stop, had to stop, wished to stop)
Use the same forms of **ansehen.**
6. Zwei Indianer **springen** aus dem Auto **heraus.** (jumped, have jumped, will jump, were about to jump, tried to jump)
7. Dann **bleibt** er eine Weile da **stehen.** (stopped, had stopped, will stop, can stop, tried to stop)

8. **Lernst** du die Stadt gut **kennen?** (were getting acquainted, did become acquainted, will get acquainted, wish to become acquainted)

9. Ich frage nur, warum Sie hier **aussteigen?** (did climb out, will be getting out, want to get out)

10. Dann **fängt** er **an** zu saugen. (began, had begun, will begin, wanted to begin)

B. Following the patterns, give German equivalents for the English sentences. Word order will be *exactly the same* as in the pattern sentences.

1. **Ist das Ihnen schon einmal begegnet?**
   A. Did it happen to him yesterday too?
   B. Has she told him about it already?
   C. Hasn't he visited you yet?

2. **Warum halten Sie den Wagen an?**
   A. Why does he wake up during the night?
   B. Why are you staring at the police car?
   C. What time are they leaving for New York?

3. **Wir stiegen dann aus, um die Gegend anzusehen.**
   A. His parents got up early in order to meet her.
   B. I came by later in order to take him along.
   C. He departed at six in order to call for his sister.

4. **Dann hat sie den Tisch abgewischt.**
   A. They called up their employees afterwards.
   B. At that moment the student looked at his watch.
   C. Mother turned off the light later.

5. **Was mußte er in den Tank stecken?**
   A. Whom was he supposed to call for in the hospital?
   B. Why do I have to call up the sawmill?

C. Verb formation.

1. Guess at the meaning of the new verbs formed with the separable and inseparable prefixes.

A. **stehen** : auf-stehen, entstehen, bei-stehen, verstehen

B. **kommen** : an-kommen, entkommen, unter-kommen, vor-kommen

C. **setzen** : ab-setzen, auf-setzen, ein-setzen, übersetzen

2. Match each German verb in the first column with an English meaning in the second column:

A	B
A. **verfolgen**	occur
B. **sich umkleiden**	decline
C. **ausschließen**	work up, arrange, revise
D. **vorkommen**	happen
E. **zunehmen**	take part
F. **hintergehen**	cheat
G. **wiederholen**	change clothes
H. **sich herablassen**	exhale
I. **ausatmen**	persecute
J. **haltmachen**	participate
K. **ablehnen**	condescend
L. **teilnehmen**	refuse
M. **stattfinden**	increase
N. **bearbeiten**	take place
	stop
	repeat
	exclude

D. Translate the following:

1. Er hat sich mit seinem Bruder in San Franzisko in Verbindung gesetzt [get in touch with].
2. Das müssen Sie aber auch in Betracht ziehen [take into consideration].
3. Auf diese Weise würden wir alle in Schwierigkeit geraten [get].
4. Bitte, nehmen Sie Platz!
5. Auf die neuen Studenten hatte er einen großen Einfluß gehabt.

6. Haben Sie das noch in Erinnerung?
7. Was hat man ihm zur Antwort gegeben?
8. Der neue Plan wurde sofort in Angriff genommen.

E. Form adjectives from the following words, using the indicated suffixes. Give a meaning for each.

1. **-bar**
    genieß(en) to enjoy
    verschieb(en) to adjust, to postpone
    erreich(en) to attain

2. **-haft**
    Beispiel example
    Grauen terror
    wohn(en) to dwell, reside
    leb(en) to live

3. **-ig**
    Gespräch conversation, talk
    Fleiß industry, eagerness
    Kraft(¨) force, power
    Ruh(e) quiet

4. **-isch**
    Künstler artist
    Chem(ie) chemistry
    Goeth(e)
    Russ(e) a Russian
    selbst self

5. **-lich**
    glaub(en) to believe
    (sich) ärger(n) to be annoyed
    König king
    Arzt(¨) physician
    Herz heart

6. **-mäßig**
    Plan plan
    Geschäft (+ s) business
    Schul(e) school
    Beruf (+ s) profession

7. **-sam**
    heil(en) to heal
    wirk(en) to have an effect
    arbeit(en) to work
    rat(en) to advise

8. -voll   **Ruhe** rest
              Bedeutung (+ s) meaning
              Sinn sense
              Trauer mourning

F. Form the negatives of the following:

1. With **-los** : ruhevoll, sinnvoll, lebhaft, ahnungsvoll.
2. With **un-** : ruhig, kriegerisch, begreifbar, absichtlich.

GRAMMAR

7.1 Inseparable verb compounds are formed with unstressed prefixes [*See 3.3 and 3.2*]. The most common such prefixes are **be-, ent-, emp-, er-, ver-,** and **zer-**; less frequent are **ge-** and **miß-**.

    ge- is not added to inseparable verbs in the past participle.

stehen	**stand**	**hat gestanden**	**steht**	stand
bestehen	**bestand**	**hat bestanden**	**besteht**	exist
entstehen	**entstand**	**ist entstanden**	**entsteht**	arise

7.1,1 Inseparable verbs may also be made with a small number of prefixes that are used in separable verbs: **durch-, über-, um-, unter-, wider-,** and **wieder-**. The position of the stress indicates whether a verb made with one of these prefixes is separable or inseparable.

    Inseparable verbs generally have a transferred meaning, **separable** verbs a literal meaning: compare **understand,** where the meaning is transferred to the mental sphere, with **stand under,** which is literal in meaning. Examples in German are:

überfallen	**überfiel**	**hat überfallen**	**überfällt**
			attack
widerstehen	**widerstand**	**hat widerstanden**	**widersteht**
			resist

7.2 In **separable verbs,** the stress falls on the prefix. In the past participle, **ge-** stands between prefix and stem.

The most common separable prefixes are prepositions, *e.g.*, **an, bei, durch, mit, unter,** and so on, and adverbs, *e.g.*, **her, hin, heran, hinunter.**

ansehen	**sah . . . an**	**hat angesehen**
		sieht an look at
herumsitzen	**saß . . . herum**	**hat herumgesessen**
		sitzt herum sit around

Verbs are also used as first elements of some compound verbs:

kennenlernen	**lernte . . . kennen**	**hat kennengelernt**
		lernt . . . kennen meet
stehenbleiben	**blieb . . . stehen**	**ist stehengeblieben**
		bleibt . . . stehen stop

A few nouns have become prefixes of separable compounds:

heimkehren	**kehrte . . . heim**	**ist heimgekehrt**
		kehrt . . . heim return
teilnehmen	**nahm . . . teil**	**hat teilgenommen**
		nimmt . . . teil participate

7.2,1 Some nouns and prepositional phrases also function like separable prefixes in that they stand at the end of their clauses. They also are translatable into English as single verbs. (Such nouns, however, are capitalized and never written together with the verbs.)

Sein Vorschlag fand unter seinen Freunden Anklang.
His suggestion was adopted (struck a responsive note) among his friends.

Cf. **zur Sprache bringen** 'discuss.'
   Man brachte seinen Vorschlag sofort zur Sprache.
      His suggestion was discussed at once.
Cf. also: **in Erinnerung haben** 'remember.'
   Einfluß haben 'influence.'

7.3 In main clauses in the present or past tense, separable prefixes stand at the end of the clause.
   Wir stehen jeden Tag um halb sieben auf.
      We get up every day at 6:30.

In subordinate clauses, the whole compound stands at the end of the clause and is written as one word:

Sie wissen doch, daß wir jeden Tag um halb sieben aufstehen.

You know, of course, that we get up every day at 6:30.

7.3,1 zu stands between the separable prefix and the infinitive in constructions that require it: **anzusehen, haltzumachen, kennenzulernen.** But it stands before inseparable verbs: **zu besehen.** Contrast:

Ich wünsche mir die Stadt anzusehen.
Ich versuche, sie heute zu besuchen.

7.4 Adjective suffixes. German, like English, has a variety of adjective suffixes. It is difficult to predict which suffix will be used to make adjectives from a specific noun or verb. Learning the suffixes, and observing words in which they occur, will, however, help in determining the meanings of new adjectives. English suffixes that resemble the German in meaning are listed below. Note that compounds are generally made with the *verb stem* alone, but with the entire *noun*.

7.4,1 Suffixes with the meaning of English *-able*, *-ible*, and *-ful*:

-bar :	**essen**	eat	**eßbar**	edible
	Furcht	fear	**furchtbar**	frightful
-haft(ig) :	**dauern**	last	**dauerhaft**	durable
	Vorteil	advantage	**vorteilhaft**	advantageous
	wahr	true	**wahrhaftig**	truthful

7.4,2 Suffixes used primarily to form adjectives from nouns (*cf.* *-y* and *-ly*):

-ig :	**Schuld**	guilt	**schuldig**	guilty
	Trauer	sadness	**traurig**	sad
-lich :	**Ende**	end	**endlich**	finally
	Freund	friend	**freundlich**	friendly
	sterben	die	**sterblich**	mortal

These adjectives are often used as stems for nouns ending in -heit and -keit:

Traurigkeit sadness **Freundlichkeit** friendliness

7.4,3 Suffixes with the meaning "characteristic of", or *-like* (*cf. -ish*):

-isch : **Kind** child **kindisch** childlike,childish
Krieger warrior **kriegerisch** warlike

-isch is also used to make adjectives denoting languages or nationalities:

	England	England	**englisch**	English
	Italien	Italy	**italienisch**	Italian
-mäßig :	**Regel**	rule	**regelmäßig**	regular
-sam :	**sparen**	save	**sparsam**	frugal

7.4,4 Suffixes with the meaning 'having' (*cf. -ful*) and 'not having' (*-less*):

-voll : **Bedeutung** meaning **bedeutungsvoll** meaningful
Geschmack taste **geschmackvoll** tasteful
-los: **bedeutungslos** meaningless **geschmacklos** tasteless

7.4,5 un-, like English *un-*, *in-*, and *non-*, is used to make the negatives of many of these adjectives:

unschuldig innocent
ungehorsam disobedient

7.5 Expressions for "time." The English word time covers a range of meanings for which German uses three different terms:

1. **die Zeit** is used for time in general:

Ich habe jetzt keine Zeit. I have no time now.
Als die Zeit der Ferien herankam,...
When vacation time came around...

2. **die Uhr** is used for telling time:

Wie viel Uhr ist es? What time is it?
Um wie viel Uhr ißt er? At what time does he eat?

3. **das Mal** refers to a specific occurrence in a sequence:

Das erste Mal, als ich ihn sah, fuhr er auf der Landstraße.
The first time I saw him he was driving on the highway.

In arithmetic, **mal** is used for English 'times.' [*See Appendix* 5.4] In combination with numerals, **das Mal** is written together with the numeral and not capitalized: **einmal, zweimal** 'once, twice.'

einmal (mal) is used idiomatically in the meanings 'once, just, sometime':

Meine Frau will, daß ich einmal nach Hause komme.
My wife wants me to come home for once (sometime).
Hören Sie mal! Just listen!

NARRATIVE

Die strenge Begleiterin

Als sie nach draußen traten, hoffte Gerald den eleganten Sportwagen wiederzusehen, den er noch so deutlich in Erinnerung hatte. Aber seine Begleiterin ging rasch auf einen alten grauen Wagen zu, der weiter unten an der Straße stand. ‚Dann ist sie es also doch nicht,' dachte er bei sich [to himself]. 5

Während der Fahrt kamen sie bald ins Gespräch. Gerald fand heraus, daß sie Margaret Brockhaus hieß, daß sie vor etwas mehr als einem halben Jahr aus Deutschland gekommen war und Verwandte in San Franzisko besaß, die ihr die Stellung im Büro verschafft hatten. „Wie gefällt Ihnen dieses Land?" 10 fragte er freundlich. „Ausgezeichnet, natürlich," gab sie ihm lachend zur Antwort. „Aber darf ich ganz offen sein? Warum nimmt man sich hier nicht etwas mehr Zeit zum Leben? Es geht alles so furchtbar schnell! Und dann die Verschwendung! Mit dem, was hier täglich verschwendet wird, kann man drüben 15 ein ganzes Land ernähren [feed]!"

Gerald sah sie von der Seite an. Er wußte nicht recht, was er darauf antworten sollte. Warum hatte sie das sagen müssen? Er konnte sie nicht verstehen. Nun gab es eine Wand zwischen

20 ihnen, die nicht so leicht zu durchbrechen [?] war. Das tat
ihm leid. Er konnte nicht jeden Tag neben einem so hübschen
Mädchen sitzen, die Klugheit und Energie so angenehm zu
verbinden wußte [knew how to combine]. Wie sicher sie durch
den Verkehr fuhr, und wie geduldig der Wagen dem leichten
25 Druck ihrer Hand zu folgen schien! Warum sollte er so schnell
in das Sägewerk zurückkehren, wo er doch nur ein ganz kleines
Rad in einer großen Maschine war? Gab es irgendeinen
Grund, weshalb er heute nicht die Freiheit noch etwas genießen
sollte? Daher konnte er dem Wunsch nicht widerstehen und
30 fragte: ,,Haben Sie wohl einen Augenblick frei zu einer Tasse
Kaffee? Wir können uns da noch etwas unterhalten, nicht
wahr? Das wäre wirklich sehr nett!"

Sein Vorschlag fand bei ihr Anklang [struck a responsive
note]. Fünf Minuten später saßen sie in einem Café. Gerald
35 hatte ein Geldstück [?] in den Spielapparat [juke-box] geworfen,
und wilde Töne kreischten [shrieked] durch den Raum.
Margaret sah ihn etwas zweifelnd an. ,,Muß das sein?
Wollten wir uns nicht unterhalten?" — Merkwürdig: Alles
was sie sagte, klang so streng und kalt. War sie vielleicht nie
40 recht glücklich gewesen? — ,,O," sagte Gerald schnell, ,,haben
Sie den neuesten Schlager [hit tune] schon gehört? Ich hatte
gehofft, er würde Ihnen vielleicht Spaß machen." — Die Platte
lief ab, aber Gerald warf kein zweites Geldstück in die Maschine.

Denn inzwischen hatten sie angefangen, von ihrem eigenen
45 Leben zu sprechen. ,,Was tun Sie eigentlich?" hatte sie ihn
gefragt. ,,Denn ich nehme an, daß Sie hier nur während der
Ferien arbeiten." Nun war Gerald glücklich, denn dies gab
ihm Gelegenheit, von seinen Autofahrten [?] zu erzählen. ,,Sie
können sich gar nicht vorstellen, wie gut ich das Land kennen-
50 lerne," sagte er. ,,Ich mag nicht herumsitzen, wie all die
anderen, die das ganze Jahr immer nur Bücher lesen." Aber
da wurde er von Margaret unterbrochen: ,,Verzeihen Sie, wenn
ich Sie etwas frage. Wie alt sind Sie eigentlich?" Und als
Gerald ihr sein Alter nannte, fuhr sie strenge fort: ,,Denken
55 Sie gar nicht an ernstere Dinge, als wie Sie andere Menschen

auf der Landstraße überholen können? An Ihrer Stelle würde
ich versuchen, sie in ihrer Arbeit zu überholen. Daher scheinen
mir Ihre Fahrten enorme Zeit- und Materialverschwendung zu
sein! — Doch es wird spät, und ich weiß, man wartet auf mich."

Als sie ihn vor seiner Wohnung aus dem Wagen ließ, lächelte 60
sie freundlich. „Nehmen Sie mir nicht übel, was ich gesagt
habe. Es hat mich gefreut, Sie erzählen zu hören. Hoffentlich
sehen wir uns bald einmal wieder!"

Gerald ging langsam in sein Zimmer. ‚Warum habe ich
immer nur von mir selbst gesprochen?' dachte er bei sich. 65
‚Jetzt weiß ich immer noch nicht, wer sie wirklich ist.'

Questions

1. Was hatte Gerald noch deutlich in Erinnerung?
2. Was stand weiter unten an der Straße?
3. Wer hatte Margaret die Stellung im Büro verschafft?
4. Was gefiel dem Mädchen in Amerika nicht?
5. Was tat Gerald leid?
6. Was für eine Autofahrerin war Margaret?
7. Warum lud Gerald das Mädchen zu einer Tasse Kaffee ein?
8. Was tat Gerald, als sie ins Café eintraten?
9. Warum warf er kein zweites Geldstück in die Maschine?
10. Warum war Margaret so streng?
11. Worüber war Gerald glücklich?
12. Was wollte Margaret wissen?
13. Was hielt sie für große Zeit- und Materialverschwendung?
14. Welchen Wunsch sprach sie schließlich aus?
15. Was wußte Gerald zuletzt immer noch nicht?

Vocabulary

die Antwort, -en answer
zur Antwort geben answer
ausgezeichnet excellent

begegnen (ist) [*dat.*]   meet; happen
die Begleiterin, -nen   companion
besitzen (-saß, -sessen)   possess
der Brennstoff, -e   fuel
deutlich   clear
der Druck   pressure
erfahren (u, a, ä)   learn, experience, find out
genießen (-noß, -nossen)   enjoy
das Gespräch, -e   conversation; ins Gespräch kommen
  get into a conversation
hoffentlich   (I) hope
keineswegs   by no means
die Leistung, -en   achievement
merkwürdig   strange, remarkable
offen   frank
die Platte, -n   phonograph record
das Rad, ⁀er   wheel
stehen-bleiben (ie, ist ie)   stop
streng(e)   strict, stern
täglich   daily
die Tasse, -n   cup
der Ton, ⁀e   tone
ungefähr   approximately, about
unten   below
die Verschwendung, -en   waste
verzeihen (ie, ie) [*dat.*]   forgive
der Vorschlag, ⁀e   suggestion
die Wand, ⁀e   wall
widerstehen (-stand, -standen) [*dat.*]   resist

Idioms

Macht das Ihnen Spaß?   Are you enjoying it?
Nehmen Sie es mir nicht übel!   Don't take offense!

Ein gutes Gewissen

Alfred Nobel, der Erfinder des Dynamits, hatte kurz vor seinem Tode einen schweren Traum. Am nächsten Morgen fragte ihn ein Freund:

„Warum so blaß, Herr Nobel? Sie sehen aus, als ob Sie Geister gesehen hätten."

„Ja," sagte Nobel, „ich möchte das nicht ein zweites Mal erleben. Mir hat nämlich geträumt, ich wäre in den Grand Canyon gestürzt. Es war mir, als fiele ich viele Meilen tief und könnte keinen Grund erreichen. Es gab nichts, woran ich mich hätte halten können. Hätte ich nur gewußt, daß es ein Traum war! Da klang eine dunkle Stimme aus der Tiefe: ‚Was hülfe es dem Menschen, wenn er die ganze Welt gewönne und nähme Schaden an seiner Seele.‘ Das hätten Sie hören sollen! Es war fürchterlich." —

In seinem letzten Willen las man, daß jedes Jahr fünf Menschen, die der Menschheit am meisten gedient hätten, aus Nobels Millionen einen Preis bekommen sollten. Seit 1901

77

gibt es einen Nobelpreis in Physik, Chemie, Medizin, Literatur
und — im Dienste des Friedens.

       blaß   pale
***der Dienst**   service
 der Erfinder   inventor
    ***erleben**   experience
    ***erreichen**   reach
***der Friede**   peace
     fürchterlich   terrible
 das Gewissen·   conscience
***der Grund**   bottom
***der Schaden**   harm, injury; **Schaden nehmen**   suffer
    injury
     schwer   bad
     stürzen   fall headlong
  die Tiefe   depth(s)
***der Tod**   death
***der Wille**   will

EXERCISES

A. Rewrite the given German sentences in the Subjunctive II
according to the forms suggested in English.

   Example: **Wir haben einen neuen Wagen.**

1. if we had   **wenn wir einen neuen Wagen hätten.**
2. as if they had   **als ob sie einen neuen Wagen hätten.**
3. they would have   **sie würden einen neuen Wagen haben.**
4. had they   **hätten sie einen neuen Wagen.**

   1. Present tense:

      A. **Er hat einen Ausweg.**

         1. if he had   3. they would have
         2. as if they had   4. had I

B. **Es gibt gar nichts.**

    1. if there were   3. there would be
    2. as if there were   4. were there

C. **Er verliert die Ruhe.**

    1. if he lost   3. she would lose
    2. as if they lost   4. were they to lose

D. **Wir laufen schnell.**

    1. if he ran   3. he would drive
    2. as if they were running   4. were we to go

E. **Ich kann es auch machen.**

    1. if we ought to   3. they should
    2. as if she could   4. were he allowed

2. Past tense:

A. **Wir fielen aus dem Bett.**

    1. if she had fallen   3. we would have fallen
    2. as if we had fallen   4. had he fallen

B. **Ich bin schon einmal da gewesen.**

    1. if they had been   3. we would have been
    2. as if we had been   4. had he been

C. **Er sah Geister.**

    1. if they had heard   3. he would have heard
    2. as if you had seen   4. had I met

D. **Ich habe es oft erlebt.**

    1. if I'd seen   3. she would have used
    2. as if you had seen   4. had we told

E. **Er hat es erzählen können.**

    1. if she had been able to   3. had we been allowed to
    2. as if they had had to

B. Following the patterns, give German equivalents for the English sentences.   Word order will be exactly the same as in the pattern sentences.

1. **Sie sehen aus, als ob Sie Geister gesehen hätten.**
   A. She acted [**tun**] as if she had forgotten him.
   B. It seemed as if he had been waiting a long time.
   C. They acted as though they had been friends.

2. **Hätte ich es gewußt, so würde ich keine Angst gehabt haben.**
   A. If he'd been in your place, he would have tried it.
   B. If they had asked us we would have done it.
   C. She'd have forgiven him if she had found it out [**erfahren**].

3. **Wenn es nur einen Ausweg gäbe!**
   A. If only I knew her name!
   B. If only he owned a car!
   C. If there were only more time!

4. **Wenn ich diese Stimme hörte, würde ich auch so aussehen.**
   A. If people took their [**sich**] time they would also live more comfortably.
   B. She would stay in America too if she had enough money.
   C. If he had the opportunity he would go there too.

5. **Dies hätte eine glückliche Stunde für ihn sein können.**
   A. That should have been an easy task for us.
   B. We should have discovered that without (any) trouble.
   C. He would have visited her yesterday.

C. Add appropriate conclusions to these statements of unreal condition.   Express the conclusions in two ways.

Example: Wenn das Leben hier nicht so teuer wäre, . . .
   . . . **würde** es mir hier viel besser **gefallen.**
   . . . **gefiele** es mir hier viel besser.

1. Wenn Gerald ein zweites Geldstück in die Maschine geworfen hätte, . . .
2. Wäre Hildebrand in Deutschland geblieben, . . .
3. Wenn ich an Geralds Stelle wäre, . . .
4. Wenn er im Krankenhaus bleiben müßte, . . .
5. Wenn er selbst die Rechnung bezahlt hätte, . . .
6. Wenn ich Verwandte hierzulande hätte, . . .
7. Wäre er nicht so schnell gefahren, . . .

GRAMMAR

8 The subjunctive mood. The German verb system, like the English, has two sets of verb forms called "moods": these are the *indicative mood* and the *subjunctive mood.* The indicative is used to express facts or positively stated opinions. The subjunctive is used to express doubt, indefiniteness, politeness, conditions contrary to fact, and so on. [*See Appendix 6.2.*]

8.1 Whereas the indicative has six tenses, the subjunctive has only four: present, past (the latter corresponding to the indicative past, present perfect, and past perfect), future, and future perfect. Each of these tenses has two sets of forms, which we call subjunctive I (primary) and subjunctive II (secondary).

The endings of the subjunctive are completely regular, except for the one form **sei.** They are:

ich/er,sie,es	-e	**wir/Sie/sie**	-en
du	-est	**ihr**	-et

8.2 Subjunctive I forms are made from the present stems of verbs (and in the compound tenses, of auxiliaries). Examples are:

Present subjunctive I:

ich/er	**mache**	**habe**	**gehe**	**werde**	**sei**
du	**machest**	**habest**	**gehest**	**werdest**	**seiest**
wir/Sie/sie	**machen**	**haben**	**gehen**	**werden**	**seien**
ihr	**machet**	**habet**	**gehet**	**werdet**	**seiet**

Past subjunctive I :

**ich habe gemacht/gehabt   ich sei gegangen/geworden/
gewesen**

Future subjunctive I :

wir werden machen/haben/gehen/werden/sein

Future Perfect subjunctive I :

**sie werden gemacht (gehabt) haben
sie werden gegangen (geworden, gewesen) sein**

8.3 Subjunctive II forms are made from the past stems of verbs (and in the compound tenses, of auxiliaries).   Strong verbs with **a, o,** or **u,** as a stem vowel modify it **(gäbe, zöge, würde),** as do **brächte, dächte, hätte, wüßte, dürfte, könnte, möchte, müßte.**   In verbs like **kennen** the stem vowel is written **e : brennte, kennte, nennte, rennte, sendete, wendete.**   Note the forms for **helfen, sterben, gewinnen : hülfe, stürbe, gewönne,** and for **stehen : stünde,** or **stände.**

Examples are:

Present subjunctive II :

ich/er	machte	hätte	ginge	würde	wäre
du	machtest	hättest	gingest	würdest	wärest
wir/Sie/sie	machten	hätten	gingen	würden	wären
ihr	machtet	hättet	ginget	würdet	wäret

Past subjunctive II :

**ich hätte gemacht/gehabt   ich wäre gegangen/geworden/
gewesen**

Future subjunctive II :

wir würden/machen/haben/gehen/werden/sein

Future Perfect subjunctive II :

**sie würden gemacht (gehabt) haben
sie würden gegangen (geworden, gewesen) sein.**

8.4 Uses of subjunctive II forms. The subjunctive II forms are used primarily in situations of uncertainty or to express conditions contrary to fact. The past-tense and past-perfect forms used in English in similar situations reflect the same usage: "If you *went* with us now, you could save a trip." "If I *had* the time, I'd go." And in past time: "If I *had* only *gone* along with you, I'd have my books now." "If you *had* only *listened* to me!" German differs from English, however, in that the present and past subjunctive II forms may also be used in the conclusion.

8.4,1 Conditions contrary to fact.

Present time: **Wenn ich das Geld hätte, gäbe ich es Ihnen.**
      or . . . **würde ich es Ihnen geben.**
      If I had the money, I would give it to you.
      Wenn ich an Ihrer Stelle wäre, verkaufte ich den alten Wagen.
      or . . . **würde ich den alten Wagen verkaufen.**
      If I were in your shoes, I would sell the old car.

Past time: **Wenn sie die Gelegenheit gehabt hätte, hätte sie es Ihnen gegeben.**
      or . . . **würde sie es Ihnen gegeben haben.**
      If she had had the opportunity, she would have given it to you.
      Wenn wir länger dort geblieben wären, wären wir verrückt geworden.
      or . . . **würden wir verrückt geworden sein.**
      If we had stayed there any longer, we would have gone crazy.

The subjunctive forms used may be summarized thus :

Time	if-*Clause*	*Conclusion*
Present	Present II	Present II or Future II
Past	Past II	Past II or Future Perfect II

8.4,2 Wishes of which the fulfillment is impossible or unlikely. These can be thought of as the *if*-clauses of conditional sentences in which the conclusion is not given, *e.g.*,

Wenn ich das nur gestern gewußt hätte!

If I had only known that yesterday!

Present time: **Wenn ich nur wüßte, daß es ein Traum war!**

If I only knew that it was a dream!

Past time: **Wenn ich nur gewußt hätte, daß es ein Traum war!**

If I had only known that it was a dream!

Nur or **bloß** is usually the cue to this construction.

8.4,3 Simple statements of which the fulfillment is unlikely or impossible. These can be thought of as the conclusions of conditional sentences in which the *if*-clause is not stated, *e.g.*, **Dies hätte eine glückliche Stunde für ihn sein können (wenn sie jene Worte nicht gesprochen hätte).**

This could have been an hour of happiness for him, if she had not said those words.

Mit dem, was hier täglich verschwendet wird, könnte man drüben ein ganzes Land ernähren.

With that (amount) which is wasted here every day one could feed an entire country over there.

8.4,4 Polite requests:

Dürfte ich um die Butter bitten?

Might I trouble you for the butter?

Hätten Sie einen Augenblick Zeit?

Would you have a minute?

8.4,5 als ob/als wenn clauses: In these, subjunctive II forms are usual, but subjunctive I forms may also be used.

Sie sehen aus, als ob Sie Geister gesehen hätten.

You look as if you had seen a ghost.

Er fuhr fort, als wenn er zu sich selber spräche (spreche).

He continued as if he were speaking to himself.

When **als** alone is used to mean 'as if,' the finite verb stands right after it.

Mir war, als fiele ich viele Meilen tief.
I felt as if I were falling miles and miles.

8.5 Word order in conditional sentences.

8.5,1 When the *if*-clause is introduced by **wenn,** the order is that of any complete sentence:

Ich würde besser schlafen, wenn ich nicht solche Träume hätte.
I would sleep better if I didn't have such dreams.

When the *if*-clause comes first, the order is again that of a simple sentence, but **so** or **dann** may stand before the finite verb of the main clause:

Wenn man sich mehr Zeit zum Leben nähme, (so) würde mir dieses Land besser gefallen.
If people would take more time to live, I'd like this country better.

When the *if*-clause precedes the main clause, the conjunction may be omitted. The verb then stands first in the subordinate clause, and the main clause is introduced by **so** or **dann.** Compare the literary English translation:

Hätte ich das gewußt, dann hätte ich mich nicht so gefürchtet.
Had I only known that, I wouldn't have been so afraid.

8.5,2 Wishes can also be expressed without **wenn,** but then they are usually accompanied by **nur** or **bloß :**

Hätte ich das nur gewußt! If I had only known that!
Cf. 'Had I but known!'

8.6 Use of **tun** and **machen.** The German verbs **tun** and **machen** are often the equivalent of their English cognates,

'do' and 'make.' However, **tun** is used when a specific activity
is thought of:

> **Was tut unser Patient auf Nummer 21?**
> What's our patient in room 21 doing?
> **Was gibt es in dieser Stadt zu tun?**
> What's there to do in in this town?

machen, which must sometimes be rendered by 'do,' is used:

A. when the status of the subject is involved:

> **Was macht unser Patient auf Nummer 21?**
> How is our patient in room 21 doing?

B. when a general activity is referred to:

> **Da läßt sich eben nichts anderes machen.**
> Nothing else can be done then.

C. in the sense of 'produce' or 'manufacture':

> **In Wolfsburg macht man Volkswagen, in Solingen macht
> man Messer.**
> In Wolfsburg they manufacture Volkswagens; in Solingen, they
> manufacture knives.

NARRATIVE

Frieden und Wohlstand

Herr und Frau Hunter waren früher als gewöhnlich von
ihren Sommerferien in Maine zurückgekehrt. Zwar wäre keine
besondere Eile nötig gewesen, denn sie hätten noch weitere
vierzehn Tage in der Stille [?] am See verbringen können —
5 fischend und schlafend und das Gespräch der Nachbarn
genießend. Aber dann hatten sie eine Nachricht erhalten, die
sie etwas beunruhigte. Das Geschäft von Herrn Hunter in
der Stadt war durch ein Feuer beschädigt worden, und der
Verlust wäre beträchtlich [considerable] gewesen, wenn der
10 Schaden nicht durch Versicherung gedeckt gewesen wäre.
Abends saßen sie schweigend auf der Veranda. Der Lärm

der Grillen [cricket] füllte [?] die Sommerluft [?]. Es war, als
ob ein Meer von Tönen durch die Bäume käme. Das Wasser der
Sprenganlage [sprinkler system] rauschte leise durch die Dunkelheit [?]. Wenn es nur einmal wieder regnen wollte! Dann 15
würde auch der Rasen gewiß wieder grün werden. Von Zeit
zu Zeit kreischten die Reifen eines Autos um die nächste
Straßenecke, und einmal läutete das Telefon: ob dies das Büro
eines Steuerberaters [tax consultant] wäre?

Herr Hunter hatte die Zeitung aus der Hand gelegt. Es 20
stand wirklich nicht viel Neues darin. Die Kurse [quotations
or prices] an der Neuyorker Aktienbörse [stock exchange] waren
etwas heruntergegangen. Wäre ein wenig mehr gehandelt
worden, dann hätten sie sich besser gehalten. Es gab wirklich
keinen Grund zur Beunruhigung; war doch überhaupt vor den 25
Wahlen kein großer Umsatz [turnover] auf dem Aktienmarkte
zu erwarten. Ein Senator ließ bekannt geben, daß er im
kommenden Wahlkampfe nur die reinsten Waffen gebrauchen
werde. In Galiläa hatte es wieder einmal Vorpostenkämpfe
gegeben; aber man hoffte, daß eine größere Krise [?] vermieden 30
werden könne.

Herr Hunter gähnte. Wo in aller Welt war Galiläa? Er
sagte zu seiner Frau: „Betty, sei doch so gut und rufe die
Griffiths an! Vielleicht hätten sie Lust zu einer Partie [game]
Karten. Und wenn ihre Tochter zu Hause ist, soll sie nur 35
mitkommen. Sie kann ja fernsehen [?], wenn sie nichts anderes
zu tun hat."

Frau Hunter kam wieder zurück: Nein, die Griffiths waren
immer noch auf Ferien. Herr Hunter gähnte wieder und sah
auf die Uhr. Es war zu früh, um schlafen zu gehen, und zu 40
spät, eines der Lichtspieltheater in der Stadt zu besuchen. Was
sollten sie tun? Es war kein schönes Gefühl, so allein zu sein.
Wenn Alice noch hier wäre, dann brächten ihre Freunde und
Freundinnen gewiß frisches [?] Leben ins Haus. Aber ihre
Tochter war seit zwei Jahren verheiratet und hatte ihre eigene 45
Familie. Und Gerald — ja, wer konnte sagen, was der Bursche
[boy] jetzt tat.

Nach einer Weile sagte Frau Hunter: „Liebster, glaubst du nicht, wir sollten wieder einmal an Jerry schreiben? Wir
50 haben schon lange nichts mehr von ihm gehört, und seit er fort ist, hat er uns noch kein einziges Mal um Geld gebeten."

Herr Hunter nickte und sagte: „Gut! Das wäre sehr nett. Schaden kann es ja nicht." Und dann gingen sie ins Haus und schrieben. Die Mutter erzählte, wie schön es in Maine
55 gewesen sei, wie sie fast täglich die Jones und die Philbricks und die Griffiths gesehen hätten, wie Papa einen zehn-pfündigen [?] Barsch [bass] aus dem See gezogen habe, und wie sie zwei Wochen länger hätten bleiben können, wenn es nicht im Geschäft gebrannt hätte. Und der Vater schrieb, wie
60 heiß und still es zu Hause sei, wie der Rasen vertrocknen würde, wenn es nicht bald Regen gäbe, wie die Aktien im Kurse gefallen und wie in Galiläa geschossen worden sei. Er schloß seinen Brief: „Ja, es ist ein Segen, daß Frieden und Wohlstand in der Welt herrschen, und wenn wir jetzt nicht alle fleißig
65 weiter arbeiteten, dann würden uns Frieden und Wohlstand wohl kaum erhalten bleiben."

Dann schlug es zehn Uhr. Herr Hunter drehte die Spreng-anlage ab, und die beiden alten Leute gingen zur Ruhe. Und die Grillen lärmten [?].

Questions

1. Was hatten Herr und Frau Hunter während der Ferien getan?
2. Welche Nachricht hatte sie beunruhigt?
3. Was hörten sie, als sie auf der Veranda saßen?
4. Worin hatte Herr Hunter gelesen?
5. Warum waren die Kurse an der Börse heruntergegangen?
6. Was war vor den Wahlen nicht zu erwarten?
7. Wo hoffte man eine größere Krise zu vermeiden?
8. Warum sollte Frau Hunter die Griffiths anrufen?
9. Warum wünschte Herr Hunter, daß Alice noch bei ihnen wohnte?

10. Was hatte Gerald seit seiner Fahrt nach Kalifornien nicht getan?
11. Welchen Erfolg hatte Herr Hunter beim Fischen gehabt?
12. Was schrieb Herr Hunter über die Arbeit?
13. Wann ging Herr Hunter schlafen?

Vocabulary

bekannt-geben (a, e, i) make known
beschädigen damage
beunruhigen disturb
blaß pale
decken cover
der **Dienst, -e** service
die **Eile** hurry
der **Frieden, -s** peace
erleben experience
erreichen reach, get to
füllen fill
gähnen yawn
der **Grund, ̈e** bottom; reason, cause
der **Lärm** noise
läuten ring
das **Lichtspieltheater, –** movie
das **Meer, -e** sea, ocean
die **Menschheit** humanity
die **Nachricht, -en** news, report
nötig necessary
der **Rasen, –** grass, lawn
der **Reifen, –** tire
rauschen rustle
rein pure
der **Schaden, ̈** harm, injury; **Schaden nehmen** suffer injury
täglich daily

der Tod death
    vermeiden, (ie, ie) avoid
    vertrocknen dry
die Waffe, -n weapon
die Wahl, -en election, choice
der Wille will
der Wohlstand prosperity

Idiom

Er hat keine Lust dazu He has no desire to (for it)

Lesson 9

USES OF SUBJUNCTIVE IN INDIRECT DISCOURSE

INDIRECT QUESTIONS

INDIRECT COMMANDS

Fliegende Untertassen

Im Jahre 1947 berichtete ein privater Flieger, er sei auf einem Fluge über die Wälder im Nordwesten mehreren unbekannten Objekten begegnet, deren Ursprung er sich nicht erklären könne. Diese Objekte hätten wie Scheiben oder Zigarren ausgesehen, seien mit enormer Geschwindigkeit geflogen und hätten mehrfach ihre Flugrichtung in einem rechten Winkel geändert.

Auf die Frage, ob er sie nicht im Radio angerufen habe, sagte er, sie seien aufgeflogen und in nordwestlicher Richtung verschwunden.

Seitdem sind viele solche Berichte in den Zeitungen erschienen. Dazu ist zu sagen, daß Objekte dieser Art uns unbekannt sind und jeder menschlichen Erfahrung und Vernunft widersprechen. Glauben wir daher nicht an diesen Unsinn!

       *die Art   sort, kind
       der Flug   flight

> **mehrfach** often
> *__menschlich__ human
> **die Scheibe** disc
> *__der Unsinn__ nonsense
> **die Untertasse** saucer
> *__der Ursprung__ origin
> *__die Vernunft__ reason
> *__widersprechen__ contradict
> **der Winkel** angle

EXERCISES

A. Use of subjunctive I.

1. If the present subjunctive I (3d person sing.) of **nehmen** is **nehme,** what are the corresponding forms for:

   geben   erscheinen   mit-nehmen
   lesen   verlassen   ab-fahren

2. If the present subjunctive I (2d person sing.) of **haben** is **habest,** what are the corresponding forms for:

   hören   besuchen   (sich) aus-ruhen
   kennen   verführen   (sich) hinüber-lehnen

3. If the present subjunctive I (3d person sing.) of **können** is **könne,** what are the corresponding forms for:

   müssen   mögen   sollen
   dürfen   wollen   wissen

4. If the present subjunctive I (3d person sing.) of **antworten** is **antworte,** what are the corresponding forms for:

   warten   berichten   an-halten
   arbeiten   begegnen   zu-wenden

5. If the subjunctive I (3d person sing.) of **sammeln** is **sammele,** what are the corresponding forms for:

   lächeln   rudern   erinnern
   wundern   verwandeln   entwickeln

6. If the past subjunctive I (3d person pl.) of **sein** is **seien gewesen,** what are the corresponding forms for:

    laufen   erscheinen   ein-schlafen
    reisen   verschwinden   nach-folgen

7. If the past subjunctive I (2d person sing.) of **machen** is **habest gemacht,** what are the corresponding forms for:

    antworten   erreichen   aus-sehen
    sprechen   gewinnen   an-schließen

B. Change the direct quotations below into indirect quotations. Be sure to keep the same tense and to make the necessary pronoun changes. Translate.

1. A. Sie hatte ihn gefragt: „Was tust du denn eigentlich?"
   B. Er fragte sie: „Was gibt es in dieser verlassenen Stadt zu tun?"
   C. Wir fragten nur: „Was erwarten sie davon?"

2. A. Dann sagte er: „Ich habe wirklich nicht immer von mir selbst gesprochen."
   B. Später erklärte sie: „Ich habe auch einmal Verwandte in San Franzisko gehabt."
   C. Nachher hatte man behauptet: „Der Wagen stand draußen vor der Tür."

3. A. Dann fragte sie ihn: „Muß das wirklich sein?"
   B. Warum fragtest du mich: „Kannst du das verstehen?"
   C. Er hat mich gefragt: „Läßt sich das wirklich machen?"

4. A. Ich sagte zu ihm: „Versuch' es noch einmal!"
   B. Er schrieb uns: „Nehmen Sie sich mehr Zeit zum Leben!"
   C. Sie antworteten: „Besuchen Sie uns bald wieder!"

5. A. Sie sagte: „Das Leben in Amerika wird mir recht gut gefallen."
   B. Wir behaupteten: „Ihm wird das nie gelingen."

6. A. Er dachte: „Ich habe schon lange keinen Brief an meine Eltern geschrieben."

   B. Sie erklärte: „Ich bin oft dagewesen."

   C. Ich antwortete: „Er hat nichts davon gewußt."

C. Following the pattern, give German equivalents for the English sentences.

1. **Der Flieger berichtete, er sei unbekannten Objekten begegnet.**
   A. People were saying he saw ghosts.
   B. The reports explained that it had never happened before.
   C. The radio reported that they disappeared at once.

2. **Er sagte, daß er ihren Ursprung nicht erklären könne.**
   A. We claimed that one shouldn't repeat such reports.
   B. She said he didn't want to see that film.
   C. I explained that you couldn't expect a payment.

3. **Man fragte ihn, ob er sie im Radio angerufen habe.**
   A. She was asked if she had found happiness in America.
   B. I asked him if he had seen it in the northwest.
   C. They asked us whether we recognized these objects in the (*am*) sky.

4. **Glauben wir nicht an solchen Unsinn!**
   A. Let's not think of things like that.
   B. Let's not go home yet.
   C. Let's not write to that address.

5. **Man sei nur vernünftig!**
   A. Just live happily!
   B. Only stand fast!
   C. Just don't laugh!

6. **Man sagte ihm, er solle das Radio abstellen.**
   A. Her husband told her to arrive on the sixteenth.
   B. I said they should enjoy life.
   C. His father told him to stay at home.

GRAMMAR

9 Indirect discourse; uses of the subjunctive.

9.1 When statements or conversations are reported, rather than quoted, their original form is modified. When a man would be quoted as saying directly "I'll come," the report of his statement would be formulated "he said that he would come." In German, the verb of the reported statement is in the subjunctive. The subjunctive always indicates uncertainty. It must not be used after verbs expressing certainty, like **wissen,** or in reporting one's own statements.

9.2 In indirect quotation, either the subjunctive I or II can be used. II forms are used whenever the subjunctive I forms are identical with the indicative; *e.g.*, **ich ginge** is preferred to **ich gehe.** On the other hand, the subjunctive I is often the distinctive form for the third person; **er mache: er̓ machte.**

9.3 Use of tenses. In indirect quotations, the *present subjunctive I* or *II* is used if the corresponding direct statement is in the present tense. The tense of the verb of reporting does not affect the choice of forms for the reported statement: **Das Objekt sieht wie eine Scheibe aus.**

Er behauptet, das Objekt sehe (sähe) wie eine Scheibe aus.
   He claims that the object looks like a disc.
Er behauptete, das Objekt sehe (sähe) wie eine Scheibe aus.
Er hat behauptet, das Objekt sehe (sähe) wie eine Scheibe aus.
   He claimed that the object looked like a disc.
Er wird behaupten, das Objekt sehe (sähe) wie eine Scheibe aus.
   He'll claim that the object looks like a disc.

9.3,1 The *past subjunctive I* or *II* is used when the verb of the original quotation is a past tense (past, perfect, or past perfect):

Das Objekt sah wie eine Scheibe aus.

> **... hat ...**   **ausgesehen.**
> **... hatte ...**   **ausgesehen.**

Er behauptet, das Objekt habe (hätte) wie eine Scheibe ausgesehen.

He claims that the object looked like a disc.

Er behauptete, das Objekt habe (hätte) wie eine Scheibe ausgesehen.

Er hat behauptet, das Objekt habe (hätte) wie eine Scheibe ausgesehen.

He claimed that the object looked (had looked) like a disc.

Er wird behaupten, das Objekt habe (hätte) wie eine Scheibe ausgesehen.

He'll claim that the object looked like a disc.

9.3,2 The *future subjunctive I* or *II* is used when the verb of the original statement is in the future tense: **Der Bericht wird morgen in der Zeitung stehen.**

Er behauptet, der Bericht werde (würde) morgen in der Zeitung stehen.

He claims that the report will be in the paper tomorrow.

Er behauptete, der Bericht werde (würde) morgen in der Zeitung stehen.

Er hat behauptet, der Bericht werde (würde) morgen in der Zeitung stehen.

He claimed that the report would be in the paper tomorrow.

Er wird behaupten, der Bericht werde (würde) morgen in der Zeitung stehen.

He'll claim that the report will be in the paper tomorrow.

9.4 Indirect statements introduced by **daß** have subordinate word order. If **daß** is not used, the order is that of a main clause: **Die Objekte sind mit ungeheurer Geschwindigkeit geflogen.**

Er berichtete, die Objekte seien (wären) mit ungeheurer
    Geschwindigkeit geflogen.
Er berichtete, daß die Objekte mit ungeheurer
    Geschwindigkeit geflogen seien (wären).
He reported (that) the objects had flown at tremendous speed.

9.5 Indirect Questions reported in indirect discourse
are introduced by the interrogative word of the direct question:

    ,,Wann haben Sie die Objekte gesehen?"
    When did you see the objects?
    Man fragte, wann er die Objekte gesehen habe.
    They asked when he had seen the objects.

    If the direct question begins with a verb, **ob** introduces the
indirect question:

    ,,Haben Sie sie im Radio angerufen?"
    Did you call them over the radio?
    Man fragte, ob er sie im Radio angerufen habe.
    They asked whether he had called them over the radio.

9.6 Indirect commands or requests are generally expressed
with subjunctive forms of **sollen** :

,,Rufen Sie das Flugzeug das nächste Mal im Radio an!"
    Next time, call the airplane over the radio.
Man sagte ihm, er solle das Flugzeug das nächste Mal
    im Radio anrufen.
Man sagte ihm, daß er das Flugzeug das nächste Mal
    im Radio anrufen solle.
They told him (that) next time he should call the airplane
    over the radio.

9.7 Where expressions beginning with *let's* are used in English,
the subjunctive I is used in German:

    Glauben wir daher nicht an diesen Unsinn!
    Let's not believe in this nonsense then.

9.8 German also uses subjunctive I forms where English has fixed phrases expressing wishes:

Es lebe der König! Long live the King!
Es lebe die Liebe! Hurrah for love!

Subjunctive I forms are also used for directions in technical writings:

Es sei x gleich 5. Let x be equal to 5.
Es sei hier daran erinnert, daß . . . Let us note here that . . .
Man bringe die Lösung zum heftigen Kochen.
Heat the solution to a vigorous boil.

NARRATIVE

Es lebe die Liebe!

Der Sommer war so gut wie vorbei. Gerald hatte noch drei Wochen, in denen er die verlorene Zeit einholen konnte, — drei Wochen, in denen er herausfinden konnte, wer Margaret wirklich war. Am 22. September sollte die Universität wieder
5 ihren Anfang nehmen [?], und daß er lange vor dem letzten Tag der Einschreibung [registration] ankommen werde, das konnte schließlich kein Mensch von ihm erwarten.

Da er während der Woche tief in den Wäldern zu arbeiten hatte, blieb ihm nur das Wochenende, um ein Wiedersehen mit
10 Margaret möglich zu machen. Am ersten Samstag gab es große Aufregung [excitement] im Büro. Es hieß, der Lohn [pay] könne nicht ausgezahlt werden, denn Reynolds, der die Lohngelder [?] aus der Stadt habe bringen sollen, sei damit verschwunden. (Später erfuhr man, daß er in Los Angeles
15 verhaftet [arrested] worden sei, nachdem er ein fröhliches Wochenende verbracht habe.) Aber da die Firma [?] versichert sei, könne die Zahlung ohne Schwierigkeit per Scheck erfolgen.

An diesem Abend besuchten Gerald und Margaret das Lichtspieltheater in einem benachbarten Städtchen. Aber da
20 weder der Film vom Bankraub im wilden Westen noch der leere, unfreundliche Raum mit den harten Sitzen [?] zu längerem Bleiben einlud, fragte Margaret ihn mit leiser Stimme, ob er

wirklich Lust habe, sich hier den ganzen Abend aufzuhalten.
Als er dies lachend verneinte, beschlossen sie, ins hellerleuchtete
[brightly lighted] Lokal nebenan [next door] zu gehen, wo sich 25
die Jugend der Nachbarschaft [?] bei Musik und Tanz zu
unterhalten pflegte. Es gebe leider nichts anderes in dieser
verlassenen Gegend.

Beim Eintreten erschraken sie fast vor dem Lärm im Lokal.
Gerald zögerte. „Gehen wir nur weiter nach hinten! Da 30
finden wir wohl noch ein Plätzchen," tröstete [comforted]
Margaret. Als sie es gefunden, waren sie froh, daß sie
niemanden erkannt hatten und von niemandem erkannt worden
waren. „Seien Sie unbesorgt, Gerald," sagte sie, „man kann
ja auch in der Menge miteinander allein sein. Es ist ja Samstag- 35
abend, und da möchte jeder die Freiheit genießen, wie er kann."
Als sie bei ihrem Glase Coca-Cola saßen, wollte Gerald sie
fragen, ob sie es wirklich gewesen sei, die vor mehr als drei
Monaten so stolz an ihm vorbeigefahren sei. Aber nach dem,
was sie neulich zu ihm gesprochen, unterdrückte [suppressed] 40
er die Frage und bat sie, etwas aus ihrer Vergangenheit zu
erzählen. Und nun hörte er, daß sie aus Dresden komme und
daß sie ihre Eltern bei einem Luftangriff [?] am Ende des
letzten Weltkrieges verloren habe.

Gerald wollte noch mehr fragen, aber Margaret sagte: „Tun 45
Sie mir den Gefallen und sprechen wir nicht mehr davon!"
Außerdem sei sie ein Kind von kaum mehr als 10 Jahren
gewesen, als das Unglück geschehen sei; daher habe sie nur
ein dunkles und undeutliches Bild jenes fürchterlichen Tages
in Erinnerung. — 50

Am nächsten Sonntag machten die beiden einen Ausflug
[excursion] nach einem tiefen und klaren See im Gebirge.
Herbst war in der Luft und die Stimme des Abschieds in ihrem
Herzen. Es war ein wundervoller Tag, und es schien, als wolle
die Sonne selbst das tiefe Wasser vergolden [gild], worüber sie 55
ruderten. Da kam ein Motorboot vom anderen Ufer gerade
auf sie zu, zog einen großen Kreis um sie, so daß Gerald kaum
das Ruderboot im Gleichgewicht [in balance] halten konnte.

Die zwei Männer im Boot stellten den Motor ab, lachten und
60 winkten ihnen zu.   Es waren Latour und Caramelli.   „So, ihr
seid's!" rief Latour fröhlich.   „Das habe ich wirklich nicht
geahnt!   Nun, es lebe die Liebe! — Wir werden im Bootshaus
auf euch warten!"   Und schon waren sie wieder davon — und
das Ruderboot tanzte auf den Wellen.   Da blieb ihnen nichts
65 übrig als freundlich zu lächeln und den Nachmittag in Gesellschaft dieser unwillkommenen [?] und doch lustigen Gesellen
zu verbringen.

Gerald und Margaret fuhren langsam nach Hause.   Sie
sprachen nicht viel.   An jeder Kurve stieg eine dunkle Frage
70 in seinem Herzen auf, welch neue Überraschung ihn am
nächsten und letzten Wochenende erwarten werde.

Questions

1. Warum kehrte Gerald nicht vor dem 22. September
   zurück?
2. Warum konnten die Lohngelder nicht gleich ausgezahlt
   werden?
3. Warum blieben Gerald und Margaret nur eine kurze Zeit
   im Lichtspieltheater?
4. Wo beschlossen sie, sich an diesem Abend zu unterhalten?
5. Warum zögerten sie, ins Lokal einzutreten?
6. Wo fanden sie ein Plätzchen?
7. Was wollte Gerald Margaret fragen?
8. Warum stellte er diese Frage nicht?
9. Was erzählte Margaret aus ihrer Vergangenheit?
10. Warum konnte sie sich an den Tag in Dresden nicht
    recht erinnern?
11. Wohin fuhren sie am folgenden Sonntag?
12. Wem begegneten sie, als sie über den See ruderten?
13. Warum mußten sie den Nachmittag mit diesen Leuten
    verbringen?
14. Woran dachte Gerald auf der Fahrt nach Hause?

Vocabulary

der **Abschied**   parting, departure
die **Art, -en**   sort, kind; manner
    außerdem   besides
der **Bankraub**   bank robbery
    beschließen (-schloß, -schlossen)   decide
    erfolgen (ist)   take place
    fürchterlich   frightful
das **Gebirge, –**   mountains
der **Herbst**   fall, autumn
    klar   clear
der **Kreis, -e**   circle
das **Lokal, -e**   place (bar, dance hall)
die **Menge, -n**   crowd
    menschlich   human
    pflegen (+ zu)   be accustomed to, be used to
    rauben   rob
    rudern (ist)   row
    stolz   proud
die **Überraschung, -en**   surprise
das **Ufer, –**   shore, bank
    unbesorgt   unconcerned
der **Unsinn**   nonsense
der **Ursprung, ⁻e**   origin
die **Vernunft**   reason
die **Welle, -n**   wave
    widersprechen (a, o, i) [*dat.*]   contradict
    winken   wave
    zahlen   pay

Idioms

Bitte, tun Sie mir den Gefallen   Please do me the favor
Hat er Lust mitzugehen?   Does he want to go along?
Da blieb ihnen nichts übrig.   There was nothing left for them.

Lesson 10

CLASSES OF NOUNS; GENDERS; PLURALS

RECOGNIZING GENDER

DER- WORDS, *EIN-* WORDS, AND ADJECTIVES

Die Feuerwehr

Herr Steffen rief eines Abends die Feuerwehr an: „Bitte, kommen Sie sofort nach West Broadway 620! Es brennt bei uns in der Küche." Die Feuerwehr raste durch die Straßen nach East Broadway 620. Als man dort keine Flammen sah, hielt man die Meldung für falsch und kehrte zur Feuerwache zurück.

Dort waren inzwischen zwei weitere Anrufe eingetroffen. Mit heulender Sirene fuhr die Feuerwehr an die richtige Adresse. Aber als sie mit größter Geschwindigkeit um eine Straßenecke bog, fiel ein Feuerwehrmann vom Fahrzeug und brach sich beide Arme. Da mußte der arme Mann erst aufgesammelt und ins Krankenhaus gebracht werden.

Als die Feuerwehrleute endlich nach einer Stunde am brennenden Hause ankamen, war nicht viel mehr zu machen. Die Flammen schlugen aus allen Fenstern, um das Haus standen neugierige Männer, Weiber und Kinder, und Herr Steffen stand auf der Straße und stammelte ungeduldige Worte!

der **Anruf** telephone call
*arm poor
auf-sammeln collect, gather up
*biegen round, bend
ein-treffen come in, arrive
*falsch false
die **Feuerwache** fire station
die **Feuerwehr** fire department
die **Meldung** report, announcement
schlagen leap
*sofort immediately

EXERCISES

A. Formation of plurals.

1. A. The genitive singular of **das Fenster** is **des Fensters**. What are the corresponding forms for:

   1. der Himmel
   2. der Zweifel
   3. der Fahrer
   4. der Straßengraben
   5. der Zuhörer
   6. der Onkel
   7. der Täter
   8. das Mädchen
   9. das Städtchen
   10. das Männlein

   B. The nominative plural of **der Lehrer** is **die Lehrer**. What are the corresponding forms for the nouns listed above?

2. A. The nominative plural of **der Kopf** is **die Köpfe**. What are the corresponding forms for:

   1. der Kampf
   2. der Ton
   3. der Kreis
   4. der Baum
   5. der Arm
   6. der Unfall
   7. der Anzug
   8. das Stück
   9. das Haar
   10. das Ding

B. The acccusative plural of **die Luft** is **die Lüfte.** What are the corresponding forms for:

1. die Kuh   4. die Wand
2. die Nacht   5. die Hand
3. die Stadt   6. die Frucht

C. The genitive plural of **das Geschäft** is **der Geschäfte.** What are the corresponding forms for:

1. das Gespräch   3. das Gewehr
2. das Gefühl   4. das Gedicht

3. A. The nominative plural of **das Feld** is **die Felder.** What are the corresponding forms for:

1. das Haus   5. das Krankenhaus
2. das Glas   6. der Geist
3. das Rad   7. der Wald
4. das Bild   8. der Irrtum

B. The dative plural of **das Feld** is **den Feldern.** What are the corresponding forms for the nouns above?

4. A. The accusative singular of **die Erde** is **die Erde.** What are the corresponding forms for:

1. die Küche   5. die Adresse
2. die Menge   6. die Stunde
3. die Kurve   7. die Straßenecke
4. die Flamme   8. die Untertasse

B. The genitive plural of **die Antwort** is **der Antworten.** What are the corresponding forms for:

1. die Arbeit   3. die Tür
2. die Uhr   4. die Frau

C. The nominative plural of **die Feder** is **die Federn.** What are the corresponding forms for:

1. die Tafel   3. die Schulter
2. die Fabel   4. die Schwester

D. The dative plural of **die Erinnerung** is **den Erinnerungen.** What are the corresponding forms for:
1. die Zeitung   4. die Wissenschaft
2. die Meldung   5. die Gesellschaft
3. die Schwierigkeit   6. die Neuigkeit

E. The accusative plural of **die Freundin** is **die Freundinnen.** What are the corresponding forms for:
1. die Begleiterin   3. die Krankenpflegerin
2. die Kellnerin   4. die Helferin

5. A. The dative singular of **der Gedanke** is **dem Gedanken.** What are the corresponding forms for:
1. der Geselle   3. der Deutsche
2. der Knabe   4. der Angestellte

B. The nominative plural of **das Bett** is **die Betten.** What are the corresponding forms for:
1. das Auge   3. das Herz
2. das Ohr   4. das Ende

C. The accusative plural of **der Mensch** is **die Menschen.** What are the corresponding forms for:
1. der Student   3. der Soldat
2. der Assistent   4. der Staat

B. Change the phrases printed in heavy type into the plural.

1. A. **Das Kind verlor** die Eltern bei einem Luftangriff.
B. **Der Angestellte verlangte** das Geld.
C. **Der Flieger hat** unbekannte Objekte gesehen.
D. **Das Bild hing** in ihrem Wohnzimmer.
E. Warum **kann das Lohngeld** nicht ausgezahlt werden?

2. A. Wer verursachte **den furchtbaren Unfall?**
B. Dann stellte er **eine schwere Frage** an sie.
C. **Welches schöne Mädchen** sahen Sie da?
D. Das Zimmer hat **keinen freien Ausgang.**
E. Das Feuer zerstörte **den Tannenwald.**

3. A. **Dem Kinde** gab er ein Spielzeug zum Geschenk.
   B. Margaret winkte **ihrer Freundin** zu.
   C. Sie flogen mit **ihrem Flugzeug** nach San Franzisko.
   D. Von **diesem schönen Tage** an war der Sommer herrlich.
   E. Was hülfe es **dem Menschen,** wenn **er** die ganze Welt **gewönne?**
4. A. **Der Vater meines Freundes erwartete** uns dort.
   B. Die Fenster **des Zimmers** waren alle geschlossen.
   C. Im Schein **der roten Lampe** betrat er den Saal.
   D. In der Mitte **einer deutschen Stadt** findet man gewöhnlich die Kathedrale.
   E. Er ärgerte sich über den Lärm **des neuen Autos.**

C. What is the difference between the two phrases in each of the following pairs?

1. dem Fräulein	den Fräulein
2. der Angestellte	die Angestellte
3. der Garten	die Gärten
4. die Deutsche	die Deutschen
5. den bösen Täter	den bösen Tätern
6. der dunklen Gestalt	der dunklen Gestalten
7. die gute . . .	die guten . . .
8. dunkles Bier	dunklen Biers
9. ein alter Tourist	eines alten Touristen
10. der Menschen	des Menschen

D. To which verbs are the following nouns related? Give the meaning and gender of each.

1. Schritt	8. Geben
2. Anzug	9. Rückgabe
3. Hoffnung	10. Druck
4. Fahren	11. Stelle
5. Anfang	12. Heulen
6. Fluß	13. Genuß
7. Folge	14. Wäsche

15. Schlag

E. Following the patterns, give German equivalents for the English sentences. Word order will be the same as in the pattern sentences.

1. **Man raste dann durch die Stadt nach East Broadway.**
   A. The young people walked slowly homeward across the fields.
   B. My relatives are driving through the mountains to Santa Fe.

2. **Inzwischen waren zwei weitere Anrufe eingetroffen.**
   A. Six other people had arrived in the meantime.
   B. Still further consequences will occur (*eintreten*) later.

3. **Die Flammen schlugen aus allen Fenstern.**
   A. The glasses were standing on a large table.
   B. His companions went into a brightly lighted bar.

4. **Er hat eine unserer schweren Fragen schon beantwortet.**
   A. She's lost some of her old friends already.
   B. Margaret found one of his expensive books there.

5. **Die Flieger begegneten mehreren unbekannten Objekten.**
   A. My brothers contradict those stupid remarks.
   B. A good boy helps such old people.

F. Replace the words in heavy type with the words in parentheses:

1. Ich habe ja auch **keinen neuen Wagen.** (a good doctor, no beautiful figure, still another question, a different job)
2. Für mich ist **mein alter Klapperkasten** noch gut genug. (my little sports car, our old house, her pretty face, this familiar place)
3. Nein, **solche Bücher** mögen die Leute nicht. (old cars, these models, difficulties like that, clever boys, new apartments)

4. Es gibt leider **keinen Kaffee** mehr. (no hope, not any money, no milk, no books, no surprises)

5. Mit unserer Hilfe bekam er **eine andere Stellung.** (lots of money, several beautiful pictures, a new car, a few new suits)

GRAMMAR

10 Classes of Nouns; genders; plurals.

10.1 German nouns can be classified into four groups according to the forms of their plurals. [*See Appendix 6.* For lists of nouns, consult the exercises in this lesson, check the vocabulary lists, and see the Appendix.] Learning nouns by classes helps one to remember their gender as well as their endings.

10.1,1 Plurals with no added endings include masculines and neuters ending in **-el, -en, -er** (often with umlaut); neuters of the **Ge . . . e** pattern; neuters in **-chen** and **-lein**; and the two feminines, **Mütter** and **Töchter** (with umlaut).

10.1,2 Plurals in -e include most monosyllabic masculines (often with umlaut), monosyllabic masculines with prefixes, (*e.g.*, **die Anzüge**), those in compounds (*e.g.*, **die Bleistifte**), and words of foreign derivation (*e.g.*, **die Apparate**); some monosyllabic feminines (*e.g.*, **die Nächte, die Städte** [always with umlaut]); and some monosyllabic neuters (*e.g.*, **die Boote, die Jahre** [no umlaut], monosyllabic neuters with prefixes (*e.g.*, **die Gesetze**), and foreign words (*e.g.*, **die Papiere**).

10.1,3 Plurals in -er include most monosyllabic neuters (*e.g.*, **die Bücher, die Gläser** [with umlaut]); some masculines (*e.g.*, **die Götter, die Männer** [with umlaut]); and nouns in **-tum** (with umlaut).

The plural of compounds with **-mann** have the form **-leute** : **die Kaufleute, die Seeleute.**

10.1,4 Plurals in -(e)n include most feminines (*e.g.*, **die Frauen, die Gaben, die Federn**), and some masculines which refer to male beings (*e.g.*, **die Menschen, die Soldaten, die Professoren**).

Some of these plurals have **-(e)n** in all cases except the nominative singular:

	der Mensch	des Menschen	die Menschen
	der Student	des Studenten	die Studenten
	der Knabe	des Knaben	die Knaben
but	der Herr	des Herrn	die Herren

A few have **-ens** in the genitive singular:

der Name   des Namens   die Namen

Like Name are: Gedanke, Glaube, Wille, Friede.

Others have **-(e)n** only in the plural:

der Professor   des Professors   die Professoren

Like Professor are: Bauer, Staat, Nachbar, See.

Some neuters like: die Augen, die Enden, die Interessen, die Ohren observe the following pattern:

das Auge   des Auges   die Augen

Note: das Herz, des Herzens, dem Herzen, die Herzen

10.2 Recognizing gender. It is possible to recognize **gender** from the form of nouns. Any genitive that ends in **-(e)s** will be masculine or neuter. Any plural ending in **-(e)n** will very likely be feminine, and any plural ending in **-er** will very likely be neuter. The genders associated with various suffixes have been given in the discussions of suffixes. The gender of compounds is determined by the gender of the final element:

die Woche + das Ende = das Wochenende

10.2,1 Genders of some nouns derived from verbs may be determined from their form. Nouns formed by capitalizing the infinitives of verbs are neuter and usually may be translated by English *-ing* nouns: **(das) Fahren macht Spaß.** 'Driving is fun.'

Many monosyllabic nouns, formed from the stems of verbs, are masculine:

present stem:	**fallen**	**der Fall**	fall, case
	kaufen	**der Kauf**	purchase
past stem:	**reiten**	**der Ritt**	horseback ride
	dringen	**der Drang**	urge
participle stem:	**gehen**	**der Gang**	passageway

with prefixes:

(hin)ausgehen	**der Ausgang**	exit
(hin)eingehen	**der Eingang**	entrance

Nouns ending in **-e** are feminine:

fragen	**die Frage**	question
annehmen	**die Annahme**	assumption, acceptance

10.2,2 Nouns taken over from other languages (*e.g.*, English and French), whose plurals end in **-s** retain this plural in German. They do not have **-n** in the dative plural.

das Auto	**des Autos**	**die Autos**
der Klub	**des Klubs**	**die Klubs**

10.3 der-words, **ein-**words, and adjectives. [*See Appendix 3*].

10.3,1 Adjectives following **der-**words (**dies-, jed-, jen-, manch-, solch-, welch-; alle** in the plural) take **e-**endings in the three nominative cases singular and in the accusative feminine and neuter; elsewhere they take **-en.**

der neue Wagen	manchen neuen Wagen
jede junge Frau	jene junge Frau
welches alte Haus	dieses alten Hauses

10.3,2 Adjectives following **ein-**words (**ein, mein, dein, sein, ihr, unser, euer, Ihr**) take the same endings as **der-**words except in those forms in which **ein-**words have no endings: the masculine nominative, the neuter nominative and accusative:

ein neuer Wagen	keinen neuen Wagen
deine junge Frau	seine junge Frau
unser altes Haus	ihr altes Haus

Note that the -er of **unser** and **euer** is not an ending but part of the stem; **unser** is an **ein**-word.

After **ein** and **kein, solcher** may be used; **beide** and **viele** may be used after the **der**-words and **ein**-words other than **ein** and **kein** in the plural:
ein solch**es** Buch   die beid**en** Wagen   die viel**en** neu**en** Wagen

10.3,3 Adjectives which are not preceded by **der**-words or **ein**-words have the endings of **dieser** (except in the masculine and neuter genitive singular, which have **-en**):
Gut**er** Rat ist teuer.   Trotz gut**en** Rats wollte er es nicht tun.
Ich gebe Ihnen gut**en** Rat.   Ich kann auf ander**e** Weise um mein Geld kommen.

Since there is no indefinite article in the plural, the endings of **dieser** are used:
Neu**e** Bücher kosten viel Geld.   Die Preise neu**er** Bücher sind hoch.

Adjectives following **andere, einige, mehrere, viele,** and **wenige** take the same endings as the word they follow:
ander**e** neu**e** Bücher   viel**er** neu**er** Wagen   an einig**en** schön**en** Tagen

After **alle,** however, the ending is always **-en :**
Alle neu**en** Bücher kosten viel.   Die Titel aller neu**en** Bücher stehen auf der Liste.

NARRATIVE

Dunkle Gestalten

„Herein, meine Damen und Herren!   Treten Sie näher, wenn Sie die Wunder [?] der Welt sehen wollen!   Hier finden Sie die großen Männer aller Zeiten, wie sie in Wirklichkeit ausgesehen haben."   Eine Masse von Menschen drängte sich vor dem Wachsfigurenkabinett [waxworks], wo Bilder in schreienden   5
Farben ausgestellt waren — Napoleon und Mussolini, Stalin und Hitler, Houdini und Mandrake mit starrenden, leblosen [?]

Augen. Im Laden daneben hieß es: „Sehen Sie Ihr wahres
Selbst und Sie können sich vor Lachen nicht halten! Eintritt
10 fünfzig Cents!" Männer und Frauen, Seeleute und Büromädchen, Alte und Junge, Touristen auf Ferien und Soldaten
auf Urlaub — alle schoben sich langsam durch die engen
Straßen der Chinesenstadt. Der Lärm der Stimmen mischte
sich mit dem Hupen [honking] der Autos. Rote und gelbe
15 und grüne Lichter blitzten [flashed] durch die Dunkelheit, und
die Polizisten hatten Schwierigkeiten, den Verkehr in beiden
Richtungen aufrecht zu erhalten [to keep straight].

In der Masse von dunklen Gestalten befanden sich auch
Caramelli und Bates. Sie waren am Nachmittag mit einem
20 Lastkraftwagen voller Bretter [planks] nach San Franzisko
gekommen, und da am Motor einige Reparaturen nötig gewesen
waren, hatten sie die Maschine in eine Garage gebracht und
beschlossen, sich einen fröhlichen Abend zu machen.

San Franzisko ist eine der schönsten Städte der Vereinigten
25 Staaten. Wer arbeiten will, findet dort etwas zu tun, und wer
das Leben genießen möchte, kommt dort auf seine Rechnung
[gets his money's worth]. Auch Caramelli und Bates. Sie
wischten sich die Tränen aus den Augen, als sie aus dem Lachkabinett heraustraten. Da gab es keine Wände im Raum, nur
30 Spiegel in allen möglichen Formen und Stellungen. So etwas
hatten sie noch nie erlebt. Der lange, dünne Caramelli hatte
ausgesehen wie ein Ei, rund und dick, und der schwerfällige
Bates hatte zwei Köpfe gehabt mit großen Ohren, die an den
Seiten saßen wie zwei riesige Griffe [gigantic handles]. Schließ-
35 lich hatten sie ihren Weg zwischen all den Spiegeln verloren
und waren auf Händen und Knieen zum Ausgang gekrochen.

„Das werde ich im Leben nicht mehr vergessen," sagte Bates,
als er wieder atmen konnte. Doch Caramelli faßte ihn am
Arm: „Sieh, ist das nicht Margaret aus dem Büro? Wie kommt
40 die hierher?" Ein Mädchen ging lächelnd an ihnen vorbei,
aber als sie sich nach ihr umdrehten, war sie schon unter den
vielen fremden Gesichtern verschwunden.

Die beiden Freunde fragten sich, ob sie nun vielleicht ins

Kino gehen sollten. Aber die Lichtreklame [advertisements]
der verschiedenen Theater machte wenig Eindruck auf sie. 45
„Goldgräber [?] in der Wüste [desert]," „Barbara und die
tausend Herzen" — das konnte man auch zu Hause sehen!
Ein Junge rief Zeitungen aus: Riesenexplosion im Orient!
Aber keiner schien es zu merken.

„Ich hab' Hunger," sagte Bates, „und es wäre wohl Zeit, daß 50
wir essen gingen." Sie blieben an einem Schaufenster [?]
stehen, aber bekamen wenig Appetit. „Das sieht ja aus wie
getrocknete Fledermäuse [dried bats]," sagte Caramelli und
wandte sich ab. Einige Schritte weiter hin war ein Lokal, wo
man importierte [?] Weine und Biere verkaufte. Wenn es 55
nicht zu teuer war, konnten sie sich ja hier ein Filet oder ein
Beefsteak leisten.

Da blieb Bates plötzlich stehen, griff in seine Hosentasche
und wurde blaß wie Papier. „Um Gotteswillen," sagte er
durch die Zähne. „Mein Geld ist weg!" Der Lärm der 60
Stimmen brauste an ihnen vorüber. Ein Straßenbahnwagen
machte seinen Weg durch die enge Straße. Und der Polizist
an der Ecke, dem Bates sein Unglück meldete, sagte: „Das tut
mir äußerst leid! Sie hätten aber besser aufpassen sollen. Vor
Taschendieben wird gewarnt. — Aber geben Sie mir Ihre 65
Adresse. Wenn wir etwas herausfinden, werden wir an Sie
schreiben." Und er fuhr fort, den Verkehr in allen Richtungen
aufrecht zu erhalten.

Questions

1. Was gab es im Wachsfigurenkabinett zu sehen?
2. Worüber gab es viel zu lachen?
3. Was für Leute drängten sich durch die Straßen in der
   Chinesenstadt?
4. Was versuchten die Polizisten?
5. Warum befanden sich auch Caramelli und Bates in dieser
   Menschenmasse?

6. Was kann jeder in San Franzisko finden?
7. Was für Wände gab es im Lachkabinett?
8. Wie sah Bates aus? wie Caramelli?
9. Warum glaubten sie Margaret unter den Leuten zu sehen?
10. Warum wollten sie nicht ins Kino gehen?
11. Warum hatten Caramelli und Bates wenig Appetit?
12. In welchem Lokal wollten sie schließlich essen?
13. Warum blieb Bates plötzlich im Verkehr stehen?
14. Wem meldete er sein Unglück?
15. Was sagte der Polizist zu ihm?

Vocabulary

arm   poor
atmen   breathe
auf-passen   pay attention
der **Ausgang, ⸚e**   exit
aus-stellen   exhibit
sich **befinden (a, u)**   be
biegen (o, ist o)   round (the corner), bend
der **Dieb, -e**   thief
sich **drängen**   shove
das **Ei, -er**   egg
der **Eindruck, ⸚e**   impression
der **Eintritt**   admission, entry
eng   narrow
falsch   false
die **Farbe, -n**   color
greifen (i, i)   grasp
das **Knie, -e**   knee
kriechen (o, ist o)   crawl
sich **leisten**   afford
die **Masse, -n**   mass
melden   announce
das **Schaufenster, –**   show window, store window

    sofort immediately
    verschieden different, various
  der Urlaub, -e leave, furlough, vacation
  die Wirklichkeit, -en reality
  das Wunder, – miracle, wonder

Idioms

Ich konnte mich vor Lachen nicht halten.
I almost died laughing.

NOMINATIVE CASE

ACCUSATIVE CASE

COMPARISON OF ADJECTIVES AND ADVERBS

Die Autoausstellung

Er: Gehen wir alle in die internationale Autoausstellung! Sie ist gleich um die Ecke. Nur diese Straße entlang.

Sie: Das können Sie meinetwegen tun, aber ohne mich. Ich mag nicht mit dem Kopf durch die Wand!

Er: Ich kauf' doch auch keinen neuen Wagen und erst recht keinen ausländischen Sportwagen. Aber Spaß macht's auf jeden Fall.

Sie: Nein, mich ärgert's jedesmal aufs neue, wenn ich die Leute sehe, die jedes Jahr ein neues Auto haben müssen. Für mich ist mein alter Klapperkasten noch gut genug. Ich kann auf andere Weise um mein Geld kommen.

Er: Sie sollten ein Buch schreiben über das Thema: ‚Wider das alljährliche Eintauschen von Wagen!' Durch ein solches Buch würden Sie noch berühmt werden.

alljährlich yearly, every year
ausländisch foreign

*die **Ausstellung** exhibit
das **Eintauschen** exchange, trade-in
   erst **recht kein** certainly not a
   *meinetwegen for all I care
das **Thema** topic
   um mein Geld kommen lose my money
   *wider against

EXERCISES

A. Replace the words in heavy type with the words in parentheses.

1. A. Gehen wir zusammen **in die Autoausstellung.** (to the office, to the movies, into the garage, behind the house, into the country, through the woods)
   B. Er kommt gerade **um die Ecke.** (through the door, across the street, into the dining room)
   C. Ich gehe lieber **an die Arbeit.** (through the park, without [a] hat, at seven o'clock)
   D. Ich mag nicht **mit dem Kopf durch die Wand.** (to bed . . . without supper, to the theater . . . every day, to the exhibition . . . without you, to work . . . at this time)

2. A. Es kommt auf **das schöne Wetter** an. (the necessary time, many other circumstances, a good topic, our hard work, the new office girl)
   B. Wir freuen uns auf **die Fahrt.** (that day, the new auto show, the yearly exchange of autos, a foreign sports car)
   C. Erinnern Sie sich an **den berühmten Mann?** (that old rattletrap, the big inflation, this excellent film, our youngest daughter, that huge crowd, her many difficulties)
   D. Mich ärgert's immer **aufs neue.** (in any case, extremely)

E. **Auf diese Weise** könnte ich **um mein Geld** kommen. (at any moment . . . my patience, through negligence . . . my job, in any case . . . my life)

3. A. San Franzisko ist die **schönste** Stadt, die ich kenne. (the most wonderful, the most interesting, the greatest, the cleanest, the oldest)

   B. Die **buntesten Bilder** waren ausgestellt. (most beautiful cars, oldest books, most interesting things)

   C. Sie hätten das **besser** gemacht. (well, best of all, extremely well)

   D. Alle schoben sich **langsam** durch die Straßen. (quickly, very slowly, extremely fast, more slowly)

   E. Es stand wirklich **nichts Neues** darin. (much that was interesting, something valuable, nothing clever, all sorts of lovely things)

   F. Jetzt besitze ich **so gut wie** nichts. (as little as you, as much as anyone [jeder])

   G. Heute war es **so herrlich wie** ein Tag im Sommer. (as hot as, as long as, as beautiful as)

   H. Sie sind **früher als gewöhnlich** zurückgekehrt. (more quickly than expected, richer than before, later than we, more often than usual)

   I. Er **arbeitet gern auf** dem Lande. (likes to live, preferred to live, likes best of all to stay, prefers to remain)

B. Translate:

1. Der Einzelne darf dem Ganzen um keinen Preis geopfert werden.
2. Es kommt darauf an, ob er das nötige Geld bei sich hat.
3. Der Mensch liest ja nichts und erst recht keine Literatur!
4. Der Stab muß um einen Zentimeter kürzer sein.
5. Worum handelt es sich eigentlich?
6. Bis zur Endstation dauert es noch einige Minuten.

7. Länger zu warten wäre Unsinn.
8. Der Enthusiast hat sich auf das neue Modell des deutschen Sportwagens sehr gefreut.

C. Following the patterns, give German equivalents for the English sentences. Word order will be exactly the same as in the pattern sentences.

1. **Gehen wir jetzt an die Arbeit!**
    A. Let's drive into the country today.
    B. Let's talk about the future then.
    C. Let's go to the auto show later.

2. **Müssen Sie jedes Jahr ein neues Auto haben?**
    A. Do they have to look for a different job every year?
    B. Can I buy something new every day?
    C. Does she want to write a long letter every month?

3. **Die Verschwendung ärgert mich immer.**
    A. Nothing surprises us now.
    B. Eating always interests him.
    C. Work doesn't please me at all.

4. **Bates redet über den starken Verkehr.**
    A. The actor is writing a book about his experience.
    B. The class was reading on that subject.
    C. The nurses were talking about his case.

5. **Die Erkältung hat nur zwei Tage gedauert.**
    A. The exhibit has lasted several days.
    B. The fire burned for six hours.
    C. It rained the whole time.

6. **Der Alte darf auf seinen Sohn stolz sein.**
    A. We can be proud of our daughter.
    B. New students must wait for their books.
    C. His parents must be happy about it.

7. **Da griff er in seine Hosentasche.**
    A. Then he drove into [the] heavy traffic.
    B. She came into the living room afterwards.
    C. On Sunday I'm going into the country.

GRAMMAR

11.1 The **nominative case** is used for the subject and the predicative nominative in German.

11.2 The **accusative case** is used for the direct object, for the object of certain prepositions, and in some expressions of time.

11.2,1 Of the prepositions which always take the accusative **(durch, für, gegen, ohne, um, wider)**, only **um** has a number of special uses:

> **um jeden Preis**   at all costs
> **um zwei Grad kühler**   cooler by two degrees
> **um sechs Uhr**   at six o'clock

The preposition **bis** 'until, by, up to' is usually used together with another preposition:

Er blieb bis zum Wochenende. He remained until the weekend.

Er fährt bis nach Garmisch. He is driving as far as Garmisch.
When **bis** is used alone, there is usually no article:

> **bis Montag**   until Monday

Some words indicating relation and governing the accusative stand after their object:

Er ging die Straße entlang. He went along the street.
Er springt die Treppen hinauf. He is running up the stairs.

11.2,2 Of the prepositions which take the accusative when location or motion to a new location is involved **(an, auf, hinter, in, neben, über, unter, vor, zwischen)**, **an, auf** and **über** have special meanings in certain phrases. In these they take the accusative:

Ich freue mich <u>auf</u> die Ausstellung. look forward to
Er freut sich <u>über</u> den neuen Wagen. is happy about
Wir ärgern uns <u>über</u> die Verschwendung. are annoyed by
Sie erinnert sich noch <u>an</u> den Tag. remembers

Es kommt auf das Wetter an. depends on
Schreiben Sie ein Buch über dieses Thema. write about
Denke an mich! think of

Auf is also used in fixed phrases:

> **aufs neue** anew
> **auf einmal** suddenly, all at once
> **auf diese Weise** ⎫
> **auf diese Art** ⎭ in this way
> **auf jeden Fall** in any case, in any event

11.2,3 The **accusative case** is used for:

recurrent time: **jedes Jahr, alle vier Wochen, jeden Monat**
duration of time: **einen ganzen Monat, den ganzen Tag**
when a fixed span of time is set, **auf** is used:

> **Ich fahre auf drei Tage heim.** for three days

11.3 Comparison of adjectives and adverbs [*see Appendix 3.2,2*]. The adjectives and adverbs used to express degrees of comparison are usually formed by the addition of suffixes to the positive form. They are sometimes also formed by a change in the stem vowel of the base form:

so klar wie	klarer als	am klarsten	(der klarste)
so lange wie	länger als	am längsten	(der längste)
groß	größer	am größten	
nah	näher	am nächsten	
hoch	höher	am höchsten	

The following have different stems for the comparative and superlative forms:

gut	besser	am besten
viel	mehr	am meisten
gern	lieber	am liebsten

The length of the word does not affect the formation of the comparative and superlative:

> interessant   interesting

interessanter   more interesting
am interessantesten   most interesting

11.3,1 The adverb **mehr** is used when attributes rather than objects are being compared:

Das Mädchen ist mehr schön als klug.
The girl is more pretty than intelligent.

11.3,2 The form **am . . . -en** is used for the superlative of the adverb and of the predicate adjective:

Am heftigsten brannte (war) das Feuer gegen Abend.
The fire burned most violently (was most violent) towards evening.
Von allen Frauen, die ich kenne, singt sie am schönsten.
Of all the women I know, she sings the most beautifully.

If two or more members of the same category are being compared, however, the form **der (die, das) . . . -ste** is used in the predicative:

Von allen Frauen, die ich kenne, ist sie die schönste.
Of all the women I know she is the most beautiful.

11.3,3 When no comparison with others is intended, the phrase **auf . . . -ste** is used. This is the equivalent of **sehr**:

Der Motor funktionierte aufs beste (= sehr gut).
The motor performed exceedingly well.

11.3,4 A few adjectives and adverbs occur only in the comparative and superlative forms. These are related to the prepositions in the first column:

in :	**der innere**	inner	**der innerste**	innermost
vor :	**der vordere**	front	**der vorderste**	farthest in front
über :	**der obere**	upper	**der oberste**	highest, upper-most
unter :	**der untere**	lower	**der unterste**	lowest
hinter :	**der hintere**	back	**der hinterste**	farthest back

From these may be formed the adverbs **innen, außen, oben, unten, hinten**. Note, however, **vorne**.

NARRATIVE

Durch den Nebel

Schon früh am nächsten Morgen wanderten [?] Caramelli und Bates nach ihrer Garage. Sie hatten die Nacht in einem billigen Hotel verbracht, um auf diese Weise den Verlust des Geldes wieder gutzumachen [?]. Die letzten Straßenreinigungsmaschinen [streetsweepers] und die ersten Milchwagen [?] 5 fuhren durch den Nebel. „Ich hasse den frühen Morgen," sagte Caramelli. „Daran kann ich mich einfach nicht gewöhnen."

Bates ging schweigend neben ihm die Straße entlang. Ihn fror. Er ärgerte sich über den Nebel, und er ärgerte sich über 10 seine eigene Dummheit. Er konnte sich einfach nicht vorstellen, wie er um sein Geld gekommen war [lost his money]. Er hätte am liebsten die ganze Sache vergessen, aber alle paar Augenblicke waren seine Gedanken wieder zu diesem Punkt zurückgekehrt. „Glaubst du nicht, daß es passiert ist, als wir 15 durch das Spiegelkabinett [hall of mirrors] krochen? Oder war's vielleicht das hübsche Mädchen? Weißt du, die hat mich so verdächtig angelacht [smiled at]."

„Was kümmert mich, wo du dein Geld verloren hast," sagte Caramelli mißmutig [peevishly]. „Auf alle Fälle ist es gut, daß 20 du mich dabei hast. Ohne mich lägest du jetzt vielleicht im Wasser."

Sie kamen in die Reparaturwerkstätte [repair shop]. Aber wider Erwarten war der Wagen noch nicht fertig. Wer darf annehmen, daß eine Firma alle Ersatzteile [spare parts] für 25 jeden Motor hat? Sie müßten mindestens noch vier Stunden auf einen neuen Vergaser warten. Inzwischen könnten sie ja in den Ausstellungsraum [?] gehen; da gebe es etwas, das sie noch nie gesehen hätten.

Und einen solchen Wagen hatten sie tatsächlich noch nie 30 gesehen. Da stand eine Maschine, die sich selber waschen

konnte! Man brauchte nur auf einen Knopf zu drücken, und
Wasserströme rauschten aus dem Dach auf alle Fenster und
Seitenwände [sides] nieder. Wenn man eine Reifenpanne [flat
35 tire] hatte, dann hob sich der Wagen von selber, streifte das
alte Rad ab [stripped off] und ersetzte es von innen durch ein
neues. Wenn einen ein Polizist auf der Landstraße anhielt,
dann genügte der Druck auf einen zweiten Knopf, um den
Führerschein mit Bild und Nummer auf einem silbernen Arm
40 durch das Fenster hinauszuschieben. Alle tausend Meilen
kündigte eine Stimme durch ein elektronisches System an:
,,Fahrer, du brauchst neue Schmiere [grease job]!,“ und alle
fünfhundert Meilen bestellte die gleiche Stimme ein Logis
[lodging] für den kommenden Abend. Statt der Hupe [horn]
45 besaß der Wagen ein Kurzwellensystem [?]. Caramelli drückte
einen dritten Knopf und eine Stimme sagte im nächsten Wagen:
,,Bitte, geben Sie den Weg frei! — Rauchen Sie Plato-Zigaretten,
die einzigen Zigaretten, deren Rauch Ihren Verstand nicht
benebelt [?]!“ Und nach einer Weile sagte die gleiche Stimme:
50 ,,Ich danke Ihnen für Ihre Liebenswürdigkeit, den Weg frei zu
geben. — Vergessen Sie nicht Ihren Beitrag für die Winternothilfe [winter relief]!“ —
    Caramelli und Bates, die erfahrenen Fahrer, machten große
Augen und schüttelten den Kopf. ,,Es ist schade,“ sagten sie,
55 ,,daß Jerry nicht dabei ist. Der würde auch diese Maschine
noch verbessern!“
    Und sie gingen langsam durch den Nebel zu ihrem Frühstück
und beachteten [paid attention to] nicht den Zeitungsjungen,
der von einer gewaltigen Explosion in Sibirien berichtete.

Questions

1. Warum verbrachten die beiden Freunde die Nacht in
   einem billigen Hotel?
2. Worüber ärgerte sich Caramelli?
3. Woran mußte Bates immer wieder denken?

4. Wie glaubte er sein Geld verloren zu haben?
5. Warum war es gut, daß Caramelli dabei war?
6. Was sollten die beiden tun, während der Wagen repariert wurde?
7. Welche technischen Verbesserungen waren an dem neuen Wagen zu finden?
8. Was gebrauchte man statt der Hupe?
9. Was bedauerten Caramelli und Bates?
10. Welche Nachricht stand in der Morgenzeitung?

Vocabulary

an-kündigen   announce
die **Ausstellung, -en**   exhibit
der **Beitrag, ⁼e**   contribution
bestellen   order
dabei   present, along
das **Dach, ⁼er**   roof
drücken   press
einzig (*adj.*)   only
ersetzen   replace, substitute
fertig   ready, finished
frieren (o, o)   freeze
das **Frühstück**   breakfast
der **Führerschein, -e**   driver's license
genügen   be enough, suffice
gewaltig   powerful
hassen   hate
der **Knopf, ⁼e**   button
kümmern   concern
die **Liebenswürdigkeit**   kindness
meinetwegen   for all I care
mindestens   at least
der **Punkt, -e**   point

schade shame; **das ist schade** that's too bad
silbern silver
der **Strom, ⸚e** stream, current
tatsächlich in fact, actually
das **Thema, Themen** topic
verdächtig suspicious
der **Verstand** understanding
wider against

DATIVE CASE

GENITIVE CASE

Der Mittelpunkt

Ein junger Mann flog eines Abends in seinem kleinen Flugzeug von Terre Haute, Indiana, nach Peoria, Illinois. Als er sich der Grenze näherte, merkte er, daß ihm der Brennstoff ausging. Aber wegen eines starken Gegenwindes gelang es ihm nicht, den nächsten Flugplatz zu erreichen, und er mußte seine Maschine in einem Wassergraben niedersetzen.

Der Bauer, dem das Land gehörte, half ihm aus dem Sumpf. Als er des Fliegers ansichtig wurde, konnte er sich des Lachens nicht erwehren. „Nehmen Sie es mir nicht übel," sagte er, „aber ist es nicht komisch, daß Sie so heil da aus der armen Maschine herauskommen? Eine höhere Kraft muß Ihnen beistehen. Ist Ihnen bekannt, wo Sie sich befinden?"

„Meiner Meinung nach in der verlassensten Gegend der Welt!"

„Nein, das nicht — sondern im Bevölkerungsmittelpunkt der Vereinigten Staaten!"

ansichtig werden   catch sight of
*der Bauer   farmer, peasant
   *bei-stehen   help, assist
der Bevölkerungsmittelpunkt   population center
sich erwehren   suppress; **er konnte sich des Lachens
      nicht erwehren**   he could not help laughing
   der Gegenwind   headwind
*die Grenze   border
*die Meinung   opinion
*sich nähern   approach, come close to
      nieder-setzen   set down
   der Sumpf   swamp
   der Wassergraben   drainage ditch

EXERCISES

A. Replace the words in heavy type with the words in parentheses.

1. Ein junger Mann flog **eines Abends** von Terre Haute nach Peoria.   (one morning, one night, one day)
2. Wegen **eines starken Gegenwindes** erreichte er den nächsten Flugplatz nicht.   (this bad weather, his late departure, a severe auto accident, many great difficulties, my stupid mistake)
3. Wir kamen in **seinem kleinen Flugzeug.**   (our new car, a fast train, her old rattletrap, the green streetcar)
4. Kam er heil aus **der Maschine** heraus?   (the accident, his difficulties)
5. Er befand sich **im Bevölkerungsmittelpunkt der Vereinigten Staaten.**   (in the middle of the room, on the bank of the lake, in front of the entrance of the theater, in his father's office, in a group of the best students)
6. Um zwei Uhr näherte er sich **der Grenze.**   (the city, the sea, a forest, our house, his garage)

7. Es gelang **ihm** nicht, den nächsten Flugplatz zu erreichen. (she, we, they, our friends, my husband, the slow flyers)

8. Der Bauer half **ihm** aus dem Sumpf. (us, me, the flyer, his friend, his friend's cows)

B. In the following sentences change the tense of the verb as suggested under A. Then change the personal pronoun as suggested under B and C.

1. **Das Land gehört mir.**

A	B	C
belonged to	her	my father
has belonged to	him	an old peasant
will belong to	us	our relatives

2. **Es gelingt ihm nicht, das zu tun.**

didn't succeed	she	the flyer
hadn't succeeded	we	a young man
will not succeed	one	his friends

3. **Der Bauer hilft ihm aus dem Sumpf.**

helped	me	his cows
is going to help	us	the man's son
could help	you	our neighbor

4. **Eine höhere Kraft steht ihnen wohl bei.**

has helped	her	our firm
will help	them	these pretty girls
must help	him	the pilot of that plane

5. **Er nähert sich ihr.**

was approaching	him	the border
is going to approach	me	the most forsaken area of the world
had drawn near	us	the population center of the United States

C. Replace the English words in parentheses by the proper prepositional phrase in German. Translate.

1. **an :**
   A. Sein Haus lag (*on the*) See.
   B. Sie fuhren langsam (*to the*) See.
   C. Gehen wir jetzt an (*the*) Tafel!
   D. Er arbeitet jetzt an (*a*) neuen Werk.
   E. Es war schon spät (*in the*) Abend.
   F. Der Bauer war reich an (*cows*).
   G. Sie leidet an (*a severe illness*).

2. **auf :**
   A. Das neue Haus ist auf (*the*) Lande.
   B. Wir wollen später auf (*the*) Land fahren.
   C. Liegt er auf (*his*) Rücken?
   D. Er freut sich auf (*the*) Ferien.
   E. Ich bin hier nur auf (*a short time*).
   F. Ein guter Student darf auf (*his work*) stolz sein.
   G. Sie mußten eine halbe Stunde auf (*a new carburetor*) warten.

3. **in :**
   A. Nachher gingen wir in (*the*) Flusse schwimmen.
   B. Sie sprangen (*in the*) Fluß, um zu schwimmen.
   C. Das Ruderboot blieb (*in the*) Sumpf stecken.
   D. Haben Sie in (*the*) Buch gesehen?
   E. Er lebte noch in (*the year*) 1847.
   F. Stecken Sie nicht die Hand in (*your*) Tasche!

4. **über :**
   A. Das Flugzeug fliegt jetzt über (*the*) Stadt.
   B. Dunkle Wolken liegen über (*the*) Gegend.
   C. Er schrieb ein Buch über (*the*) alljährliche Eintauschen von Wagen.
   D. Über (*all*) Gipfeln ist Ruh'.
   E. Das geht über (*all reason*).
   F. Kommen Sie heute über (*a week*).

5. **vor** :

   A. Man trete jetzt vor (*the*) Laden.

   B. Ein Lehrer muß immer vor (*the*) Klasse stehen.

   C. Vor (*a*) Monat habe ich es schon getan.

   D. Warum hat er vor (*his father*) Angst?

   E. Wir sollen vor (*that time*) da sein.

   F. (*A short time ago*) flogen wir nach San Franzisko.

D. Following the patterns, give German equivalents for the English sentences. Word order will be exactly the same as in the pattern sentences.

1. **Aber wegen eines Gegenwindes gelang es ihm nicht, den nächsten Flugplatz zu erreichen.**

   A. They won't succeed in getting to the next town, however, because of the accident.

   B. But because of his laziness he didn't succeed in getting another A.

2. **Der Bauer, dem das Land gehörte, half ihm dann aus dem Sumpf.**

   A. The policeman who assisted the woman is now following her across the street.

   B Caramelli, whom the workers thanked, helped them out of their difficulties then.

3. **Das ist mir gar nicht bekannt.**

   A It certainly wasn't easy for her.

   B. That's completely new to us.

   C. It never was too much for us.

4. **Der junge Mann flog dann mit dem Flugzeug von Terre Haute nach Peoria.**

   A. The pretty girl was riding in a bus from New York to San Francisco.

   B. Many old people still take the train from one town to the other.

GRAMMAR

12.1 The **dative case** is used as the case of the indirect object, after certain prepositions, with certain verbs, and with certain adjectives.

12.1,1 The position of the indirect object varies according to that of the direct object; if the direct object is a noun, the indirect object precedes it. (Compare English: I'm giving the man the book—I'm giving it to the man.)

> Er gibt dem Mann das Geld.
> Er gibt ihm das Geld.
> Er gibt es dem Mann.
> Er gibt es ihm.

12.1,2 The dative case is always used after the prepositions **aus, außer, bei, mit, nach, seit, von, zu.**

In the meaning 'according to,' **nach** can stand after its object, as in the common phrase **meiner Meinung nach** 'in my opinion.'

The words **entgegen** and **gegenüber** also follow their objects:

> **Mir gegenüber saß eine schöne Dame.**
> A pretty woman sat opposite me.

12.1,3 The nine prepositions **an, auf, hinter, in, neben, über, unter, vor,** and **zwischen** govern the dative in space relationships when the sentence does not express motion to a new position or change to a new state. They are also usually followed by the dative in expressions of time: **vor einer Stunde, in zwei Stunden, am nächsten Tage** (but note **über acht Tage).**

Some of these prepositions are used in fixed phrases with certain verbs. One must learn whether the verb and the preposition are used with the dative or the accusative in each such phrase. The two prepositions most often used with the dative are **an** and **vor**. Selected examples are:

an :

> **Er leidet an einer unheilbaren Krankheit.**
> He suffers from an incurable illness.
> **Alle nahmen an dem Schauspiel teil.**
> Everybody took part in the play.

vor :

> **Ich habe Angst vor einem neuen Krieg.**
> I'm afraid of a new war.
> **Ich sterbe vor Hunger.** I'm dying of hunger.

12.1,4 The following verbs take their only object in the dative: **antworten, begegnen, danken, fehlen, folgen, gefallen, gehören, helfen,** and **widersprechen.**

In some verbs, the prefix makes the use of the dative mandatory:

> **Er entkommt den Flammen.** He escapes the flames.
> **Er winkt dem Mädchen zu.** He nods to the girl.
> **Gott steh' mir bei!** God help me!

The dative is also used as the case of the person or thing to which the verbal phrase refers:

> **Es bleibt mir nichts anderes übrig, als zu gehen.**
> There is nothing left for me to do but go.
> **Es ging ihm der Brennstoff aus.** He ran out of fuel.

12.1,5 The dative case goes with adjectives where the meaning 'to' or 'for' is present:

> **Ist Ihnen das bekannt?** Are you acquainted with that?
> **Das ist mir aber zu viel.** That's just too much for me.
> **Es ist mir nicht möglich, ihn heute abzuholen.**
> I can't possibly call for him today.

12.2 The **genitive case** is used to indicate possession or relationship, after certain prepositions, after certain verbs and adjectives, and as the case of indefinite time.

12.2,1 To show possession or relationship, the genitive may precede or follow the noun it governs:

Die Wohnung des Mädchens   the girl's apartment
Margarets Wohnung   Margaret's apartment
Die Geschwindigkeit seines Wagens   the speed of his car

12.2,2 Common prepositions followed by the genitive are **statt (anstatt), trotz, während, wegen,** and prepositions of place ending in **-halb** and **-seits.** In addition, formal written German uses a great many prepositions with the genitive: **mittels** 'by means of,' **zwecks** 'for the purpose of,' **angesichts** 'in view of,' and **infolge** 'as a result of.'

12.2,3 In formal and older German there occur a number of syntactical situations in which the genitive is used where a prepositional phrase is more normal in modern conversational style:

Er erinnerte sich der Sache.   He remembered the matter.
　　　　　　an die Sache.

Ich freute mich des Wiedersehens   I was happy about
　　　　　über das Wiedersehen.   [meeting again.

In other phrases only the genitive can be used, but these constructions are avoided in conversation:

　　sich (einer Sache) rühmen   to boast of
　sich (des Lachens) erwehren   to keep from
　　sich (eines Hundes) annehmen
　　take charge of, take into one's care

Adjectives are also used with the genitive:

　Ich bin mir meiner Schwäche wohl bewußt.
　　I am quite aware of my weakness.
Er wurde des Fliegens müde.   He grew tired of flying.

12.2,4 The genitive case is used for indefinite time: **eines Tages** 'one day'; **eines Abends** 'one evening.' From this usage have come such adverbial forms as **morgens, abends, nach-mittags,** and **spätestens.**

NARRATIVE

Enttäuschungen

Gerald konnte das Ende der kommenden Woche gar nicht abwarten [?]. Gewiß — er war stolz darauf, daß er, den seine Freunde „Die Schnecke" nannten, eine Verabredung mit dem schönsten Mädchen der Gegend hatte. Aber er konnte sich doch einer dunklen Ahnung nicht erwehren [get rid of]. Was würde in Zukunft aus ihm werden? Würde er diesem Mädchen jemals wieder begegnen? Sie war ihm so ans Herz gewachsen, daß er sich ein Leben ohne sie einfach nicht vorstellen konnte. — Die Woche verging ihm zu langsam, und doch wußte er, daß der Tag mit Margaret zu schnell vergehen würde.

Am Samstag nachmittag hielt sein Wagen, gewaschen und poliert [?], vor Margarets Wohnung, und Gerald, rote Rosen in der Hand, sprang leichtfüßig [with light steps] die Treppe hinauf. An der Tür erschien Margarets Hauswirtin, gab ihm einen Brief, und Gerald las:

Lieber Gerald!

Es tut mir von ganzem Herzen leid, daß ich Dich enttäuschen muß. Mein Onkel in San Franzisko ist einem Herzschlag erlegen [succumbed to] und ich muß am Samstag seiner Beerdigung [funeral] beiwohnen. Was aus mir werden wird, weiß ich nicht. Ich glaube, meine Verwandten werden nach dem Osten gehen, nach Detroit oder Pittsburgh, und da sie alles für mich tun, werde ich ihnen dahin wohl folgen müssen. Es war mir furchtbar lieb, Dich kennengelernt zu haben, und ich hoffe sehr, daß ein gutes Schicksal uns eines Tages wieder zusammenführen wird.

In Eile
Margaret.

Gerald sagte kein Wort. Die Hauswirtin sah ihm kopfschüttelnd [?] nach, wie er schweigsam [?] die Treppe hinunter-

ging und durch die enge Haustür verschwand. Eine Stunde
fuhr er in der Gegend herum, ohne ein Ziel. Er fuhr die
Landstraße entlang, der untergehenden [?] Sonne entgegen,
35 die sich blendend auf den Wellen des Ozeans spiegelte [was
reflected]. Und er fuhr unter den Tannen [fir trees] dahin,
die sich hinter und über ihm zu einem dunklen Gewölbe [arch]
zusammenschlossen. Gegen Abend, als er des Fahrens müde
war, trat er in ein Café.
40 An einem der Tische saß Hildebrand, alt und allein, bei
einem Glas Wein. Er winkte, daß Gerald sich zu ihm setzen
sollte. — „Morgen werde ich abfahren," sagte Gerald. — „So?"
sagte Hildebrand. „Haben Sie hier gefunden, was Sie gesucht
haben?" „Ich wollte mir während der Ferien etwas Geld
45 verdienen, und das habe ich verdient." — „Gut, junger Mann,
da sind Sie auf dem richtigen Wege. Wenn man an sich selbst
denkt, ist man immer auf dem richtigen Wege. Wenn man
sich auf andere verläßt, wird man bald selbst verlassen sein." —
„Das klingt ja, als ob Sie andere Menschen nicht gern hätten."
50 Hildebrand lachte bitter. „Andere Menschen gern haben!
So reden nur Pastoren und Professoren, und wer glaubt noch
den Professoren? Meiner Meinung nach liebt jeder Mensch
nur sich selbst. Ein Mensch baut sich ein Haus, ein zweiter
kauft sich einen Wagen, ein dritter erfindet eine Maschine,
55 eine Methode. Jeder liebt nur sein Haus, seinen Wagen, seine
Methode. Im Grunde aber liebt jeder nur sich selbst. Und
alle lieben das Geld." —
Gerald hatte zwar viel darauf zu entgegnen, aber er sagte nur
kleinlaut [meekly]: „Mir gefällt das Leben."
60 Da fuhr Hildebrand um so heftiger fort: „So? Das ist ja
reizend! Da sitzt ein junger Herr und sagt, daß ihm das Leben
gefalle! Und er weiß immer noch nicht, was er werden soll!
Hat man Ihnen jemals geholfen? Hat man Ihnen in der Schule
jemals geraten, welchen Beruf Sie ergreifen [take up] könnten?
65 Betrogen hat man Sie! Man hat Sie lernen lassen, was Sie
wollten und was Sie schon wußten, nicht was Sie wissen sollten!
Ja, der junge Herr ist ein Narr! Man hat die Energie seiner

Jugend verschwendet. Da sitzt er und nimmt sich eines heulenden Hundes an [devotes himself to] und einer kreischenden Maschine! Aber daß er einmal eine große Aufgabe erfüllen 70 könnte, das fällt dem jungen Manne nicht ein!"

Gerald wußte nicht, wie er auf die Straße gekommen war. Als er in seinem Wagen saß, sagte er zu sich selbst zwischen den Zähnen: „Der alte Hildebrand ist ein Teufel!" — Wenige Stunden später fuhr er in der Nacht über die Berge nach dem 75 Osten.

Er sagte sich, daß er vorläufig keine weiteren Veränderungen an dem alten Wagen vornehmen wolle. Der Motor summte [hummed] und trieb ihn vorwärts. Auf dem Gebirge fiel der erste Schnee. Da der Donner Pass wegen des Eises gesperrt 80 war, nahm er seinen Weg über Echo Summit.

Questions

1. Warum freute sich Gerald auf das kommende Wochen-ende?
2. Welche dunkle Ahnung konnte er aber nicht loswerden?
3. Welche Vorbereitungen machte Gerald für das Wochen-ende?
4. Warum hatte Margaret abreisen müssen?
5. Welchen Wunsch sprach sie in ihrem Brief aus?
6. Wohin fuhr Gerald während der nächsten Stunden?
7. Wohin ging er gegen Abend?
8. Warum glaubte Gerald, daß Hildebrand andere Menschen nicht gern hätte?
9. Welche Meinung hatte Hildebrand von anderen Menschen?
10. Warum hielt Hildebrand Gerald für einen Narren?
11. Warum hielt Gerald Hildebrand für einen Teufel?

Vocabulary

ab-fahren (u, ist a, ä) depart
der **Bauer, -n** farmer, peasant
bei-stehen (-stand, -standen) [*dat.*] help, assist
bei-wohnen [*dat.*] attend
der **Beruf, -e** profession
betrügen (o, o) deceive, cheat
blenden blind
dahin there, along
ein-fallen (ie, ist a, ä) [*dat.*] occur to
das **Eis** ice
entgegnen [*dat.*] answer, reply
enttäuschen disappoint
erfinden (a, u) invent
die **Grenze, -n** border
die **Hauswirtin, -nen** landlady
heftig violent; **um so heftiger** all the more violently
der **Herzschlag** heart attack
die **Meinung, -en** opinion
sich **nähern** [*dat.*] approach, come close to
der **Narr, -en** fool
raten (ie, a, ä) [*dat.*] advise
reizend charming
sperren close
der **Teufel, –** devil
die **Verabredung, -en** date
sich **verlassen (ie, a, ä) (auf)** [*acc.*] rely (on)
vorläufig for the time being
sich **vor-nehmen (a, -nommen, -nimmt)** undertake
wachsen (u, ist a, ä) grow
wählen choose, elect

Lesson 13

PERSONAL PRONOUNS

DEMONSTRATIVE PRONOUNS

INTERROGATIVE PRONOUNS

REFLEXIVE PRONOUNS

IMPERSONAL VERBS

Ein Geschäftsbrief

Freitag, den 13. April

Herrn Joachim A. Kaufmann
Buchhandlung
Stuttgart S.
Untere Badgasse 72/A

Sehr geehrter Herr Kaufmann!

Dankend bestätige ich den Eingang Ihrer Büchersendung vom 3. April. Ich bedauere, Sie darauf aufmerksam machen zu müssen, daß Ihnen in der Sendung ein Fehler unterlaufen ist. Wie Sie sich vielleicht erinnern, bestellte ich am 27. vorigen Monats 250 Exemplare von ,,Deutsch für Ausländer,'' neu, zu DM 8.30 das Stück, und 75 Exemplare von ,,Unserer Sprache'', neu, zu DM 8.67 das Stück. Statt dessen enthielt Ihre Sendung 250 gebrauchte

Exemplare des zweiten Titels und 75 Exemplare eines mir unbekannten Buches. Ich bin daher gezwungen, die Sendung zurückgehen zu lassen und sehe Ihrer Berichtigung derselben mit großem Interesse entgegen.

Ihr sehr ergebener
Hans Apfelkern

*aufmerksam attentive; **einen auf etwas aufmerksam machen** to call someone's attention to something

*der Ausländer foreigner

*bedauern be sorry

die Berichtigung correction

*bestätigen confirm

*die Buchhandlung book store

DM Deutsche Mark

*der Eingang arrival, receipt

entgegen-sehen await, look forward to

*enthalten contain

ergeben devoted; **Ihr sehr ergebener** yours very truly

*das Exemplar copy

die Gasse street

geehrt honored; **sehr geehrter Herr ...** Dear Mr. ...

die Sendung shipment

*die Sprache language

der Titel title

*vorig last, preceding

*zwingen compel

EXERCISES

A. Read aloud and translate the following expressions:

1. A. den 4. Juli
   B. den 30. IV.
   C. vom 17. Mai
   D. den 11. November 1918
   E. am 26. März 1956
   F. vom 20. bis 21. Mai

2. A. $6 + 5 = 11$ G. $367 - 145 = 100 + 122$
   B. $17 - 12 = 5$ H. $1/3 \cdot 2/3 = 2/9$
   C. $10 \cdot 2 = 20$ I. $3/15$
   D. $132 : 11 = 12$ J. $32\ 1/2$
   E. $0,08$ K. $3\ 100\ 240$
   F. $2/5 = 0,40$ L. $165,45$
          $16\ 545$

3. A. der dritte Mann   D. mit dem ersten
   B. im sechsten Bezirk   E. zweiter Klasse
   C. ein zweiter Brief   F. ein fünftes Mal
        G. zum viertenmal

B. Following the patterns, give German equivalents for the English expressions.

1. **Am 27. vorigen Monats**
   A. on the 13th of that month
   B. on the 3d of the previous month
   C. on the 30th of the same month

2. **zu DM 8.30 das Stück**
   A. for 16 marks per book
   B. at six and a half francs (*fr.*) a picture
   C. for a thousand dollars per share (die Aktie)

3. **fünfundsiebzig Exemplare des zweiten Titels**

   A. one hundred and fifty-six copies of the fourth book

   B. sixty-two pages of the first chapter (das Kapitel)

   C. one thousand and three copies of the first title

C. Address a letter, following "Ein Geschäftsbrief" as a model, to Miss Elsie Schmidt, assistant at the Institute for Foreign Languages, which is located on New Market Street, number 16-B, in North Hannover, Germany.

D. Following the patterns, give German equivalents for the English sentences.

1. **Wozu hat er sich entschlossen?**

   A. What did they decide?

   B. When is she going to make up her mind?

2. **Wie lange werden Sie sich da aufhalten?**

   A. Where did you stay there?

   B. How long have I stayed here?

3. **Wir unterhielten uns gut.**

   A. They were talking freely (with one another).

   B. I am enjoying myself.

4. **Dann hab' ich mich furchtbar geärgert.**

   A. Why was he so awfully annoyed?

   B. Afterwards she got terribly angry.

5. **Ließ sich das leicht verändern?**

   A. Can't that simply be changed?

   B. It couldn't be altered at all.

6. **Wir baten Sie, sich uns anzuschließen.**

   A. They came in order to join our friends.

   B. I asked him to join me.

7. **Ich lasse mich alle zwei Jahre untersuchen.**

   A. We have ourselves examined every six months.

   B. She had an examination last month.

8. **Der kann es sich kaum vorstellen.**
   A. I imagined it differently.
   B. Just (= nur einmal) imagine that!

9. **Wie befinden Sie sich?**
   A. How was she?
   B. Where is it now?

10. **Wir kauften uns ein neues Haus auf dem Land.**
    A. I'm going to purchase that new book by Maugham.
    B. What did she buy?

11. **Ich erinnere mich an die schönen Feiertage.**
    A. They don't remember anything.
    B. He remembered his mother, but not his father.

12. **Seitdem hat er sich daran gewöhnt.**
    A. We shall get used to it in (mit der) time.
    B. I've finally gotten used to her.

E. Complete the following pairs by translating the English sentences.

1. Caramelli verlor sein Geld. Did you lose yours too?
2. Er ließ sich seinen Motor reparieren. Must she also have hers repaired?
3. Haben Sie Schwierigkeiten bei solcher Arbeit? Certainly, I have many.
4. Der Mann kam mit seinem Sohn. The latter was very short, the former quite tall.
5. Erinnert er sich an ihn? Yes, he remembers this man and his brother as well.
6. Haben Sie von der Neff gehört? Of course; she's (*emphatic*) a famous German actress.
7. Mancher versteht es nicht trotz der Erklärung. In spite of what explanation?
8. Ich schreibe morgen an meinen Vater. When are you going to write to yours?

9. Mir ist ein Wagen zu wenig.   But for her one is enough.
10. Mir widerspricht er immer.   But he never contradicts those who lend him money.

GRAMMAR

13.1 Numerals and Pronouns [*see Appendix 4 and 5*].

13.1,1 Personal pronouns.   Although German has a complete set of personal pronouns [*see Appendix 4.1*], the genitive forms are used only after prepositions that govern the genitive and with verbs and adjectives that are accompanied by the genitive.

13.1,2 The emphatic pronoun **selbst (selber)** is indeclinable and is used with nouns, personal pronouns, and reflexive pronouns:
Er sagte es zu sich selbst (selber).   He said it to himself.
Der Vater selbst (selber) hat es gesagt. *or* **Der Vater hat es selbst gesagt.**   Father said it himself.

13.1,3 The demonstrative pronouns **dieser** 'this one' and **jener** 'that one' are also used for "the latter" and "the former":
Ich habe dieses schon gelesen, jenes aber noch nicht.
I have already read this one [the latter], but not that one [the former].
Hans und Fritz sind Brüder.   Dieser ist der ältere.
Hans and Fritz are brothers.   The latter is the older.

13.1,4 Forms of **der, die,** and **das** are often used as demonstrative pronouns or as stressed personal pronouns:
Hermann ist hier gewesen.   Den mag ich nicht.
Herman was here.   I don't like him.
In all forms of the genitive and in the dative plural **(s)en** is added to these:

	Masc.	*Fem.*	*Neut.*	*Pl.*
G.	dessen	deren	dessen	deren
D.	(dem)	(der)	(dem)	denen

Ich kenne Herrn Schmidt. Dessen (= seine) Frau war gerade hier.

The form **derer** 'of those' is used only as the antecedent before relative pronouns:

Die Namen derer, die an dem Stück teilnehmen, sind wohl bekannt.

The names of those who are taking part in the play are well known.

When a relative clause follows, **derjenige, diejenige,** and so on are also used as demonstrative pronouns. Both parts of the word are inflected:

Die Namen derjenigen, die an dem Stück teilnehmen, sind wohl bekannt. The names of those . . .

13.1,5 The **ein**-words are also used pronominally. The forms are the same as those of **dieser** :

Ich habe keinen Bleistift. Hier ist einer (meiner, deiner, etc.)

Hier ist mein Buch. Wo ist Ihres?

13.2 For a discussion of interrogative pronouns [*see Appendix 4.2*].

13.3 Reflexive pronouns are used far more frequently in German than in English. Very few reflexive verbs are translated with reflexive pronouns in English.

Ich ärgere mich. I am annoyed.

Er gewöhnte sich an das Leben dort. He got used to the life there.

Sie unterhielten sich darüber. They were talking about that.

Reflexive pronouns or **einander** are used for 'each other.'

Sie lieben sich. Sie lieben einander. They love each other.

Reflexive pronouns occur in the dative case also as pronouns of reference. These are usually not translated:

Ich kann mir das gut vorstellen. I can well imagine that.

Du kannst dir kein Beefsteak leisten. You can't afford a steak.

Sie nehmen sich keine Zeit zum Leben. They don't take
time to live.

13.4 Impersonal Verbs. German, like English, has **impersonal verbs**—verbs referring to natural phenomena that
have an impersonal subject, **es** 'it.'

Es regnet hier jeden Tag. Hier regnet es viel.
It rains here every day. Here it rains often.

Other examples are: **es donnert, es blitzt, es schneit, es
hagelt.**

In addition to these, German has many impersonal verbs
which are not translated as such in English:

Es friert mich. *or* **Mich friert.** I am cold.

Other examples are: **mich hungert, mich schläfert, es freut
mich, es wundert mich, es gefällt mir, es gelingt mir,
es tut mir leid.**

13.4,1 Es is also used to anticipate the subject: ·

Es brach ein Waldbrand aus. A forest fire broke out.
When the subject begins the sentence, **es** is not used:

Ein Waldbrand brach aus.

13.4,2 Both **es ist (es sind)** and **es gibt** are translated as
'there is (are).' A specific situation calls for **es ist (es sind):**

Es sind nur dreizehn Studenten in meiner Klasse.
There are only thirteen students in my class.

When a generalized statement is being made **es gibt** is used:

Es gibt Studenten, die das nicht wissen.
There are students who don't know that.

Es gibt is also used with reference to programs, menus, or other
scheduled items and events:

Was gibt es zu essen? What is there to eat?
Es gibt einen guten Film im Roxy.
There's a good movie at the Roxy.

Note that **es gibt** is always followed by the accusative case.

NARRATIVE

Ankunft zu Hause

Am Dienstag, den 22. September, abends um zehn Uhr, kam Gerald im Haus seiner Eltern, Ahorn [Maple] straße 128, an. Es war das erste Mal, daß er rechtzeitig zum Schulbeginn [?] erschien. Seine Mutter saß noch unter der Lampe im Wohnzimmer, als er, von der Garage kommend, durch die 5 Küchentür [?] eintrat.

„Mein Gott, Jerry, du bist aber braungebrannt [?]," sagte sie und schloß ihn in die Arme. Und Gerald lächelte und meinte, daß man nach zwölf Wochen Arbeit in den Wäldern leicht sonnverbrannt [?] sein könne. „Dein Vater hat sich 10 schon hingelegt [gone to bed]," sagte sie. „Er hat einen schweren Tag im Büro gehabt." — „Ich wäre früher gekommen, wenn es nicht in Iowa und Illinois ganz fürchterlich geregnet hätte," sagte Gerald, als ob er sich entschuldigen wollte. „Morgen wird es wohl auch hier anfangen." — „Wann bist du 15 in San Franzisko abgefahren," erkundigte sie sich vorsichtig. — „Samstag nachmittag," sagte Gerald etwas prahlerisch [boastfully]. — „Was? Dann hast du die zweieinhalb tausend Meilen in drei Tagen zurückgelegt [covered]! Junge, wenn dir etwas passiert wäre! Hast du denn nicht einmal Halt 20 gemacht [?] und geschlafen?" — „Doch. Am Sonntag abend habe ich mir ein Zimmer genommen, in Salt Lake City. Aber ich hab' doch nicht recht schlafen können und bin schon früh wieder weiter gegondelt [shoved off]." — „Dann geh nur gleich zu Bett und schlafe dich einmal gründlich aus," sagte seine 25 Mutter. Und sie saßen noch lange zusammen und plauderten. Sie bereitete ihm ein schlichtes Abendessen, und er erzählte ihr mit dröhnender [resounding] Stimme von seinen Erlebnissen des Sommers. —

Am Morgen regnete es in Strömen. Schon in der Nacht 30 war ein schweres Gewitter [thunderstorm] vorübergegangen, und als es unaufhörlich blitzte und donnerte, hatte Frau Hunter

ihrem Manne erzählt, wie kräftig [?] Gerald geworden sei und wie sehr er gereift scheine. „Das werden wir ja sehen," hatte
35 Herr Hunter gesagt.

Um acht Uhr wollte Herr Hunter seinen Sohn aufwecken, aber seine Frau bat: „Laß den Jungen doch ruhen! Er hat den Schlaf so nötig. Erinnerst du dich, wie müde du gestern abend warst? Stelle dir doch nur vor, wie du dich nach drei
40 Tagen Autofahrt fühlen würdest!" Dann hatte Herr Hunter nach der Zeitung gegriffen und nicht gemerkt, wie es neun Uhr wurde. Er sah zum Fenster hinaus und freute sich über den Regen. Die Wasserrechnung der letzten drei Monate hatte sich schon auf vierundzwanzig Dollar belaufen!
45 Um zehn Uhr kam Gerald herunter. „Da bist du ja wieder," sagte sein Vater und schüttelte ihm die Hand. Es freute ihn, seinen Sohn wiederzusehen. Ja, er schien reifer geworden zu sein. Aber warum mußte er sich so sehr von ihm unterscheiden? Er sah ihn einen Augenblick prüfend an. Dann
50 setzte er sich zu ihm und unterhielt sich ernst mit ihm über die Pläne für das kommende Jahr. Erstens sollte Gerald fleißig studieren; zweitens wäre es Zeit, sich mit dem Problem der Berufswahl [?] einmal gründlich auseinander zu setzen; und drittens sollte er nicht so viel Geld und Zeit mit seinem Wagen
55 verschwenden. —
Gerald kam erst spät am Nachmittag wieder zurück. Ja, er hatte sich eingeschrieben [registered]. Er hatte aber auch Robert, Heinrich und Willi wieder gesehen, und am zweiten, dritten und vierten Wochenende hatten sie Exkursionen [?] in
60 die Nachbarschaft geplant. Aber Pech muß ein Mensch haben: Gerade als Gerald in ihr Grundstück einfahren wollte, war ein Wagen hinter ihm vorbeigefahren. Er schaut sich um, und die Fahrerin lächelt ihn an! Bei Gott, es ist Margaret! Er reißt das Steuerrad herum; doch es ist zu spät. Schon ist der
65 Wagen gegen den Rinnstein [curb] gefahren und hat sich die Achse [?] gebrochen. . .
Es bestand kein Zweifel, daß das Leben mit all seinem Lärm wieder in das Haus Ahornstraße 128 zurückgekehrt war!

Questions

1. Was geschah bei Geralds Rückkehr in diesem Jahre zum ersten Mal?
2. Warum saß seine Mutter allein im Wohnzimmer?
3. Warum hatte Gerald nicht früher kommen können?
4. Warum war er nicht lange in Salt Lake City geblieben?
5. Warum ging Gerald nicht gleich zu Bett?
6. Wovon sprachen die Eltern während des Gewitters?
7. Warum weckte Herr Hunter seinen Sohn nicht auf?
8. Wovon sprachen Vater und Sohn am nächsten Morgen?
9. Was tat Gerald am Nachmittag?
10. Welcher Unfall geschah bei seiner Rückkehr?
11. Worüber bestand kein Zweifel?

Vocabulary

die **Ankunft, ⸚e**   arrival
aufmerksam   attentive; **einen auf etwas aufmerksam machen**   call someone's attention to something
sich **auseinander-setzen**   face (discuss and come to terms with)
der **Ausländer, –**   foreigner
bedauern   be sorry
sich **belaufen (ie, a, äu) (auf)**   amount (to)
bestätigen   confirm
die **Buchhandlung, -en**   bookstore
der **Eingang, ⸚e**   arrival, entry, receipt
enthalten (ie, a, ä)   contain
sich **erkundigen**   inquire
erstens   firstly
das **Exemplar, -e**   copy
fürchterlich   terrible

die **Lampe, -n**   lamp, light
    Pech haben   have bad luck
    prüfen   examine, test
    rechtzeitig   promptly, on time
    reifen (ist)   mature
    schlicht   smooth, plain
die **Sprache, -n**   language; speech
das **Steuerrad, ⁼er**   steering wheel
der **Titel, –**   title
    unaufhörlich   unceasing
sich **unterscheiden (ie, ie)**   be different
    vorsichtig   careful
    zwingen (a, u)   compel, force

Idioms

es **blitzt**	there's lightning
es **donnert**	it is thundering
es **regnet**	it is raining
es **schneit**	it is snowing

RELATIVE PRONOUNS

PARTICIPLES AS ADJECTIVES

Unfall

In dem erst vor zehn Tagen eröffneten Park passierte gestern abend ein Unfall, der leicht tragische Folgen hätte haben können. Ein mit zehn jungen Leuten besetztes Motorboot stieß in der Dunkelheit mit einem Ruderboot zusammen, in welchem sich eine Familie mit vier Kindern befand. Der Zusammenstoß war so heftig, daß nicht nur die Insassen des Ruderboots, sondern auch mehrere der im Motorboot befindlichen Leute. von denen keiner des Schwimmens fähig war, ins Wasser stürzten. Es gelang einigen herbeigeeilten Polizisten, die sofort ins Wasser sprangen, die Verunglückten zu retten. Wen die Schuld an diesem Unfall trifft, ist nicht festzustellen. Jedoch wurde der Besitzer des Motorboots, dessen Sohn das Fahrzeug lenkte, wegen fehlender Rettungsgürtel zur Anzeige gebracht.

die Anzeige notice; **zur Anzeige bringen** arraign
*besetzen occupy

eröffnen open
*__fähig__ able, capable
*__das Fahrzeug__ vehicle
*__fest-stellen__ establish, determine
*__die Folge, -n__ consequence
herbei-eilen hurry to the scene
der Insasse, -n occupant
lenken steer
der Rettungsgürtel life belt
*__die Schuld__ blame, guilt
der Verunglückte victim
*__zusammen-stoßen__ collide

EXERCISES

A. Supply the correct form of the relative pronoun and translate the following sentences.

1. A. Der junge Mann, ——— kein Flugzeug besitzt, muß einfach mit dem Auto fahren.

   B. Das hübsche Mädchen, ——— Caramelli im Spiegel-kabinett anblickte, hatte ihm wohl das Geld gestohlen.

   C. Die schöne Dame, ——— jetzt bei uns wohnt, ist uns sehr ans Herz gewachsen.

   D. Dem alten Hildebrand, ——— so bitter sprach, gefiel das Leben nicht mehr.

   E. Der Professor wollte sich ein Haus bauen, ——— für die ganze Familie groß genug sein würde.

2. A. Hat man Ihnen in der Schule, ——— alle jungen Leute einmal besuchen müssen, jemals gut geraten?

   B. Mit dieser Maschine, ——— er neulich von einem seiner Freunde kaufte, will er nächstes Jahr nach Kalifornien fahren.

   C. Er wußte, daß er sich auf das Geld, ——— er während des Sommers im Sägewerk verdient hatte, verlassen konnte.

D. Im Restaurant, in ——— er eintrat, saß Hildebrand allein bei einem Glas Wein.

E. Mein Sohn, auf ——— ich wirklich stolz bin, hat mir neulich geschrieben, er werde uns in ein paar Wochen mit einigen seiner Freunde besuchen, ——— er in San Franzisko kennengelernt habe.

F. Du wirst doch wohl nicht die Verabredung, an ——— ich dich noch vor einer Woche erinnert habe, ganz und gar vergessen haben.

G. Seine Gewohnheiten, um ——— du dich so viel kümmerst, gehen dich doch gar nichts an.

H. Nach seiner Meinung, ——— er so heftig ausdrückte, sollte jeder Mensch nur das Geld lieben.

3. A. Mein Vater, ——— Zunge immer scharf war, gab mir eine verneinende Antwort.

B. Meine Mutter aber, an ——— Gesicht ich noch mit Freude denke, war mir immer gut.

C. Danach mußte der Präsident,——— Herzkrankheit nicht so ernst war, wie man zuerst geglaubt hatte, mehrere Monate in Ruhe und arbeitsloser Stille verbringen.

D. Plato Zigaretten sind die einzigen, ——— Rauch den Verstand nicht benebelt.

E. Diese Menschen, auf ——— Liebenswürdigkeit wir uns jetzt verlassen, werden uns wohl beistehen.

F. Der neue Wagen, ——— Geschwindigkeitsrekord bis jetzt noch keiner geschlagen hat, besitzt ein Kurzwellensystem.

G. Das Lachen, ——— er sich nicht erwehren konnte, hörte man auch im Zimmer nebenan.

4. A. Als die Jungen den Bauer erblickten, ——— das Land gehörte, liefen sie schnell weg.

B. Der Lehrer, ——— ich nicht antwortete, stellte seine Frage noch einmal.

C. Hätte nur Jerry, ——— es gewiß nie einfiel, ein paar Worte darüber gesagt!

D. Die Zeitungsjungen, ——— ich immer ein bißchen Extrageld gebe, berichteten von einer neuen Explosion in Sibirien.

E. Aber dieser Narr, ——— wir alles erzählten, verstand kein Wort davon.

F. Die Stühle, auf ——— man im Klassenzimmer sitzen muß, sind furchtbar unbequem.

G. Die Werkstätte, in ——— er im Augenblick arbeitet, ist zu klein.

H. Mit dem Gelde, mit ——— er sich eine Eintrittskarte fürs Kino kaufte, hätte er auch etwas zu essen bekommen können.

5. A. Alles, ——— man Sie hat lernen lassen, ist Unsinn.

B. Ob ich eine große Aufgabe erfüllen werde, ——— mir im Augenblick sehr zweifelhaft scheint, läßt sich erst in Zukunft feststellen.

C. Bei der Versammlung gestern erfuhr ich etwas, ——— Sie bestimmt interessieren wird.

C. Explain the use of the pronouns in the following sentences.

1. A. Was der Mensch liebt, das sucht er.
   B. Was sucht der Mensch?
   C. Sucht der Mensch nur das, was er liebt?

2. A. Wer hat es Ihnen geraten?
   B. Wer es Ihnen riet, war ein Narr.
   C. Der ist ein Narr, der es Ihnen rät.

3. A. Er weiß immer noch nicht, was er werden soll.
   B. Und was er werden soll, weiß er noch nicht.
   C. Was soll er werden?
   D. Was er auch werden will, er wird doch arbeiten müssen.

4. A. Wessen Hund ist es, der jede Nacht heult?
   B. Wessen Hund das auch sei, der jede Nacht heult, er muß doch mal zum Schweigen gebracht werden!
   C. Der Mann, dessen Hund jede Nacht heult, muß diesen einmal zum Schweigen bringen.

D. Reword the following sentences to express the long attribute as a relative clause.

Example: **Der in einem beinahe auseinanderfallenden Wagen fahrende Mann** mußte in Terre Haute Halt machen.

Der Mann, der in einem beinahe auseinanderfallenden Wagen fuhr, mußte in Terre Haute Halt machen.

1. Dem in so viele Schwierigkeiten geratenen Menschen kann nur Gott helfen.

2. Auf diese von ihm vielleicht nur im Spaß ausgedrückte Meinung läßt sich keine Antwort geben.

3. Eine vom Himmel kommende höhere Macht muß Ihnen wohl beistehen.

4. Er wollte in einem mit kaltem Bergwasser gefüllten See baden.

5. Wenden wir uns zunächst einmal dem zu untersuchenden Experiment zu.

E. Follow the patterns of the German examples in translating the English sentences below.

1. **Gestern sahen wir einen Unfall, der tragische Folgen hatte.**
   A. Later he bought a machine which had a short-wave system.
   B. In the café we saw Hildebrand sitting alone at a table.

2. **Ein Motorboot stieß mit einem Ruderboot zusammen, in welchem sich eine ganze Familie befand.**
   A. Gerald departed on a plane on which there were thirty other people.
   B. He attended the meeting, at which several of my friends were present.

3. **Die sechs Leute, von denen keiner schwimmen konnte, stürzten ins Wasser.**
    A. Various people, all of whom wanted to help, replied to her questions.
    B. The new professors, none of whom was able to stay, went out of the room.

4. **Wer die Schuld daran trägt, soll sich sofort melden.**
    A. Whoever has any recollection of it is to inform the police immediately.
    B. Whoever is proud of it should express himself clearly.

5. **Den Polizisten, die sofort ins Wasser sprangen, gelang es, die Verunglückten zu retten.**
    A. My friends, who climbed the mountain yesterday, didn't succeed in reaching the top (= der Gipfel).

GRAMMAR

14.1 Forms of the relative pronoun. The relative pronoun has the same forms as the definite article when the latter is used as a demonstrative pronoun [*see 13.1,4*]. Forms of **welch-** may be used for all cases except the genitive.

14.1,1 In English, relative pronouns can be omitted when they function as the object; in German, however, they must be used.

The man we met yesterday talks a great deal.
Der Mann, den [welchen] wir gestern kennenlernten, spricht viel.

14.1,2 was and **wer** are used as relatives in the following ways. **was** is used as a relative pronoun:

1. when the antecedent is a whole clause:

Gerald verbrachte die Ferien zu Hause, was seinen Eltern sehr gefiel.
Gerald spent his vacation at home, which pleased his parents very much.

2. when the antecedent is **alles; was** or **das** is used when the antecedent is **etwas** or **nichts :**

Das ist alles, was ich besitze.   That is all I own.

Es gab nichts, das er nicht schon getan hatte.

There was nothing (that) he had not already done.

wer is used as relative pronoun when no antecedent is stated.

Wer nicht aufpaßt, hat oft Pech.

[He] who doesn't pay attention often has bad luck.

When a change of case is involved in the two clauses, a demonstrative is used in the main clause:

Wen Gott lieb hat, dem schickt er ein großes Glück.

God sends much happiness to the one he loves.

14.1,3 Compounds with wo- as relative pronouns.   When the relative is the object of a preposition and the antecedent is not a living being, compounds consisting of **wo-** plus preposition are used.   [Before prepositions beginning with vowels, **wor-** is used.]

Sein Wagen, womit kaum noch etwas anzufangen war, . . .

His car, with which scarcely anything could be done, . . .

Such compounds are also used as **interrogatives :**

Womit hat er das gemalt?   What did he paint that with?

14.2 We have already encountered **participles as predicate adjectives** and as **attributive adjectives :**

die Tür ist geschlossen   die geschlossene Tür

In both English and German these adjectives can in turn be modified by adverbs, *e.g.*, 'the swiftly falling snow.'   In German, however, more and longer modifiers are customarily allowed to stand between the article and the participle than in English. Modified participle constructions correspond to that of relative clauses:

**der Park, der vor zehn Tagen geöffnet wurde =
der vor zehn Tagen geöffnete Park
ein Motorboot, das mit zehn jungen Leuten besetzt war =**

ein mit zehn jungen Leuten besetz<u>tes</u> Motorboot
mehrere Leute, die sich im Motorboot befanden =
mehrere sich im Motorboot befindend<u>e</u> Leute

Note that participles in the attributive position have the same
endings as any other adjectives. Adjectives other than participles
can also be modified in this way:

mehrere im Motorboot befindliche Leute

Participles are used without limiting adjectives (articles, etc.)
just as are other adjectives:

„Margaret!" rief er <u>mit</u> vor Freude erstickter Stimme.
"Margaret!" he called in a voice (which was) choked with joy.

14.2,1 It is best to begin by translating all **modified participle
constructions** by relative clauses. The stem verb of the
participle is used as the verb of the relative clause:

Das von der Mutter <u>gekochte</u> Abendessen schmeckte gut.

The supper *which* his mother had *cooked* tasted fine.

If the modified adjective is not a participle, the verb 'to be' is
used in translation:

die des Schwimmens unfähigen Leute.
the people *who were* unable to swim.

NARRATIVE

Das Wiedersehen

Wen Gott lieb hat, dem schickt er von Zeit zu Zeit eine
kleine Warnung [?] und ein großes Glück. Gerald erfuhr
beides am Tag nach seiner Rückkehr in die Heimat.

Als sein Wagen über den dummen Rinnstein lief und dann
5 hilflos wie ein gestrandetes [?] Schiff auf dem Rasen liegen blieb,
hielt er den Atem an. Aber was ihm wirklich das Herz in die
Kehle trieb, war die Begegnung mit Margaret, wo er sie am
wenigsten erwartete, — die plötzliche Verwirklichung [real-

ization] eines heimlichen [secret] Wunsches, an dessen Erfüllung
er kaum zu glauben gewagt hatte.   10

„Margaret!   Wie kommst du hierher?" rief er mit vor Freude
erstickter [choked] Stimme und wollte ihre Hand nicht wieder
loslassen, die sie ihm entgegengestreckt hatte. — „Das wollte
ich dich fragen," entgegnete sie lächelnd. „Ich wohne hier
nämlich." Bei den gleichen entfernten Verwandten, die sie 15
eingeladen hatten, nach Amerika zu kommen — lieben und
freundlichen alten Leuten, die sich etwas einsam fühlten, nachdem ihre Kinder sich verheiratet und sie verlassen hatten, Leuten,
denen es gut ging und die jeden Winter nach Florida reisten.

Gerald wußte kaum, was er sagen sollte.   Seine Augen ruhten 20
glänzend [sparkling] auf ihrer Gestalt, und sie streiften [roamed]
mit Sehnsucht und schwermütigem Neid über ihren Wagen.
Es war derselbe elegante Sportwagen, in welchem sie vor
mehreren Monaten an ihm vorbeigefahren war. — „Du hast
einen kleinen Unfall gehabt?" fragte sie und nickte nach seiner 25
Maschine hinüber. — „Ja, ich habe nicht aufgepaßt auf den
Wagen, der hinter mir herfuhr," sagte er und sah sie lachend
an. „Ein trauriger Anblick, nicht wahr? Das ist alles, was
ich besitze."

Die letzten Worte hätte er nicht sagen sollen.   Denn Gerald 30
merkte, wie er rot wurde — und beide brachen in ein Lachen
aus, worin sie sich näher fühlten als je zuvor. (Die weitere
Unterhaltung war die gleiche, die so oft unter Liebesleuten [?]
stattfindet, und wir tun gut, die beiden Leutchen in dem von
ihnen geführten Gespräch allein zu lassen.)   35

Von diesem Nachmittag an war Gerald wie verwandelt.
Morgens kam er singend und pfeifend die Treppe herunter,
und oft war er schon aus dem Haus, bevor er das Frühstück,
das seine Mutter ihm hingestellt [placed before], gegessen hatte.
Sein Wagen, womit kaum noch etwas anzufangen war, saß noch 40
immer auf dem Rasen des Vordergartens [?] — wie zur
Erinnerung an längst vergangene Zeiten und ein Dorn [?] im
Auge seines „alten Herrn," dem diese unvorhergesehene [?]
und durch nichts zu rechtfertigende Verschönerung [?] seines

45 Besitztums keineswegs angenehm war. Aber er sagte nichts,
denn Gerald begann davon zu reden, daß er Geologie studieren
wolle, weil dieses Gebiet eine große, noch nicht erforschte
Zukunft habe. „Es hat keinen Zweck," sagte Gerald, „mich
mit dem zu beschäftigen, was ich schon weiß. Und in der
50 Schule hat man mir doch nie beigebracht [taught], was ich
wirklich wissen sollte."

Wenn das Telefon läutete, war es Gerald, nach dem
verlangt wurde. Abends spielte er auf dem Grammophon die
neuesten Platten, die sich durch einen fremden, ja bedrohlichen
55 [threatening] Rhythmus auszeichneten. Und ehe ein Monat
vorüber war, hatte er seinen Eltern Margaret vorgestellt, seine
hübsche Verlobte, die er in Kalifornien gefunden hatte. Ja, es
herrschte wieder Leben im Haus, und es schien nichts zu geben,
das Gerald von dem von ihm gewählten Wege hätte abdrängen
60 können.

Questions

1. Was erfuhr Gerald am Tag nach seiner Rückkehr?

2. Woran hatte er kaum zu glauben gewagt?

3. Wie kam es, daß auch Margaret nach Geralds Heimat-
stadt gekommen war?

4. Welchen Wagen erkannte Gerald wieder, als er mit
Margaret sprach?

5. Warum bot alles, was er besaß, „einen traurigen Anblick"?

6. Wieso war Gerald von jetzt ab wie verwandelt?

7. Was gefiel Geralds Vater nicht?

8. Warum wollte Gerald jetzt Geologie studieren?

9. Welche Meinung hatte er von seiner Schule?

10. Wodurch zeichneten sich Geralds Grammophonplatten
aus?

11. Was geschah noch vor Ende eines Monats?

Vocabulary

	ab-drängen	force off
der	**Anblick**	sight
sich	**aus-zeichnen**	be distinguished
	besetzen	occupy
das	**Besitztum, ⁼er**	property
	entfernt	distant
die	**Erfüllung**	fulfillment
	erforschen	investigate
	fähig	capable, able
das	**Fahrzeug, -e**	vehicle
	fest-stellen	establish, determine
die	**Folge, -n**	consequence, result
das	**Gebiet, -e**	field
die	**Heimat**	home, native country
	hübsch	pretty
die	**Kehle**	throat
	lieb	dear; **lieb-haben** like, love
der	**Neid**	envy
	rechtfertigen	justify
die	**Rückkehr**	return
die	**Schuld**	guilt
die	**Sehnsucht, ⁼e**	longing, yearning
	statt-finden (a, u)	take place
die	**Unterhaltung, -en**	conversation
die	**Verlobte, -n**	fiancée
	wagen	dare
	am wenigsten	(the) least
	zusammen-stoßen (ie, ist o, ö)	collide
	zuvor	before

Idiom

ein Gespräch führen   carry on a conversation

Kritik

A. Darf ich Sie fragen, wie Ihnen diese Geschichte gefällt?

B. Nur ziemlich gut; denn die darin vorkommenden Gestalten sind nicht wirklich.

C. Vor allem das Mädchen zeichnet sich dadurch aus, daß sie zu kalt ist und immer zu kritisieren hat.

A. Glauben Sie nicht, daß es manches im Leben zu kritisieren gibt?

C. Freilich. Aber kann man denn nicht auch etwas lesen, was die angenehmeren Seiten des Lebens ausdrückt?

B. Und ohne daran erinnert zu werden, daß das Leben nicht immer so ist, wie es sein sollte.

A. Aber wenn Ihnen das Leben gefällt, wie es ist, brauchen Sie ja nicht zu lesen oder ins Kino zu gehen.

B. So?

*aus-drücken express
kritisieren criticize
*vor-kommen appear; happen
*ziemlich rather

162

EXERCISES

A. Dependent word order.

1. Make a dependent clause from the second sentence of each of the following pairs, using the conjunctions given under A.

    Example: Ich frage ihn: „Gehen Sie nach Hause?"

        A. **wann**

        Ich frage ihn, wann er nach Hause geht.

2. Vary the verb of the dependent clause as suggested under B. Repeat the whole clause each time.

    Example: Ich frage ihn: „Haben Sie diese neue Geschichte gelesen?

        A. **has read**

        Ich frage ihn, wann er diese neue Geschichte gelesen hat.

1. Ich frage Sie: „Gefällt Ihnen diese Geschichte?"

    A. **wie**

    B. has pleased, can please, has been able to please.

2. Er glaubt nicht. Es gibt manches im Leben zu kritisieren.

    A. **daß**

    B. there was, there has been, there will be.

3. Sie brauchen heute nicht zum Arzt zu gehen. Es geht Ihnen wieder gut.

    A. **da**

    B. he has no time, he was called away, he is said to be very busy.

4. Wir standen auf der Straße. Gestern passierte ein Unfall.

    A. **wo**

    B. had happened, could have happened, was supposed to have happened.

5. Es war schon sechs Uhr. Er kam in die Stadt.

    A. **als**

    B. visited a sick person, drank a glass of beer.

6. Ein Monat war vorbei. Er hatte seinen Eltern Margaret vorgestellt.

   A. **ehe**

   B. had wanted to introduce, had been able to introduce, could introduce.

B. Translate.

1. Noch ein Geldstück in die Maschine werfend, ließ er die neue Schallplatte von Liane spielen.
2. Mit der Reparatur seines alten Motors beschäftigt, merkte er nicht, wie spät es geworden war.
3. Der untergehenden Sonne entgegenfahrend, wurde er so geblendet, daß er den Weg nicht mehr finden konnte.
4. Sich die Tränen aus den Augen wischend, schwor das Mädchen, daß sie ihnen das Geld nicht gestohlen hätte.
5. Am frühen Morgen in San Franzisko angekommen, suchten sich seine Eltern zuerst ein Hotel.
6. Auf das im Sommer verdiente Geld rechnend, plante er, das nächste Jahr in Europa zu verbringen.
7. Singend und pfeifend die Treppe herunterkommend, trat Gerald aus dem Haus, bevor er gegessen hatte.
8. Mit ihrer Geschichte fortfahrend, erzählte Margaret ihm von ihren letzten Tagen in Deutschland.
9. Sich auf die Freigebigkeit seiner Eltern verlassend, kaufte sich Gerald einen neuen Wagen.
10. Von einer solchen Hypothese ausgehend, würde es niemandem gelingen, die Wahrheit zu erreichen.

C. Translate.

1. Gewiß war er stolz darauf, daß er eine Verabredung mit dem schönsten Mädchen der Gegend hatte.
2. Man machte mich darauf aufmerksam, daß ich die Rückreise noch nicht bezahlt hatte.
3. Es handelt sich nämlich darum, ob wir uns rechtfertigen können.

4. Es kommt eben darauf an, ob er die Sache überhaupt versteht.

5. Er fürchtete sich davor, daß sie zu frühzeitig zurückkehren würde.

6. Das Läuten des Telephons erinnerte ihn daran, daß er um sechs eine Verabredung mit seiner Verlobten hatte.

7. Ich habe dich deswegen darum gebeten, weil ich es mir selbst nicht verschaffen konnte.

8. Das wird man erst dann verstehen, wenn es in klarem Englisch ausgedrückt ist.

D. Following the patterns, give German equivalents for the English sentences.

1. **Darf ich Sie fragen, wie Ihnen diese Geschichte gefällt?**
   A. Could I explain to you why you don't like this country?
   B. Should she tell him how the sight pleased her?

2. **Das Mädchen zeichnet sich dadurch aus, daß sie zu kalt ist.**
   A. His warning was characterized by the fact that it was so threatening.
   B. He became conspicuous to us because he was so tall.

3. **Ohne sich damit näher zu beschäftigen, gab er das Schreiben einfach weiter.**
   A. Instead of being annoyed with it (any) longer, we simply accepted it.
   B. In order to get used to it, he took it home with him.

4. **Das Leben ist nicht immer so, wie es sein sollte.**
   A. People did not act at all in the way we had expected.
   B. The countryside never before looked like it does now.

5. **Entweder weiß man es oder man weiß es nicht.**
   A. Either she loves him or she doesn't.
   B. A person either likes the cold or he doesn't.

GRAMMAR

15.1 The **position of the verb** in German clauses is a highly important indication of the meaning of the clause.

15.1,1 If the verb stands in first place, the clause is generally a question, request, or wish.

> **Darf ich Sie fragen?** May I ask you?
> **Laß den Jungen doch ruhen!** Let the boy relax!
> **Hätte ich nur nicht immer von mir gesprochen!**
>> Had I only not always talked about myself!

Two infrequent constructions also have the verb in first place:

A. Explanatory sentences following a statement: **doch** serves as cue to this usage.

> **Denn dies hätte eine glückliche Stunde für ihn sein können.**
> **Hatte er <u>doch</u> nie neben einem so schönen Mädchen gesessen.**
>> For this could have been a very happy hour for him.
>> *After all*, he had never sat beside such a pretty girl before.

B. Concessive clauses: **auch noch** serves as cue to this construction.

> **Saß er <u>auch noch</u> so gerne neben ihr, jetzt mußte er fort.**
>> No matter how much he liked sitting near her, he had to leave now.

15.1,2 When the verb stands in second place, the clause is an independent statement. The first element may be a word, a phrase, or an entire clause.

> **Wenn Ihnen das Leben so gefällt, <u>brauchen</u> Sie ja nicht Bücher zu lesen.**
>> If you like life the way it is, you really don't have to read books.

15.1,3 When the verb stands at the end of its clause, the clause is dependent. Such clauses are introduced by subordinating conjunctions and relative pronouns.

Es war das erste Mal, daß er sich zum Schulbeginn rechtzeitig einfand.
It was the first time that he arrived on time for the opening of school.

15.2 End of clause material. The end of the German clause is an important position. Non-finite verb forms, adverbs, adjectives, prefixes, and objects which deeply affect the meaning of the sentences are found here. Since these stand earlier in the English clause than in the German, one must read through an entire German clause or sentence before one can determine its meaning.

15.2,1 Position of non-finite verb forms.

A. Dependent infinitives and participles in compound tenses normally stand at the end of the main clause:

Das kann ich auch nicht recht verstehen.
Das habe ich auch nicht recht verstanden.

Occasionally prepositional phrases or **wie** or **als** phrases stand after the dependent verb form:

Der lange, dünne Caramelli hatte ausgesehen wie ein Ei, rund und dick.

B. The "double infinitive" stands at the very end of the sentence:

Das habe ich nicht recht verstehen können.
I haven't been able to understand that.

It is preceded by the auxiliary **haben** and **werden**:

Das würde ich auch nicht haben verstehen können.

I wouldn't have been able to understand that either.
In subordinate word order, the double infinitive is preceded by the finite verb:

Er sagte, daß er das nicht habe verstehen können.
He said he couldn't understand that.

15.2,2 When the **finite verb** is used in **subordinate clauses,** it normally stands at the end of the clause. (The "double infinitive" construction has just been noted as an exception to this.)

Es war das erste Mal, daß er sich zum Schulbeginn rechtzeitig <u>einfand.</u>

It was the first time he showed up promptly at the beginning of school.

Gerade als Gerald in ihr Grundstück <u>einfahren wollte,</u> ...

Just as Gerald was about to drive into their lot, ...

Exceptions to this order are also admitted in clauses containing prepositional phrases and **wie** and **als** phrases (see 15.2,1 above).

15.2,3 Participle absolute. Both the present and the past participles are used without auxiliaries in adverbial phrases. They normally stand at the end of their phrases:

Von oben <u>gesehen,</u> sah die Gegend wie eine endlose Wüste aus.

When viewed from above, the area looked like an endless desert.

..., als er, von der Garage <u>kommend,</u> durch die Küchentür eintrat.

..., when, coming from the garage, he stepped through the kitchen door.

15.2,4 Other elements which occur at the end of clauses are:

A. Adverbs:

Das ganze Gespräch mit der jungen Dame gefiel ihm nicht.
Das ganze Gespräch mit der jungen Dame gefiel ihm sehr.

He did not like the whole conversation with the young lady.
He liked very much the whole conversation with the young lady.

B. Adjectives:

Dies wurde aus ihren Worten durchaus nicht klar.

This did not become clear at all from her words.

Denn die darin vorkommenden Gestalten sind meiner Meinung nach nicht wirklich.

For the figures which appear there are, in my opinion, not real.

C. Prefixes, objects, and prepositional phrases:

Er geriet wegen seiner Leidenschaft für Sportwagen immer wieder in Schwierigkeiten.

He was constantly getting into trouble because of his passion
for sports cars.

15.3 In spoken German, stress and intonation are used as
cues to indicate the nature of the following material.

In writing and in formal speech, certain cue words are used
that are not usually translated into English:

A. **zwar** 'to be sure' for adversative statements introduced
by **aber :**

Er fährt zwar schnell, aber nicht zu schnell.

He does drive fast (to be sure), but not too fast.

B. **dann** for expressions of time introduced by **als** and **wenn :**

**Er verringerte nur dann seine Geschwindigkeit, wenn
Hunde und Frauen mit kleinen Kindern über die Straße
liefen.**

He decreased his speed only when dogs and women with small
children were crossing the street.

Es fiel ihm erst dann ein, als es schon zu spät war.

It did not occur to him until it was too late.

C. **dort** for clauses indicating location or spatial relationship:

**Er war immer dort zu finden, wo das Leben am brau-
sendsten war.**

He was always to be found where life was most uproarious.

D. **darum, deswegen** and **deshalb** for causal clauses:

**Es war mir deshalb unmöglich, ihm zu helfen, weil er
sich selbst nicht helfen wollte.**

It was impossible for me to help him, because he didn't want
to help himself.

15.3,1 The anticipation of following **daß**-clauses by **da(r)-**
compounds in the main clause presents a special problem in
translation. This can be met by translating the **da-** compound
with the preposition plus "the fact that":

**Nur der aus dem Wolkenmeer ragende „Teufelsberg“
machte darauf aufmerksam, daß eine Weltstadt hier
unter dem Nebel verborgen war.**

Only Mt. Diablo, which jutted out of the sea of clouds, called one's attention *to the fact that* a metropolis lay hidden under the fog.

Sometimes it is possible to avoid this clumsy circumlocution:

Das Mädchen zeichnet sich dadurch aus, daß sie zu kalt ist und immer zu kritisieren hat.

The girl is characterized *by being* too cold and *by* always *having* something to criticize.

15.3,2 da- compounds are also used to anticipate infinitive phrases with **zu :**

Wir wollten ihn dazu überreden, mit uns nach Kalifornien zu fahren.

We wanted to persuade him to drive to California with us.

NARRATIVE

Das letzte Spiel

Die Morgennebel rollten [?] vom Meer herein und hüllten die Stadt in solch undurchdringliche [impenetrable] Dunkelheit, daß die Straßenlampen länger als gewöhnlich brannten. Von oben gesehen, sah die Gegend wie eine endlose weiße Wüste

5 aus, und nur der aus dem Wolkenmeer [?] ragende „Teufelsberg" [Mt. Diablo] machte darauf aufmerksam, daß eine Weltstadt hier unter dem Nebel verborgen war. In höchster Höhe [?] zogen zwei Düsenjäger [jet fighters] weiße Linien durch den klaren Morgenhimmel.

10 Da geschah etwas Schreckliches. Bald zitterte die Erde und bald schüttelte sie sich derartig, daß Berge sich spalteten und Felsen ins Tal [valley] rollten. Und ein Licht erschien im Himmel, heiß und blendend, als ob die Sonne selber über dieser Gegend in tausend Feuer zersprungen [?] sei. (Später,

15 als alles vorüber war, wußte kein Mensch, woher dieses Licht gekommen war, ob es aus dem Himmel gefallen war oder aus der Erde heraufgestiegen.) Diejenigen, die es sahen, bedeckten ihr Gesicht oder warfen sich auf die Erde, nur um von fallenden

Häusern begraben zu werden. Während das Meer kochte und
wütende [raging] Wellen die Ufer überschwemmten [over- 20
flowed], mischte sich der Dampf mit dem Staub der zer-
fallenden [?] Stadt, und eine braune Wolke des Unheils [disaster]
erhob sich bis in die dünnsten Schichten [layers] der Atmosphäre. —

Und eine Stimme sprach durch den Staub: „Es brennen 25
die Berge, kein Baum bleibt auf der Erde stehen; die Wasser
vertrocknen, das Meer verdunstet [evaporates], der Himmel
glüht in Flammen; der Mond fällt aus dem Himmel, kein Stein
bleibt stehen; wenn der letzte Tag ins Land fährt, um mit
Feuer die Menschen heimzusuchen [punish], dann vermag 30
keiner seinem Mitmenschen [?] zu helfen vor dem Brande der
Welt." —

Erst spät am Nachmittag, nachdem Rauch und Staub sich
etwas verzogen [dispersed] hatten, gelangten [reached] die
ersten Menschen, denen es gelungen war sich zu retten, in 35
höher gelegene Orte der Umgebung. Graue, erschöpfte
Gestalten tauchten aus der Tiefe auf; einige brachen zusammen,
die anderen schleppten [dragged] sich weiter, ohne zu wissen,
wohin. Alle aber wollten so schnell wie möglich fort von
dem, was verwirrende Gerüchte [rumors] ihnen vorflüsterten
— von einer Explosion im Hafen, von einem Erdbeben [earth-
quake], von der Bildung eines neuen Vulkans [volcano].

In einem Feldlazarett [field hospital] wurde fieberhaft [?]
gearbeitet. Ambulanzen kamen an und rasten fort mit
kreischender Sirene; und kaum war in zehn Fällen Hilfe gereicht 45
[tendered], als in hundert neuen Fällen Hilfe notwendig wurde
und Tausende unter Ruinen [?] lagen und schrieen.

In einem einzigen Augenblick der Stille inmitten [?] der
allgemeinen Verwirrung wurden zwei Gesichter in Dämmerlicht
[dusk] der Empfangsstation [receiving station] sichtbar — eine 50
junge Helferin, der man trotz ihrer Erschöpfung ihre Anmut
[charm] ansah, und ein Ambulanzfahrer, der kaum unter dem
Schatten seines Stahlhelms [steel helmet] zu erkennen war:

„Diese zwei kennst du," sagte er. „Sie sind schrecklich

55 verbrannt, aber sie leben noch. — Ich fahre noch einmal hinunter und suche nach den andern."

Sie nickte. „Ja. Ich weiß, daß es sein muß. Aber komme wieder, sobald du kannst."

Er nahm sie in die Arme und küßte sie. „Ich weiß nicht, 60 wann ich wieder zurück sein werde. Jetzt kommt es nur darauf an, wievielen wir helfen können. Aber wir alle leben in immerwährender [continual] Gefahr. Von nun an wird das Leben eine atemlose Jagd [chase] sein. Wie wir in Zukunft leben werden, das hängt ganz davon ab, ob wir stärker als die 65 Erde und stärker als die Atome sein werden." —

Das Bild im Fernsehapparat verschwand unter lebhafter [?] Musik, und Herr Hunter drehte das Licht an. Gerald und Margaret standen auf und machten sich zum Weggehen bereit. Nur Frau Hunter sagte: „Die ganze Zeit hab ich euch in diesem 70 Spiel zu sehen geglaubt. War das nicht merkwürdig?" — Gerald lachte laut auf. Aber dann sah er Margaret an, blickte tief in ihre Augen und dachte nach.

Questions

1. Warum brannten die Straßenlampen noch am Morgen?
2. Was war im klaren Morgenhimmel zu sehen?
3. Was geschah auf der Erde?
4. Was geschah im Himmel?
5. Was geschah auf dem Meer?
6. Wohin retteten sich die Menschen?
7. Was war die Ursache des Unglücks?
8. Welche zwei Gesichter waren in der Verwirrung zu erkennen?
9. Was sollte der junge Mann noch einmal tun?
10. Was sagte er vom Leben in der Zukunft?
11. War dies ein wirkliches Unglück gewesen?
12. Was taten die vier Leute am Ende des Programms?

Vocabulary

ab-hängen (i, a) (von) depend (on)
allgemein general
auf-tauchen (ist) appear, show up
aus-drücken express
begraben (u, a, ä) bury
die **Bildung, -en** formation
der **Dampf** steam
derartig in such a way
endlos infinite
sich **erheben (o, o)** rise
erschöpfen exhaust
der **Fels, -ens, -en** rock
die **Gefahr, -en** danger
der **Hafen, ⸗** harbor
hüllen hide, envelop
kochen boil, cook
die **Linie, -n** line
notwendig necessary
der **Ort, -e** place, locality
ragen jut
der **Schatten, –** shadow
sichtbar visible
sich **spalten** split
der **Staub** dust
die **Umgebung, -en** surroundings, environs
verbergen (a, o, i) hide, conceal
verbrennen (-brannte, -brannt) burn
vermögen (-mochte, -mocht, -mag) be able
vor-kommen (a, ist o) appear; happen
ziemlich rather
zittern tremble

GRAMMATICAL APPENDIX

Grammatical Appendix

1 The Sounds of German

The general manner in which any language is pronounced differs from that of any other. To achieve success in speaking a new language, you must be aware of the way in which you pronounce your own language in addition to knowing the rules for pronouncing the language you set out to master. Americans who are learning German will find the following rules helpful.

German is more sharply articulated than is American English. Vowels are drawled in English; in German they are pronounced tensely, even when they are long. During the pronunciation of any German vowel, the position of the vocal organs is maintained steadily. Similarly, the consonants must be energetically articulated, especially [p, t, k] sounds in the middle or at the ends of words.

Further, German makes sharp distinction between short and long vowels. In English there is no complete set of long vowels as opposed to short vowels; the so-called "short vowels" are often held as long as the "long vowels."   In German the short vowels are really short, approximately one-half the length of corresponding long vowels; compare **Stadt : Staat.**

In German, unstressed syllables are more clearly enunciated than they are in English.   Speakers of English must accordingly be careful not to slur over unstressed syllables.

1.1 Vowels.   The German sound system, especially the vowel system, is simpler and more symmetrical than that of English. Vowels occur in long and short pairs, whereas in English the essential differences between pairs of vowels are in quality, not length.   However, the German consonant system, with a few exceptions, is much like that of English.

When pronouncing a German vowel, one must maintain a steady position of the speech organs; in English, on the other hand, there is motion during the production of most vowels. For this reason German pronunciation can be described as a vowel sound plus a hold (indicated by a colon in notations of pronunciation); the English pronunciation is interpreted as a vowel followed by a consonant.   (Notations in brackets [ ] indicate *pronunciation.*)   Compare:

	German				*English*		
lieg	[li:k]	**lug**	[lu:k]	**leek**	[liyk]	**luke**	[luwk]
leg	[le:k]	**log**	[lo:k]	**lake**	[leyk]	**woke**	[wowk]
lag	[la:k]			**lock**	[lahk]		

Besides the long vowels above, German has two long umlaut vowels (as in **lügen, lögen**) for which English has no equivalents.

German also has seven short vowels; these resemble English vowels more than the long vowels do, but they must be pronounced shorter than the English vowels.   Compare:

ißt [ist]	**Lust** [lust]	**list** [list]	**look** [luk]
eßt [est]	**Rost** [rost]	**lest** [lest]	
Ast [ast]		**Lost** [last]	

Besides these short vowels, German has two short umlaut vowels (as in **Rücken, Röcke**) which have no counterparts in English.

In addition to these fourteen vowels German has three diphthongs; these are similar to English diphthongs but are more tensely articulated.   Compare:

Eis [ays]	**ice** [ays]
Haus [haus]	**house** [haus]
neu [nöü]	**annoy** [ənoy]

These fourteen vowels and three diphthongs of German occur most often in stressed syllables.   Syllables of weakest stress generally have a short vowel similar to that in the second syllable of **Boston** (*cf.* **paßten**) or the first syllable of **alone** (*cf.* **belohnen**).

The complete systems compare as follows (long vowels are given first):

biete	bitte	Hüte	Hütte	rußte	mußte
bete	bette	Gœthe	Götter	Bote	Lotte
		raten	Ratten		

beat					boot
bit				book	
bait	but		boat		
bet	bought				
bat	bot				

The German long vowels [i: e: a: o: u:] are pronounced like the corresponding English vowels, but without a following glide. Contrast:

biet beat	**lud** loot
Beet bait	**Boot** boat
kam calm	

The German long vowels ü and ö are pronounced with the tongue position of i and e; the lips must be rounded, however, as they are for u and o.   Contrast:

Tür Tier	**hören Heeren**
Bühne Biene	**Söhne Sehne**

The German short vowels [i e a o u] are pronounced like the German long vowels, but are held for a much shorter time. Contrast:

biete	**Bitte**	**Hüte**	**Hütte**	**flucht**	**Flucht**
Beet	Bett	Höhle	Hölle	Hofe	hoffe
		kam	Kamm		

Some German speakers produce an additional vowel by distinguishing between long **ä** and long **e,** as in

gäbe   gebe

The German diphthongs **ai/ei, au,** and **eu** differ slightly from the corresponding diphthongs in English.   In English **ai** begins with a vowel sound like that of **hot** and continues with one like that of **heat** (*e.g.*, as in **height**); the German **ai** begins with a vowel sound somewhat like that of **hats.**   Contrast:

mein   mine   **Teil**   tile

The English **au** diphthong, on the other hand, begins with a vowel sound similar to that of **hat** and continues with one like that of **hoot** (*e.g.*, as in **out**); the German **au** begins with a vowel sound like that of **hot.**   Contrast:

Haus   house   **laut**   loud

The German **eu** diphthong is much like that of English, except that both the first and second parts are rounded.   Contrast:

Heu   ahoy   **keusch**   coy

The typical German vowel of unstressed syllables, [ə], is pronounced like its counterpart in English.   Compare:

Nickel   nickel   **vergeben**   forgive

1.2 Consonants.   The consonant systems of the two languages differ in that German has the additional combinations **pf** and **ts** and the [ch]-sound, while English has the combinations [tš] and [dž] and the [w, θ, and ð] sounds.   Compare:

German			*English*				
Paar	**T**or	kahl	par	tar	car		
bar	dar	gar	bar	**d**oor	gore		
lah**m**	**L**ah**n**	lang	lame	lawn	long		
fein	hei**ße**	fi**sch**reich	fine	**th**igh	sign	shine	
Wein	leise	**G**arage	vine	**th**y	resign	vision	

Pfeife **Z**eit .... judge church

helfen help

rein -**l**ein **J**ahr wine **Rh**ine line you

The German consonants are produced much like English consonants, and are therefore not difficult to pronounce accurately.

German [p b m] are like English [p b m]:

Paß pass **Baß** bass **Mann** man
Oper opera **Bibel** bible **Kamm** comb

German [t d n] are like English [t d n], but in German the tip of the tongue must touch the upper teeth:

Tee tea **Dame** dame **neun** nine
Punkt point **Ende** end **in** in

German [k g ŋ] are like English [k g ŋ]:

küssen kiss **Garten** garden **singen** sing
Haken hook **mager** meager **Gesang** song

German [f s š] are like English [f s sh]:

Fisch fish **scheinen** shine
sanft soft **Haus** house **waschen** wash

German [v z ž] are like English [v z ž]:

Vase vase **sie** [zi:]
Revue review **Busen** bosom **Garage** garage

The sound of the German **ch** is not found in standard English. It is produced by raising the tongue as for **k** and keeping the passage between the tongue and the roof of the mouth slightly open so that friction results. Scottish English has this sound in **Loch.** Standard English has a similar sound in such

words as **huge** and **hue,** but the German **ch** is pronounced
with more friction.   The place at which the friction is produced
varies with the preceding vowel; if an $\begin{bmatrix}ü\end{bmatrix}$ or $\begin{bmatrix}ö\end{bmatrix}$ vowel
$\begin{bmatrix}i\end{bmatrix}$ $\begin{bmatrix}e\end{bmatrix}$
precedes **ch,** it is produced closer to the front of the mouth.
Compare:

Front :	**Licht**	**brechen**	**welcher**
Back :	**Buch**	**kochen**	**machen**

Although some German dialects have a **ch** sound which is
very much like the **sch** sound, American speakers should avoid
confusing the two.   Contrast:

> **Kirche : Kirsche   Löcher : löschen**

The German [pf] and [ts] are consonant combinations which
are also found in English, as in **cupfuls** and **cuts,** and are therefore easy to produce.   In German, however, they commonly
occur initially as well as finally; one must practice them in the
initial position so that they are pronounced with no trace of a
vowel between them.   (An example of this pronunciation in
English is **tsetse.**)

> **Apfel   Katze**
> **Topf   setz'**
> **Pfennig   zu**

German **h** is like English **h,** and it too occurs only initially:

> **Hand** hand   **hohl** hollow

German **l** is like some English l-sounds.   It is pronounced
in the front of the mouth and has a clear sound; most American
speakers produce a dark or back **l,** especially at the ends of
words.   There is, therefore, a sharp distinction between the
words in these pairs:

> **Ball** ball   **Meile** mile

When they are initial, the l's of the two languages are similar:

> **lang** long   **Liter** liter

German **r** is quite unlike English **r.**   English **r** is produced
with the tongue curled slightly backward and differs little from

a vowel (compare **sofa** and **loafer**). There are two widely
used varieties of German **r**. The **r** most widely used is made
by trilling the uvula. Some teachers have their students learn
this **r** by making them simulate gargling. The other **r** is made
by trilling the tip of the tongue. The usual tongue-trilled **r**
is made by flipping the tongue rapidly against the roof of the
mouth. Most Americans pronounce in this way the **t** of **pity,
Betty** and **water**. This **t** serves as a good **r** in such words as
Beere (*cf.* **Betty**). If it can be produced in this word, it can
be carried over to others:

Jahre   ihre   rot   rund

After vowels, the **r** is often a glide that is almost an **h :**

Bier   Herr   Zucker

German **j** [y] is like the corresponding English sound:

Jahr year   **jung** young

Combinations of [š] plus **l m n r w p** and **t** are frequent
in German. Of these, only [šr] is found in English. Except
before **p** and **t,** where **s** is used, [š] is written **sch.**

schreiben	schreien	schlafen	schmerzen	schnell
Schwester	spät	sprechen	Stadt	streng

1.3 Stress and sentence melody. The stress of most
German words falls on the first syllable as in **Schnélligkeit,
Fúßballspiel.** In several groups of words, however, the stress
falls on a later syllable. One such group is the inseparable
verbs — **besétzen, versétzen, überréden,** and so on. The
second large group is made up of words adopted from other
languages; many of these resemble English words, *e.g.*,
Proféssor, Mathematík, Rakéte, interessíeren, and all
verbs in **-ieren.** One must learn the position of the stress as
one learns each word in this group.

In sentences, the placement of stress and the modulations of
the voice indicate the sentence's meaning as a whole. Some
sentence melodies of German are much like those of English;

for example, a drop in pitch at the end of a German sentence indicates completeness or assurance, *e.g.*,

Wir haben Anna gestern gesehen.　We saw Anna yesterday.

as opposed to:

Wir haben Anna gestern gesehen?　We saw Anna yesterday? The rise in pitch of this second sentence indicates doubt.　This rise is also heard in questions that are not introduced by an interrogative, *e.g.*,

　Ist er gestern gekommen?　Did he come yesterday?

German sentence melodies vary from dialect to dialect.　It is best to imitate those of a native speaker, listening carefully and repeating sentences after him.

1.4 German orthography.

1.4,1 The basic German alphabet is the same as that of English. Most books were formerly printed in an ornate typeface known as Fraktur or Gothic.　If one can already read German, Fraktur will cause few difficulties, for similar ornate fonts have occasionally been used in printing English.　Formerly a distinctive script was used in writing German, but today German handwriting is much like that used in English-speaking countries.

　In addition to the 26 letters of the English alphabet, German uses four modified letters: the 3 umlaut vowels **ä, ö,** and **ü,** and **ß.**　The latter, a form of double **s,** is used after a long vowel or a diphthong, at the end of a syllable and before final **t.** Besides the **ß,** some German type fonts have special combinations for **ch, ck,** and **tz.**

　The names of the German letters are pronounced as follows:

a	A	[a:]	f	F	[ef]	k	K	[ka:]	p	P	[pe:]	u	U	[u:]
b	B	[be:]	g	G	[ge:]	l	L	[el]	q	Q	[ku:]	v	V	[fau]
c	C	[tse:]	h	H	[ha:]	m	M	[em]	r	R	[er]	w	W	[ve:]
d	D	[de:]	i	I	[i:]	n	N	[en]	s	S	[es]	x	X	[iks]
e	E	[e:]	j	J	[jot]	o	O	[o:]	t	T	[te:]	y	Y	[üpsilon]
												z	Z	[tset]

In general, German spelling is regular and the sound value of the symbols is consistent. The following rules apply, however, to the pronunciation of consonants.

At the ends of words, **b d g** are pronounced like **p t k,** *e.g.*, **gab, lud, lag, Bild, Hand, Talg.** This rule holds if the **b d g** is followed by **t** or **s,** as in **gabt, Stadt, lagt, gab's.** The combination **chs** is pronounced [ks], as in **sechs.** (Speakers from north Germany often pronounce final **g** like **ch; Tag** then rimes with **Aach**-en).

The **-ig** suffix is pronounced to rime with **ich,** as in **billig.**

p before **s** is pronounced: *e.g.*, **Psychiater.**

k before **n** is pronounced. Contrast **Knie:** knee; **Knoten:** knot.

qu is pronounced [kv], as in **quer.**

th is pronounced [t]; **Goethe, Thema.**

At the beginnings of words and when single between vowels (as in **weise**) **s** is pronounced [z], as in **sein;** when **s** stands before consonants or at the ends of words or when it is doubled, it is pronounced [s], as in **ist, uns,** and **Wasser.** Initially before **p** and **t, s** is pronounced [š], as in **spielen** and **stehen.**

z is pronounced [ts], as in **Zeit.** In the suffix **-tion, t** is also pronounced [ts], *e.g.*, in **Multiplikation.** In the middle of a word, **tz** is used to spell [ts], *e.g.*, as in **nützen.**

v is pronounced [f], as in **viel.** In words adopted from other languages it may be pronounced [v], as in **November.**

w is pronounced [v], as in **wie.**

The appearance of a single vowel may indicate that pronunciation is short, especially if two consonants follow, *e.g.*, **bitte, Betten, hatte, Bombe, Bund, Hütte,** and **Hölzer.** Long vowels may be indicated by the presence of **h** after the vowel symbol, as in **ihm, sehr, Fahrt, Sohn, Huhn, Söhne,** and **Hühner.**

Other indications of long vowels are the spellings **ee, aa, oo,** and **ie (ieh),** as in **Beet, Saat, Boot, sie,** and **sieht.** It should be noted that frequently long vowels are spelled with single vowel symbols, especially if other forms of the word have only a single consonant after the vowel: for example,

gebt has a long **e** like **geben, gabt** as well as **gaben** has a long **a, rot** and **rote,** have a long **o, gut** and **gute** have a long **u.**

The combinations **eu** and **äu** are used to spell [oü], as in **neu, Mäuse; ei** and **ai** are used to spell [ai], as in **ein** and **Saite,** although **ey** and **ay** may also be used in names, as in **Geyser, Bayreuth.**

1.4,2 Syllabication. In German, syllables are divided between vowels and consonants, *e.g.,* **la-den, Au-ge, (hei-ßen), ko-chen, wa-schen.** Like **ch** and **sch, st** and **th** are not separated in dividing a word.

If two or more consonants stand after a vowel, the last alone follows the hyphen, *e.g.,* **war-nen, Höl-zer.** If in printing it is necessary to divide **ck** at the end of a line, it is written **-k-k-,** *e.g.,* **trok-ken.**

Compounds are divided according to their simple elements: **Haus-tier, Holz-ofen, un-er-bitt-lich.**

1.4,3 Punctuation. The simple marks of punctuation—the period, comma, question mark, and colon—are used in German as in English, with a few exceptions.

The comma is used much more frequently than in English; it must be placed before any dependent clause in the middle of the sentence, as in **Der Junge, der spät kam, war Heinrich.** 'The boy who came late was Henry.' In general, commas replace English semicolons. Commas also are used to mark infinitive phrases which have modifiers, as in **Es gefiel ihm nicht, den Wagen zu verkaufen.** 'He didn't like to sell the car.' Commas are also used for decimal points, *e.g.,* **1,3 (eins Komma drei)** = English 1.3. On the other hand, spacing alone is used to set off thousands; **152 643 721** = English 152,643,721.

Periods are used to indicate that a numeral is an ordinal: **den 8. Juni (den achten Juni)** = June 8.

Exclamation points are used after imperatives, *e.g.,* **Geben Sie ihm das Heft!** 'Give him the notebook.' They are also used after the salutation in a letter [*see page 139.*]

Hyphens are used to show that the second part of a compound will appear in a following word, *e.g.*, **Näh- und Schreibmaschinen waren nicht zu finden.** 'Sewing machines and typewriters could not be found.'

1.4,4 Capitalization and spacing of letters.

All nouns are capitalized.

Forms of the pronoun **Sie** 'you' are capitalized, but not **sich : Bitte, setzen Sie sich nicht auf Ihre Bücher, Herr Professor!** 'Please don't sit on your books, professor!'

Forms of the pronoun **ich** are not capitalized, nor are adjectives referring to nationalities: **Er hat mich gefragt, ob ich einen italienischen Brief übersetzen könnte.** 'He asked me if I could translate an Italian letter.'

In letters, the pronouns of address are capitalized: **Du, Ihr,** etc., as well as **Sie.**

Italics are rarely used in German. Instead, words are printed with extra space between letters. This device is employed in dictionary entries, for example: **d u m m, unklug : du bist dumm . . .** Occasionally this method is used to distinguish **e i n** 'one' from **ein** 'a, an.'

2 The Noun.

Nouns are words which are inflected for case, gender, and number. They are always capitalized in German texts.

For most forms of nouns, case is indicated only by the preceding **dieser**-word, **ein**-word, or adjective.

Gender, also, is usually to be determined from the preceding words, although nouns of specific genders are more predominant in some classes; *e.g.*, most nouns with the **-en** ending in the plural are feminine, most with **-er** in the plural are neuter.

Gender may also be determined from the form of some nouns: All nouns ending in **-er** which denote an agent are masculine, *e.g.*, **der Lehrer** 'the teacher.' Most nouns ending in **-e** are feminine, *e.g.*, **die Lehre** 'the doctrine', as are nouns ending in **-ei, -heit /keit, -ie, -schaft, -tät,** or **-ur**, most of which are abstract in meaning: **die Wahrheit** 'the truth.' Nouns ending in **-chen** and **-lein** are neuter, *e.g.*, **das Väterchen** 'the dear father'; further, most nouns ending in **-tum** and those beginning with **Ge-**, *e.g.*, **das Gebirge** 'the range of mountains' are neuter.

Number can often be determined from the plural ending. Although nouns must have a fixed gender and must stand in a definite case in a given sentence, they are not necessarily to be inflected in singular and plural; **der Osten** 'the east' is singular only, and **die Leute** 'the people' is plural only.

2.1 Forms of the noun.   There are several general rules of inflection:

1. The genitive singulars of most masculine and neuter nouns end in **-(e)s;** the other forms of the singular are generally the same as the nominative.

2. Feminine nouns have the same form throughout the singular.

3. The nominative, accusative, and genitive plural forms of all nouns are alike.

4. All nouns add **-(e)n** in the dative plural unless the plural already ends in **-n** or unless they make their nominative plural in **-s,** as does **den Autos.**

2.1,1 Class 1 nouns : no ending in the plural.

Since there are distinct forms only for the nominative, accusative, and dative singular, the genitive singular, the nominative, accusative and genitive plural, and the dative plural, we shall list only four forms for nouns in this class:

Sg. Nom., Acc., Dat.:	der, den, dem	Vater
Gen.:	des	Vaters
Pl. Nom., Acc., Gen.:	die, die, der	Väter
Dat.:	den	Vätern
Sg. Nom., Acc., Dat.:	das, das, dem	Mädchen
Gen.:	des	Mädchens
Pl. Nom., Acc., Gen.:	die, die, der	Mädchen
Dat.:	den	Mädchen

Sg. Nom., Acc., Dat.: die, die, der	Mutter
Gen.: der	Mutter
Pl. Nom., Acc., Gen.: die, die, der	Mütter
Dat.: den	Müttern

2.1,2 Class 2 nouns : -e in the plural.

Since these nouns may have **-e** in the dative singular, an additional form is listed.—Masculines of this class may take umlaut in the plural, feminines usually do, and neuters do not.

Sg. Nom., Acc.:	der, den	Punkt	Zug
Dat.:	dem	Punkt(e)	Zug(e)
Gen.:	des	Punkts	Zugs
Pl. Nom., Acc., Gen.:	die, die, der	Punkte	Züge
Dat.:	den	Punkten	Zügen
Sg. Nom., Acc.:	das, das	Jahr	die, die Kraft
Dat.:	dem	Jahr(e) der	Kraft
Gen.:	des	Jahrs der	Kraft
Pl. Nom., Acc., Gen.:	die, die, der	Jahre	Kräfte
Dat.:	den	Jahren	Kräften

2.1,3 Class 3 nouns : -er in the plural.

Both neuter and masculine nouns in this class take umlaut.

Sg. Nom., Acc.:	der, den	Mann	das, das Volk
Dat.:	dem	Mann(e)	Volk(e)
Gen.:	des	Manns	Volks
Pl. Nom., Acc., Gen.:	die, die, der	Männer	Völker
Dat.:	den	Männern	Völkern

2.1,4 Class 4 nouns. (1) With -(e)n in the plural.

These are chiefly feminine; there is no umlaut.

Sg. Nom., Acc., Dat., Gen.:
die, die, der, der Frau   Gabe   Lehrerin   Nadel
Pl. Nom., Acc., Dat., Gen.:
die, die, den, der Frauen   Gaben   Lehrerinnen   Nadeln

190 *Grammatical Appendix*

Sg. Nom.

der Mensch Knabe Herr

Acc., Dat., Gen.:

den, dem, des Menschen Knaben Herrn

Pl. Nom., Acc., Dat., Gen.:

die, die, den, der Menschen Knaben Herren

(2) **Class 4 nouns with** $\begin{cases} \text{-(e)s} \\ \overline{\text{-(e)ns}} \end{cases}$ **in the genitive singular.**

Sg. Nom. (Acc.):

der Professor Name das, das Auge Herz

(Acc.) Dat.:

den, dem Professor Namen dem Auge Herzen

Gen.:

des Professors Namens des Auges Herzens

Pl. Nom., Acc., Dat., Gen.:

die, die, den, der Professoren Namen Augen Herzen

2.1,5 Nouns with -s in the plural.

Sg. Nom., Acc., Dat.: das, das, dem Auto

Gen.: des Autos

Pl. Nom., Acc., Dat., Gen.: die, die, den, der Autos

2.2 Uses of the noun forms, including lists of prepositions.

2.2,1 The **nominative** is used (*a*) for the subject, (*b*) for address, and (*c*) in the predicate after **sein, werden, bleiben, heißen**:

(*a*), (*b*): **Herr Schmidt, Ihr Name kommt mir sehr bekannt vor.** Mr. Smith, your name seems very familiar to me.

(*c*): **Er wird wohl der Letzte sein.** He will probably be the last one.

2.2,2 The **accusative** is used (*a*) for the object of transitive verbs, (*b*) to indicate definite time or duration of time, and (*c*) after certain prepositions.

The accusative is always used after the following prepositions:

bis	until	**ohne**	without
durch	through, by	**um**	around, about, concerning
für	for	**wider**	against
gegen	against		

The accusative is used after the following prepositions when change of place is involved and when the meaning is figurative:

an	at, on, to, along	**über**	over, above, about
auf	on, in, to	**unter**	under, below, among
hinter	behind, after	**vor**	in front of, before
in	in (to)	**zwischen**	between, among
neben	beside, near		

(*a*), (*b*): **Den ganzen Tag hat er den Studenten besucht.**
He visited the student for the whole day.

(*c*) **Die Platte habe ich für ihn auf den Tisch gelegt.**
I laid the record for him on the table.

2.2,3 The **dative** is used (*a*) for the indirect object, (*b*) after certain prepositions, (*c*) for the only object after certain verbs, (*d*) with some adjectives, and (*e*) for the person or thing to which an action refers.

The dative is always used after the following prepositions:

aus	out of, from	**mit**	with
außer	besides	**nach**	after, according to, to
bei	at, near, at the house of, in the case of		[*may stand after noun*]
		nächst	next to
		nebst	besides
entgegen	in contrast with, toward, against	**samt**	together with
		seit	since, for
		von	from, by, about
gegenüber	opposed to [*often stands after noun*]	**zu**	to, at

The dative is used after the second group of prepositions in **2.2,2** above when change of place is not involved.

The most common verbs after which the dative alone is used are:[1]

antworten	answer	**gehören**	belong
begegnen	meet	**gelingen**	succeed
danken	thank	**glauben**	believe
einfallen	occur to	**gleichen**	resemble
fehlen	lack	**helfen**	help
folgen	follow	**passen**	fit
gefallen	please	**widersprechen**	contradict
		widerstehen	resist

Adjectives with which the dative is used are:

ähnlich	similar	**möglich**	possible
angenehm	pleasant	**nützlich**	useful
bekannt	known	**treu**	faithful
gleich	similar	**verwandt**	related
leicht	easy		

(*a*): **Schicken Sie mir das Buch später!** Send me the book later.

(*b*): **Bei ihnen im Haus wird er nicht lange bleiben.** He won't stay long in their house.

(*c*): **Er entkam den Flammen.** He escaped from the flames.

(*d*): **Ist es Ihnen bekannt?** Do you know (it)?

(*e*): **Nimm es mir nicht übel!** Don't take offense at it (with regard to me).

2.2,4 The **genitive** is used (*a*) to indicate possession or relationship, (*b*) after certain prepositions, (*c*) after some verbs, especially in more formal writing, and (*d*) after some adjectives.

Prepositions after which the genitive is used are:

außerhalb	outside of	**statt/anstatt**	instead of
diesseit(s)	this side of	**trotz**	in spite of
innerhalb	inside of	**unterhalb**	below
jenseit(s)	that side of	**während**	during
mittels	by means of	**wegen**	on account of
oberhalb	on top of, above	**um... willen**	for the sake of

Verbs after which the genitive is used are:

sich erinnern remember   **bedürfen** need
sich freuen   rejoice at   **gedenken** think of
sich rühmen boast of

Adjectives after which the genitive is used are:

bewußt aware of   **müde**   tired of
fähig   capable of   **würdig** worthy of

(*a*), (*b*): **Ihres Vaters Haus liegt außerhalb der Stadt.**
Her father's house is situated outside of the city.

(*a*), (*b*): **Wegen meiner Krankheit schmeckte mir der Inhalt der Flasche nicht.** The contents of the bottle didn't taste good because of my illness.

(*c*): **Er erinnerte sich der Sache [an die Sache] zu spät.** He remembered the thing too late.

(*d*): **Er wurde des Fliegens müde.** He grew tired of flying.

3 The der-words, ein-words, and Adjectives.

Words which modify nouns may be divided into two groups:

(1) **der**-words and **ein**-words: these are always inflected in a certain way, and adjectives standing after them require a certain set of endings.

(2) adjectives: these may be inflected variously, depending on what precedes them.

3.1 The **der**-words are inflected like **dieser**. In addition to **dieser**, they are **jeder, jener, mancher, solcher,** and **welcher.** [*For the inflection of* **der, die,** *and* **das,** *see* 3.2 *below*.]

	M.	F.	N.		
Sg. Nom.	dieser	diese	dieses	Pl.	diese
Acc.	diesen	diese	dieses		diese
Dat.	diesem	dieser	diesem		diesen
Gen.	dieses	dieser	dieses		dieser

The **ein**-words are inflected like **kein.** The others are **mein, dein, sein, ihr, sein, unser, euer, ihr,** and **Ihr.** Note that the -**er** of **unser** and **euer** is not an ending but belongs to the stem; in inflection, the -**e**- of these two **ein**-words often drops out, as in **unsre, euren.**

		M.	F.	N.		
Sg.	*Nom.*	kein	keine	kein	*Pl.*	keine
	Acc.	keinen	keine	kein		keine
	Dat.	keinem	keiner	keinem		keinen
	Gen.	keines	keiner	keines		keiner

3.2 Adjectives are inflected variously, depending on the preceding word.

3.2,1 Adjectives standing after **der**-words or **ein**-words have -**en** endings in all forms but five in the singular — the masculine nominative, the feminine nominative and accusative, and the neuter nominative and accusative.

After **der**-words, these five forms have the ending -**e** :

		M.			F.	
Sg.	*Nom.*	der	junge Mann	die	junge Frau	
	Acc.	den	jungen Mann	die	junge Frau	
	Dat.	dem	jungen Mann	der	jungen Frau	
	Gen.	des	jungen Mannes	der	jungen Frau	

		N				
Sg.	*Nom.*	das junge Kind	*Pl.*	die	jungen Leute
	Acc.	das junge Kind		die	jungen Leute
	Dat.	dem jungen Kind		den	jungen Leuten
	Gen.	des jungen Kindes		der	jungen Leute

After **ein**-words the masculine nominative has -**er**, the feminine nominative and accusative again have -**e**, and the neuter nominative and accusative have -**es** :

		M.			F	
Sg.	*Nom.*	ein	junger Mann	eine	junge Frau	
	Acc.	einen	jungen Mann	eine	junge Frau	
	Dat.	einem	jungen Mann	einer	jungen Frau	
	Gen.	eines	jungen Mannes	einer	jungen Frau	

N

Sg.	*Nom.*	ein	jung**es** Kind	*Pl.*	keine	jung**en** Leute
	Acc.	ein	jung**es** Kind		keine	jung**en** Leute
	Dat.	ein**em** jung**en** Kind			kein**en** jung**en** Leuten
	Gen.	ein**es** jung**en** Kind**es**			kein**er** jung**en** Leute

Adjectives which are not preceded by **der**-words or **ein**-words have the endings of **dieser** except the masculine and neuter genitive singular, which have **-en**

		M		F	
Sg.	*Nom.*	grün**er**	Tee	dick**e**	Milch
	Acc.	grün**en**	Tee	dick**e**	Milch
	Dat.	grün**em**	Tee	dick**er**	Milch
	Gen.	grün**en**	Tees	dick**er**	Milch

N

Sg.	*Nom.*	frisch**es**	Brot	*Pl.*	jung**e**	Leute
	Acc.	frisch**es**	Brot		jung**e**	Leute
	Dat.	frisch**em**	Brot		jung**en**	Leuten
	Gen.	frisch**en**	Brot**es**		jung**er**	Leute

If two or more adjectives are used before one noun, they all have the same ending. Adjectives which follow **andere, einige, mehrere, viele** and **wenige** have the same ending as these.

3.2,2 Comparative and superlative forms of adjectives :

To make the comparative form, **-er** is added to adjectives, and **-(e)st** is added to make the superlative: **jung, jünger, jüngst-.** Like **jung,** most monosyllabic adjectives take umlaut when they become comparatives. When the adjective ends in **t, s, z, ß,** or **sch, -est** is added: **alt, älter, ältest-.**

Unless the superlative is used after a **der**-word or an **ein**-word, it is preceded by **am** (*i.e.,* as predicate adjective and adverb). Examples are:

jung	jünger	der jüngste	am jüngsten
alt	älter	der älteste	am ältesten
gut	besser	der beste	am besten
viel	mehr	der meiste	am meisten
hoch	höher	der höchste	am höchsten

Karl sieht jung aus.	Karl looks young
Hans sieht jünger aus.	Hans looks younger.
Fritz sieht am jüngsten aus.	Fritz looks youngest.

No German adjective, including participles, uses adverbs in comparison (as English **more interesting, most pressing**):

interessant	interessanter	interessantest-
dringend	dringender	dringendst-

When no comparison is intended in the use of the superlative, the phrase **aufs- ...te** is used ; this is equivalent to the English 'very ...':

Er ging aufs schnellste. He walked very fast.

When comparing two or more objects, the following phrases are generally used:

so (gut) wie   **(besser) als**

Karl ist so jung wie Anna.   **Anna ist älter als Hans.**

(der beste) von ...

Fritz ist der jüngste von allen.

3.2,3 Adjectives used as nouns. Adjectives, including participles, may be used as nouns, but in this use they retain their adjective inflections: **der Einsame** 'the lonesome (man)'; **die Empfindliche** 'the sensitive (woman)'; **das Schöne** 'the beautiful'; **ein Einsamer** 'a lonesome (man)'; **eine Empfindliche** 'a sensitive (woman)'; **ein Deutscher, eine Deutsche; der Verwandte, ein Verwandter,** etc.; **ein Einsamerer** 'a more lonesome (man).'

4. Pronouns.

Pronouns are used in place of nouns to refer to persons or things which have already been mentioned or which are clear from the context. They are inflected for case and number, but not throughout for gender.

4.1 Personal pronouns; reflexives.

4.1,1 The German personal pronouns are:

Nom.	ich	er	sie	es	du	Sie
Acc.	mich	ihn	sie	es	dich	Sie
Dat.	mir	ihm	ihr	ihm	dir	Ihnen
Gen.	meiner	seiner	ihrer	seiner	deiner	Ihrer

Nom.	wir	sie	ihr	Sie
Acc.	uns	sie	euch	Sie
Dat.	uns	ihnen	euch	Ihnen
Gen.	unser	ihrer	euer	Ihrer

The genitive forms are used only in formal style. As the pronoun of address, **Sie** is most common; **du** and **ihr** are used to members of one's family, to close friends, to servants and animals, and to God in prayer.

4.1,2 When a pronoun refers to the same person or thing as does the subject, it is reflexive. The dative and accusative of personal pronouns are used in reflexive constructions except in the third person and with **Sie,** where **sich** is used for both dative and accusative. (Note that **sich** is not capitalized when used with **Sie.**)

Er nahm sich ein Exemplar. He took a copy for himself.

Setzen Sie sich, bitte! Sit down, please.

As in this example, many reflexives occur in verb phrases that are not translated with pronouns in English; the reflexive may be dative with some verbs:

Ich kann mir das kaum vorstellen. I can hardly imagine that.

4.1,3 Reflexives or **einander** are used interchangeably for the meaning 'each other, one another' (reciprocal relation):

Wir haben uns/einander dort gesehen.

We saw each other there.

4.1,4 selbst and **selber** are used as emphatics with nouns, personal pronouns, and reflexives; they are undeclined.

Der Junge selbst ist mitgegangen.

Der Junge ist selbst mitgegangen.

The boy himself went along *or* The boy too went along.
Selbst may precede the word to which it applies, and then
can be translated 'even': **Selbst der Professor verstand
nichts.** Even the professor didn't understand anything.
Selbst in der Ecke fand man keinen Staub. Even in the
corner there was no dust to be found.

4.2 Interrogatives. The interrogatives **wer** and **was** correspond to 'who' and 'what'; **was** is used only in the nominative
and accusative, **wer** in all four cases: nom. **wer,** acc. **wen,**
dat. **wem,** gen. **wessen.**

Welcher, a **der**-word, is used as an interrogative adjective
or as an interrogative pronoun in the meaning 'which one':

Welches Mädchen hätte mitkommen sollen?
Which girl should have come along?
Welche ging mit?   Which one went along?

When interrogatives plus prepositions refer to things rather
than persons, compounds of **wo(r)-** plus the preposition are
used:

Wovon erzählte er?   What did he tell about?
Worüber unterhielten Sie sich?   What did they discuss?
(Compare the older English "*Whereof* did they speak?")   The
-r- is used when prepositions begin with a vowel.

4.3 Relative Pronouns. The usual relative has the same
form as the definite article, except that in the four genitive
forms and the dative plural **-(s)en** is added:

Sg.	der	die	das	*Pl.*	die
	den	die	das		die
	dem	der	dem		denen
	dessen	deren	dessen		deren

Forms of **welcher** may be used for all forms but the genitive.

Relatives refer to a word or statement preceding them (their
antecedent) and must agree grammatically with that antecedent
in number and gender; the case of a relative is determined
by its function in the clause.

Er erzählte von einem Unfall, der leicht tragische Folgen hätte haben können.

He told of an accident that could easily have had tragic results. In this sentence, the relative **der** is singular and masculine because its antecedent is **der Unfall,** but it is nominative because it is the subject of its own clause.

4.3,1 When no antecedent is stated, **wer** and **was** are used as relatives:

Wer das Fenster zerbrochen hat, sollte auch dafür bezahlen.
Whoever broke the window should also pay for it.
Aber was ihm wirklich das Herz in die Kehle trieb, war die Begegnung mit Margaret.
But what really drove his heart into his throat was the meeting with Margaret.

was is also used as a relative pronoun when:

(1) the antecedent is a complete statement:

Er schickte mir das Geld, was ich auch erwartet hatte.
He sent me the money, which I had expected anyway.

(2) the antecedent is **alles, etwas, nichts** or **das** (**das** may also be used as relative after the last three):

Ist das alles, was er kann? Is that everything he can do?
Nichts, was ich getan habe, scheint richtig zu sein.
Nothing that I've done seems to be right.

4.3,2 When relatives plus prepositions do not refer to persons, compounds of **wo(r)-** plus the preposition are used:

Er schickte mir das Geld, womit ich die Reise bezahlen sollte.
He sent me the money with which I was to pay for the trip.
Ist das alles, worüber Sie schreiben können?
Is that all you can write about?

4.4 Demonstratives and possessives. The articles **der, die,** and **das** may be used as pronouns. When so used they correspond to "that [one], he," and are spoken with strong stress. In this use they take the **-en** forms in the genitive and the dative plural (*cf.* the relative pronoun).

Der ist nicht mehr hier. He is no longer here.

Von der weiß ich sehr wenig. I know little about her.

If such a demonstrative is used in the genitive plural as the antecedent of a relative, **derer** is substituted for **deren :**

Die Namen derer, von denen wir eben gesprochen haben,
sollten wir nicht weitergeben.

We ought not communicate elsewhere the names of those
whom we have just been talking about.

The other **der**-words may also be used as pronouns. **Dieser** and **jener** are particularly common in this use: **jener** corresponds to 'the former,' **dieser** to 'the latter':

Unter allen Studenten hatte er vielleicht Hans und Willi
am liebsten, aber jener hatte sich kaum ausgezeichnet.

Among all the students he probably liked Hans and Willi best;
the former, however, had hardly distinguished himself.

derjenige, diejenige, and **dasjenige** are also used as demonstratives, especially as antecedents of relative clauses. The **der-, die-,** and **das-** of these compounds are inflected like the definite article, **-jenige** like an adjective:

Die Namen derjenigen, von denen . . .

The names of those about whom . . .

ein-words are also used as demonstratives. In this use, the three forms without endings, (the masculine nominative, the neuter nominative and accusative) have the endings of the **der**-words. **Ein**-words other than **ein** and **kein** are often known as possessive pronouns.

Keiner hatte so einen Wagen wie Hans, und seiner war
nur ein Porsche.

No one had such a car as Hans, and his was only a Porsche.

ein- is used in the nominative, accusative, and dative for the number pronoun 'one' and the pronoun form of the indefinite article:

Er hat zwei Wagen, ich nur einen.

He has two cars, I only one.

Karl hat einen Porsche; sein Vater hat auch einen.

Karl has a Porsche; his father also has one.

Ein- is also used in the accusative and dative for the indefinite pronoun **man :**

Und das erzählt man einem nicht!

And that they don't tell anybody!

Other indefinite pronouns are **jemand** 'someone', **niemand** 'no one', **jedermann** 'everybody'; these are inflected only in the singular of the masculine.

5. Numerals and Their Uses

Cardinal and Ordinal Numbers

0 Null

1 eins	erst-	19 neunzehn	neunzehnt-
2 zwei	zweit-	20 zwanzig	zwanzigst-
3 drei	dritt-	21 einundzwanzig	einundzwanzigst-
4 vier	viert-	22 zweiundzwanzig	zweiundzwanzigst-
5 fünf	fünft-	23 dreiundzwanzig	dreiundzwanzigst-
6 sechs	sechst-	30 dreißig	dreißigst-
7 sieben	sieb(en)t-	40 vierzig	vierzigst-
8 acht	acht-	50 fünfzig	fünfzigst-
9 neun	neunt-	60 sechzig	sechzigst-
10 zehn	zehnt-	70 siebzig	siebzigst-
11 elf	elft-	80 achtzig	achtzigst-
12 zwölf	zwölft-	90 neunzig	neunzigst-
13 dreizehn	dreizehnt-	100 hundert	hundertst-
14 vierzehn	vierzehnt-	1000 tausend	tausendst-
15 fünfzehn	fünfzehnt-		
16 sechzehn	sechzehnt-		
17 siebzehn	siebzehnt-		
18 achtzehn	achtzehnt-		

1 000 000	eine Million	millionst-
1 000 000 000	eine Milliarde	milliardst-
1 000 000 000 000	eine Billion	billionst-

The ordinal numbers up to and including 19 are formed by adding **-t-** to the cardinal number. (Note, however, **erst-,**

dritt-.) From 20 on, **-st-** is added to the cardinal number. Ordinal numbers are used as adjectives and have regular adjectival endings: **der erste Mann, Friedrich der Zweite (II.), zum ersten Mal.** They have adverbial forms ending in **-ens,** which are used in listings: **erstens** 'firstly, in the first place', **zweitens,** etc.

The form **zwo** 'two' is used for clarity on the telephone and elsewhere in listing figures.

5.1 Dates and the calendar. The names of the days of the week and of the months are all masculine:

Montag	Januar (Jenner)	Juli
Dienstag	Februar (Feber)	August
Mittwoch	März	September
Donnerstag	April	Oktober
Freitag	Mai	November
Sonnabend (Samstag)	Juni	Dezember
Sonntag		

The names of the seasons are also masculine: **der Frühling, der Sommer, der Herbst, der Winter.**

In giving a date one says: **Heute ist der dreizehnte (13.) April** *or* **Heute haben wir den dreizehnten April.**

In the heading of a letter the accusative is used:

Freitag, den (d.) 13. April 1956

In referring to the date of a correspondent's letter of the same month, one writes: **In Ihrem Brief vom 20. ds.** 'In your letter of the 20th of this month.' Here **ds.** stands for **dieses Monats; ds. M.** is also used.

In stating the year of an event one says: **Im Jahre 1492 entdeckte Columbus Amerika** *or* **1492 entdeckte Columbus Amerika.** (Not: 'In 1492' as in English.)

5.2 Telling time. Germans use both the twelve-hour and the twenty-four-hour clock. Time may be counted *toward* the approaching hour, thus:

Es ist viertel vier (3:15).
Es ist halb fünf (4:30).
Es ist drei viertel sechs (5:45).

However, Germans also say: **drei Uhr fünfzehn, vier Uhr dreißig, viertel nach drei, viertel vor sechs, viertel vor [der Stunde]**, and so on.

The following expressions are commonly used in giving the time:

Ich habe noch eine halbe Stunde Zeit.
I still have half an hour.

Es hat anderthalb (1 1/2) Stunden gedauert.
It lasted 1 1/2 hours.

Er hat fünf viertel (1 1/4) Stunden geredet.
He talked 1 1/4 hours.

Es ist zwölf Minuten achtzehn Sekunden nach siebzehn Uhr.
It is 12 minutes and 18 seconds after 5 p.m.

5.3 Decimals and fractions. The English decimal point is replaced by a comma, and the number is read aloud accordingly: **eins Komma fünf (1,5).**

Fractions are formed by adding the suffix **-el** to ordinal numbers, thus: **drittel, viertel, sechzehntel,** etc.

5.4 Arithmetical processes. (For more details refer to *Der Sprach-Brockhaus* or the *Bilderduden*, under the heading *Rechnungsarten*.)

Addition (Zusammenzählung) – addieren, zusammenzählen
   zwei + (und or **plus) drei = ist** or **(gleich) 5**
Subtraktion (Abziehen) – subtrahieren, abziehen
   fünf – (weniger or **minus) zwei = (gleich) drei**
Multiplikation (Vervielfachung) – multiplizieren, vervielfachen
   zwei × (mal) drei = (gleich) sechs

Division (Teilung) – dividieren, teilen
neun : (geteilt durch or dividiert durch) drei = (gleich)
drei.

Potenzieren, Wurzelziehen

$\sqrt{4}$ **Wurzel aus vier**   ist zwei
2^2 **zwei hoch zwei**   ist vier
2^5 **zwei hoch fünf**   ist zweiunddreißig

6. The Verb

German verbs are either weak (regular) or strong (irregular). Weak verbs add **-te** in the past, **-t** in the past participle; strong verbs change the vowel of the stem in the past and often also in the past participle and add **-(e)n** in the past participle.

Strong verbs are divided into three groups in accordance with vowel changes:

1. In group A, the vowel of the past participle is the same as that of the past tense: *e.g.*, **bleiben, blieb, geblieben**; **bieten, bot, geboten.**

2. In group B, the vowel of the past participle differs from that of the past and present forms, *e.g.*, **finden, fand, gefunden**; **sterben, starb, gestorben.**

3. In group C, the vowel of the past participle is the same as that of the present: *e.g.*, **geben, gab, gegeben**; **fahren, fuhr, gefahren**; **lassen, ließ, gelassen.**

To make the various forms of any verb, one must know the three or four forms called the *principal parts*. These are the infinitive, the 3d person singular past, the 3d person singular present perfect, and, for some verbs, the 3d person singular present. The principal parts of the most frequently used simple verbs are listed at the end of this chapter.

As weak verbs are regular, the principal parts can be readily made from any infinitive; forms of weak verbs which have some irregularities are listed with the strong verbs.

Verbs whose stem ends in **d, t,** a consonant (other than **l** or **r**) plus **m** or **n,** add **-e-** before endings beginning with **t** or **st**: *e.g.*, **finden, findest, findet** – **wartet, wartete, gewartet.** (Strong verbs, however, usually add — **st** directly to the stem in the past, *e.g.*, **fandst.**)

ge- must be added to participles of verbs, unless they begin with an unstressed syllable. Two groups of verbs do not add **ge-**: (1) those with inseparable prefixes, *e.g.*, **bestehen, bestand, bestanden**; (2) those with the suffix **-ieren**, *e.g.*, **reparieren, reparierte, repariert.** If verbs have an accented prefix (*e.g.*, **auf-stehen**), **ge-** is placed between the prefix and the stem, as in **aufgestanden.** Such verbs also put **zu** in this position when used in constructions requiring **zu** in the infinitive, *e.g.*, **aufzustehen.**

6.1 Categories of inflection. Verbs are inflected for:

1. Active and passive voice: **Er kauft das Buch.** 'He buys the book.' **Das Buch wird verkauft.** 'The book is (being) sold.'

2. Indicative, subjunctive, or imperative mood: **Er ist hier.** 'He is here.' **Wenn er nur hier wäre.** 'If only he were here.' Imperative mood: **Lesen Sie!** 'Read.'

3. Tense: present, past and the compound tenses: present perfect, past perfect, future, and future perfect.

4. Person: In the second person, the **du** and **ihr** forms are used only when speaking to members of the family, to children and servants, to animals, and to God in prayer. The usual form of address is the same as the third person plural.

6.2 Lists of forms

Since the compound tenses are inflected only in the auxiliary, full lists of their forms are not included here. The forms of compound tenses can be determined by reviewing the inflections of the present and past of **sein, haben,** and **werden.**

Present Indicative				Present Subjunctive I		
ich	bin	habe	werde	sei	habe	werde
du	bist	hast	wirst	seiest	habest	werdest
er	ist	hat	wird	sei	habe	werde
wir	sind	haben	werden	seien	haben	werden
ihr	seid	habt	werdet	seiet	habet	werdet
sie	sind	haben	werden	seien	haben	werden

ich	kaufe	falle	kaufe	falle
du	kaufst	fällst	kaufest	fallest
er	kauft	fällt	kaufe	falle
wir	kaufen	fallen	kaufen	fallen
ihr	kauft	fallt	kaufet	fallet
sie	kaufen	fallen	kaufen	fallen

Past Indicative				Present Subjunctive II		
ich	war	hatte	wurde	wäre	hätte	würde
du	warst	hattest	wurdest	wärest	hättest	würdest
er	war	hatte	wurde	wäre	hätte	würde
wir	waren	hatten	wurden	wären	hätten	würden
ihr	wart	hattet	wurdet	wäret	hättet	würdet
sie	waren	hatten	wurden	wären	hätten	würden

ich	kaufte	fiel	kaufte	fiele
du	kauftest	fielst	kauftest	fielest
er	kaufte	fiel	kaufte	fiele
wir	kauften	fielen	kauften	fielen
ihr	kauftet	fielt	kauftet	fielet
sie	kauften	fielen	kauften	fielen

Present Perfect
ich habe gehabt, gekauft
ich bin gewesen, geworden,
gefallen

Past Perfect
ich hatte gehabt, gekauft
ich war gewesen, geworden,
gefallen

Future
ich werde sein, haben
werden, kaufen, fallen

Future Perfect
ich werde gehabt, gekauft
haben
ich werde gewesen,
geworden, gefallen sein

Past Subjunctive I
ich habe gehabt, gekauft
ich sei gewesen,
geworden, gefallen

Past Subjunctive II
ich hätte gehabt, gekauft
ich wäre gewesen,
geworden, gefallen

Future Subjunctive I
ich werde sein, haben
werden, kaufen, fallen

Future Subjunctive II
ich würde sein, haben,
werden, kaufen, fallen

Future Perfect Subjunctive I
ich werde gehabt,
gekauft haben
ich werde gewesen,
geworden, gefallen sein

Future Perfect Subjunctive II
ich würde gehabt,
gekauft haben
ich würde gewesen,
geworden, gefallen sein

Imperative

Sei!	Werde!	Kaufe!
Seid!	Werdet!	Kauft!
Seien Sie!	Werden Sie!	Kaufen Sie!

6.3 Reflexives. Phrases consisting of a verb plus a reflexive pronoun often correspond in meaning to an English intransitive verb: *e.g.*, **sich fürchten** 'to fear,' 'to be afraid.' The verb itself is inflected normally. The reflexive occupies the position of an object. Examples are:
Ich fürchte mich. I am afraid.

Amüsierst du dich?   Are you enjoying yourself?
Hat er sich erholt?   Has he recovered?
Sie hatte sich erkältet.   She had caught a cold.
Wir werden uns dafür interessieren.   We'll be interested in that.

6.4 Modals.   Modals are inflected like weak verbs, except in the present tense; the present-tense forms must be noted separately.   They are:

	dürfen	können	mögen	müssen	sollen	wollen
ich/er, sie, es	darf	kann	mag	muß	soll	will
du	darfst	kannst	magst	mußt	sollst	willst
wir/sie, Sie	dürfen	können	mögen	müssen	sollen	wollen
ihr	dürft	könnt	mögt	müßt	sollt	wollt

For the principal parts, see the list of forms at the end of the chapter.

When the modals are used with another infinitive, the infinitive of the modal is used in place of the participle.   Compare:

Sie hat früher gehen wollen.   She wanted to go earlier.
Sie hat das nicht gewollt.   She didn't want that.
Double-infinitive constructions are also used with **hören, lassen,** and **sehen.**

6.5 The passive.   The passive construction is made up of a verbal phrase consisting of forms of **werden** and past participles. (In compound tenses, the participial form of **werden** does not add **ge-**.)   Examples are:

Ich werde gefragt.   I am asked.
Wurdest du eingeladen?   Were you invited?
Ist das beschrieben worden?   Was that described?
Waren sie da eingeladen worden?   Had they been invited there?
Wird das auch unterstützt werden?   Will that also be supported?
To indicate the agent performing an action, **von** is used; to indicate a means, **durch.**

Wurdest du vom Lehrer eingeladen?
Were you invited by the teacher?
Waren Sie durch einen Brief eingeladen worden?
Had you been invited by means of a letter?

6.6 Impersonal constructions. In these, **es** is used as the subject of a small number of verbs:

es friert	It is freezing.	**Es geht mir gut.**	I am fine
es regnet	It is raining.	**Es tut mir leid.**	I am sorry
es schneit	It is snowing.		

With verbs referring to the weather, **it** may be translated literally, as in the examples above; with many other verbs, however a different English construction is used. To indicate that something exists or is present, **es ist/es sind** 'there is/are' is used in referring to a specific situation, **es gibt** to a general situation:

Es waren drei Männer im Eßsaal.
There were three men in the dining-room.
Es gibt heute genug zu tun.
There is enough to do today.

6.7 Uses of verb forms. German has only one form of a verb for each tense; progressive forms ('he is walking'), emphatic forms ('he does walk'), and simple forms ('he walks') are all translated **er läuft.** This applies to the past tense and to the compound tenses as well.

The present tense is used as it is in English. It may be used for future time, especially when the sentence includes an adverb of time: **Ich gehe morgen.** Compare the use of the English progressive 'I am going tomorrow.'

The past tense is rarely used except in exposition. In everyday speech it is replaced by the present perfect in most constructions.

The present perfect corresponds in use to the English present perfect and is also used to correspond to the English past: **Gestern ist er zurückgekommen.** He came back yesterday.

The other compound tenses — the past perfect, the future, and the future perfect — are used as these tenses are in English. The future, however, is not used as widely as in English because it is often replaced by the present.

For the uses of the passive, see lesson 5. For the uses of the subjunctive, see lessons 8 and 9.

6.8 Principal parts of selected **irregular verbs** (strong verbs):

Infinitive	*Past*	*Past Participle*	*3d Sg. Pres.*
befehlen command	**befahl**	**befohlen**	**befiehlt**
beginnen begin	**begann**	**begonnen**	**beginnt**
beißen bite	**biß**	**gebissen**	**beißt**
betrügen deceive	**betrog**	**betrogen**	**betrügt**
beweisen prove	**bewies**	**bewiesen**	**beweist**
biegen bend	**bog**	**gebogen**	**biegt**
bieten offer	**bot**	**geboten**	**bietet**
binden tie	**band**	**gebunden**	**bindet**
bitten ask	**bat**	**gebeten**	**bittet**
bleiben remain	**blieb**	(ist) **geblieben**	**bleibt**
brechen break	**brach**	**gebrochen**	**bricht**
brennen burn	**brannte**	**gebrannt**	**brennt**
bringen bring	**brachte**	**gebracht**	**bringt**
denken think	**dachte**	**gedacht**	**denkt**
dringen push	**drang**	(ist) **gedrungen**	**dringt**
dürfen be permitted	**durfte**	**gedurft/ dürfen**	**darf**
empfangen receive	**empfing**	**empfangen**	**empfängt**
erscheinen appear	**erschien**	(ist) **erschienen**	**erscheint**
erschrecken be frightened	**erschrak**	(ist) **erschrocken**	**erschrickt**
essen eat	**aß**	**gegessen**	**ißt**
fahren drive	**fuhr**	(ist) **gefahren**	**fährt**
fallen fall	**fiel**	(ist) **gefallen**	**fällt**

Infinitive		Past		Past Participle	3d Sg. Pres.
fangen	catch	fing		gefangen	fängt
finden	find	fand		gefunden	findet
fliegen	fly	flog	(ist)	geflogen	fliegt
fliehen	flee	floh	(ist)	geflohen	flieht
fließen	flow	floß	(ist)	geflossen	fließt
frieren	freeze	fror		gefroren	friert
geben	give	gab		gegeben	gibt
gefallen	please	gefiel		gefallen	gefällt
gehen	go	ging	(ist)	gegangen	geht
gelingen succeed		gelang	(ist)	gelungen	gelingt
genießen	enjoy	genoß		genossen	genießt
geschehen	happen	geschah	(ist)	geschehen	geschieht
gestehen	confess	gestand		gestanden	gesteht
gewinnen	win	gewann		gewonnen	gewinnt
gießen	pour	goß		gegossen	gießt
gleichen	resemble	glich		geglichen	gleicht
gleiten	glide	glitt	(ist)	geglitten	gleitet
graben	dig	grub		gegraben	gräbt
greifen	grasp	griff		gegriffen	greift
haben	have	hatte		gehabt	hat
halten	hold	hielt		gehalten	hält
hängen	hang	hing		gehangen	hängt
heben	lift	hob		gehoben	hebt
heißen	be called	hieß		geheißen	heißt
helfen	help	half		geholfen	hilft
kennen	know	kannte		gekannt	kennt
kommen	come	kam	(ist)	gekommen	kommt
können	be able	konnte		gekonnt/ können	kann
laden	load	lud		geladen	lädt
lassen	let	ließ		gelassen/lassen	läßt
laufen	run	lief	(ist)	gelaufen	läuft
leiden	suffer	litt		gelitten	leidet
leihen	lend	lieh		geliehen	leiht

Infinitive	Past	Past Participle	3d Sg. Pres.
lesen read	las	gelesen	liest
liegen lie	lag	gelegen	liegt
messen measure	maß	gemessen	mißt
mögen like	mochte	gemocht/ mögen	mag
müssen have to	mußte	gemußt/ müssen	muß
nehmen take	nahm	genommen	nimmt
nennen name	nannte	genannt	nennt
pfeifen whistle	pfiff	gepfiffen	pfeift
raten advise	riet	geraten	rät
reißen tear	riß	gerissen	reißt
reiten ride	ritt	(ist) geritten	reitet
rennen run	rannte	(ist) gerannt	rennt
riechen smell	roch	gerochen	riecht
rufen call	rief	gerufen	ruft
saugen suck	sog	gesogen	saugt
schaffen create	schuf	geschaffen	schafft
scheiden separate take leave	schied	(ist) geschieden	scheidet
scheinen seem	schien	geschienen	scheint
schieben shove	schob	geschoben	schiebt
schießen shoot	schoß	geschossen	schießt
schlafen sleep	schlief	geschlafen	schläft
schlagen strike	schlug	geschlagen	schlägt
schleichen sneak	schlich	(ist) geschlichen	schleicht
schließen close	schloß	geschlossen	schließt
schneiden cut	schnitt	geschnitten	schneidet
schreiben write	schrieb	geschrieben	schreibt
schreien cry	schrie	geschrieen	schreit
schreiten stride	schritt	(ist) geschritten	schreitet
schweigen be silent	schwieg	geschwiegen	schweigt
schwimmen swim	schwamm	(ist) geschwommen	schwimmt

Infinitive		*Past*		*Past Participle*	*3d Sg. Pres.*
schwinden		schwand	(ist)	geschwunden	schwindet
disappear					
schwingen	swing	schwang		geschwungen	schwingt
schwören	swear	schwor		geschworen	schwört
sehen	see	sah		gesehen/sehen	sieht
sein	be	war	(ist)	gewesen	ist
senden	send	sandte		gesandt	sendet
singen	sing	sang		gesungen	singt
sinken	sink	sank	(ist)	gesunken	sinkt
sitzen	sit	saß		gesessen	sitzt
sollen	should	sollte		gesollt/sollen	soll
sprechen	speak	sprach		gesprochen	spricht
springen	spring	sprang	(ist)	gesprungen	springt
stehen	stand	stand		gestanden	steht
stehlen	steal	stahl		gestohlen	stiehlt
steigen	climb	stieg	(ist)	gestiegen	steigt
sterben	die	starb	(ist)	gestorben	stirbt
stoßen	push	stieß		gestoßen	stößt
tragen	carry	trug		getragen	trägt
treffen	meet	traf		getroffen	trifft
treiben	drive	trieb		getrieben	treibt
treten	step	trat	(ist)	getreten	tritt
trinken	drink	trank		getrunken	trinkt
tun	do	tat		getan	tut
verbergen	hide	verbarg		verborgen	verbirgt
verbieten	forbid	verbot		verboten	verbietet
verderben	spoil	verdarb	(ist)	verdorben	verdirbt
vergessen	forget	vergaß		vergessen	vergißt
verlieren	lose	verlor		verloren	verliert
vermeiden	avoid	vermied		vermieden	vermeidet
vermögen	be able	vermochte		vermocht	vermag
verzeihen	forgive	verzieh		verziehen	verzeiht
wachsen	grow	wuchs	(ist)	gewachsen	wächst
waschen	wash	wusch		gewaschen	wäscht
wenden	turn	wandte		gewandt	wendet

Infinitive		*Past*		*Past Participle*	*3d Sg. Pres.*
werden	become	**wurde**	(ist)	geworden	**wird**
werfen	throw	**warf**		geworfen	**wirft**
wissen	know	**wußte**		gewußt	**weiß**
wollen	want	**wollte**		gewollt/wollen	**will**
ziehen	pull; move	**zog**	(ist)	gezogen	**zieht**
zwingen	compel	**zwang**		gezwungen	**zwingt**

7. Conjunctions. Six conjunctions have no effect on the word order: **aber, allein** 'but,' **denn, oder, sondern, und.** All other conjunctions are followed by transposed word order. Among the more common are **als, als ob, bevor, da, damit, daß, indem** 'while,' **nachdem, ob, obgleich, sobald, während, weil, wenn,** and **wie.**

8. Adverbs. In German, adverbs are simply uninflected forms of adjectives, *e.g.* **gut** 'well,' derived from **gut** 'good.'

A few words are used only as adverbs:

bald	soon	**eher**	**am ehesten**
gern(e)	gladly	**lieber**	**am liebsten**

Some common adverbs end in **-e** when the corresponding adjective ends in a consonant, *e.g.*, **lange** as compared with **lang.**

9. Word Order. The key element in the order of the German sentence is the verb. From its position we can determine what kind of sentence we are dealing with. The verb may stand initially, in second position, or at the end of its clause.

It stands initially in:

1. questions that do not begin with an interrogative: **Kommt sie?** 'Is she coming?'

2. commands and requests: **Kommen Sie bitte mit!** 'Please come along.'

3. conditional clauses not introduced by **wenn**: **Kommt sie nicht, so fahren wir doch nach Madison.** 'If she doesn't come, we'll drive to Madison nonetheless.'

4. explanatory sentences with **doch : Hat er doch selber nichts davon gewußt.** Why, he didn't know about it himself.

It stands in second place in:

1. most independent sentences, *e.g.*, statements: **Sie kommt morgen.** 'She's coming tomorrow.'
2. questions with interrogatives: **Wann kommt sie?** 'When is she coming?'
3. statements introduced by. adverbs, objects, or entire clauses: **Morgen kommt sie. Wenn sie Zeit hat, kommt sie morgen.** 'If she has time, she'll come tomorrow.'

It stands in final position when the clause is introduced by subordinating conjunctions or by relative pronouns: **Es ist Geralds Mutter, die morgen kommt.** 'It's Gerald's mother who is coming tomorrow.' **Es sieht so aus, als ob sie mitkommen möchte.** 'It looks as if she would like to come along.'

If **als** is used in the sense of 'as if,' the verb must follow **als : Es sieht so aus, als möchte sie mitkommen.**

If a clause contains the double-infinitive construction, the infinitives must stand at its end and the finite verb directly before them: **Es sah so aus, als ob sie hätte mitkommen wollen.**

Unlike English, German requires infinitives and participles to stand at the end of the clause. It is important to be aware of the kinds of words that generally occur last in clauses; for a discussion of these, see lesson 15.

The order of adverbial elements in the clause is restricted.

(1) Time adverbs stand before place adverbs: **Er war vorige Woche hier.** 'He was here last week.'

(2) General time adverbs stand before specific time adverbs: **Er war vorige Woche zwei Tage hier.** 'He was here two days last week.'

Indirect-object nouns stand before direct-object nouns: **Sie gab ihrem Freund das Buch.** 'She gave the book to her friend.'

Direct-object pronouns stand before indirect objects: **Sie gab es ihm/dem Freund.** 'She gave it to him/her friend.'

10. Formation of Words. See the pertinent materials in the first chapters of this text.

GERMAN—ENGLISH VOCABULARY

ENGLISH—GERMAN VOCABULARY

German—English Vocabulary

This vocabulary includes all words used in the text except words for numerals and time units (days, months), possessive adjectives, and personal pronouns. These are to be found in the Grammatical Appendix (see Index). The principal parts of strong and irregular verbs are given with the stem verb only. Compound strong and irregular verbs are marked with an *. (When in doubt, check the list of such verbs in the Appendix, pages 210 to 214. Complete mastery of this list is essential.)

Words which do not belong to the student's required vocabulary are accordingly not included in this vocabulary but are glossed in the lessons. Words in the narrative portions of lessons that are marked with a question mark are mainly cognate or compound words. These add to the student's vocabulary at little expense of effort and should be learned. This is also true of many compound words not marked in any way in the text.

Separable compound verbs are hyphenated.

A

ab-drängen force off
ab-drehen turn off
der Abend, -e evening;
    abend(s) in the evening(s);
    heute abend this evening
das Abendessen dinner, evening
    meal
der Abendsonnenschein evening sunshine
    aber but, however
ab-fahren* (ist) depart,
    leave
ab-fliegen* (ist) fly away
ab-hängen* (von) depend
    (on)
ab-holen call for
ab-laufen* (ist) run down
ab-lehnen decline, refuse
ab-reisen (ist) leave
der Abschied, -e parting, departure
ab-schneiden* cut off
absichtlich intentional
absorbieren absorb
ab-stellen turn off
ab-streifen strip off
ab-tasten feel, run one's
    fingers over
ab-warten wait for
sich ab-wenden* turn aside
ab-wischen wipe off
ach oh
die Achse, -n axle
die Achtung attention; alle
    Achtung! Well done!
die Adresse, -n address
ahnen suspect
die Ahnung, -en foreboding;
    ahnungsvoll full of foreboding, suspicious
der Ahorn maple
die Aktie, -n stock
die Aktienbörse, -n stock exchange

der Aktienmarkt, -̈e stock market
die Aktualität actuality
all all
allein alone
alles everything
allgemein general
alljährlich yearly, every year
als when; as; than
also therefore; so, then
alt old
der Alte, -n old man
das Alter age
älter older, elderly
die Ambulanz, -en ambulance
der Ambulanzfahrer ambulance driver
der Amerikaner American
    [*male*]
die Amerikanerin, -nen American [*female*]
amerikanisch American
    [*adj.*]
an [*dat.*] at, near, by, on;
    [*acc.*] to, up to, on
der Anatom, -en anatomist
der Anblick sight
an-blicken look at
ander- other; different
ändern change, alter
anders otherwise, differently
an-drehen turn on [*a light,
    etc.*]
aneinander past, by, to
    one another
der Anfang, -̈e beginning
an-fangen* begin, start; do
angeln fish
angenehm [*dat.*] pleasant
angesichts in view of
der Angestellte, -n employee
der Angriff, -e attack; in Angriff nehmen* take up

die **Angst, ⁼e** fear, anxiety
an-halten* stop
an-hören listen to
der **Anklang, ⁼e** accord; **bei einem Anklang finden*** strike a responsive note
an-kommen* (ist) arrive; **auf etwas ankommen** depend on
an-kündigen announce
die **Ankunft, ⁼e** arrival
an-lächeln smile at
an-lachen laugh at
die **Anmut** charm
die **Annahme, -n** assumption; acceptance
an-nehmen* assume; accept; **sich annehmen** [gen.] devote oneself to
an-rufen* call up, telephone
der **Anruf, -e** telephone call
sich **an-schließen*** [dat.] join, connect
die **Anschrift, -en** address
an-sehen* look at, regard; **ansichtig werden** [gen.] catch sight of
anstatt instead of
die **Anthropologie** anthropology
die **Antwort, -en** answer; **zur Antwort geben*** answer
antworten [dat.] answer
die **Anzeige, -n** notice; **zur Anzeige bringen*** arraign
der **Anzug, ⁼e** suit
der **Apparat, -e** apparatus
der **Appetit** appetite
die **Arbeit, -en** work
arbeiten work
der **Arbeiter, -** worker
arbeitslos unemployed, inactive
die **Arbeitsstellung, -en** job, position
ärgern annoy; **sich ärgern** [über + acc.] be annoyed (at)
arm poor

der **Arm, -e** arm
die **Armee, -n** army
die **Art, -en** sort, kind; manner
die **Artillerie** artillery
das **Artilleriefeuer** artillery fire
der **Arzt, ⁼e** physician, doctor
die **Asche, -n** ash, ashes
der **Assistent, -en** assistant
die **Ästhetik** aesthetics
der **Atem** breath; **atemlos** breathless
atmen breathe
die **Atmosphäre, -n** atmosphere
das **Atom, -e** atom
auch too, also; even; either [in negative sentence]; **auch wenn** even if
auf up, upon, on, at
auf-binden* untie
auf-fallen* (ist) [dat.] notice
auf-fliegen* (ist) fly away
die **Aufgabe, -n** lesson, task, assignment, mission
auf-geben* give up
sich **auf-halten*** stay, spend time
auf-lachen laugh aloud
aufmerksam attentive; **jemand auf (etwas) aufmerksam machen** call someone's attention to (something)
auf-passen [auf + acc.] pay attention (to)
aufrecht erect; **aufrecht erhalten*** keep straight
die **Aufregung** excitement
sich **auf-richten** sit up
auf-sammeln collect, gather up
auf-schrecken (ist) startle
auf-springen* (ist) jump up
auf-stehen* (ist) get up, arise
auf-steigen* (ist) rise
auf-tauchen (ist) appear, show up

auf-wachen (ist) [*intrans.*]
  wake up
auf-wecken [*trans.*] wake up
das Auge, -n eye
der Augenblick, -e moment
  aus out of, from
  aus-atmen exhale
  aus-brechen*(ist) break out
  aus-breiten spread
die Ausbreitung spread
  aus-brennen* (ist) burn out
  aus-drehen turn off [*a
  light, etc.*]
  aus-drücken express
  auseinander-fallen* (ist)
  fall apart
sich auseinander-setzen (mit),
  face, discuss, come to terms
  (with)
der Ausflug, ⸚e excursion
der Ausgang, ⸚e exit
  aus-gehen* (ist) run out,
  proceed
  ausgezeichnet excellent
der Ausländer, - foreigner
  ausländisch foreign
die Ausnahme, -n exception
  aus-rücken (ist) move away
  aus-rufen* call out

sich aus-ruhen rest
  aus-schlafen* have one's
  sleep out
  aus-schließen* exclude
  aus-sehen* look, appear
  außen outside
  außer besides, except
  außerdem besides, more-
  over
  äußerst extreme
  aus-sprechen* express
  aus-steigen* (ist) get out
  aus-stellen exhibit
die Ausstellung, -en exhibit
der Ausstellungsraum, ⸚e exhibition hall
der Ausweg, -e way out
  aus-zahlen pay (out)
sich aus-zeichnen be distinguished
das Auto, -s automobile
die Autoausstellung, -en automobile exhibit
die Autobahn, -en super-highway
der Autofahrer, - driver
die Autofahrt, -en car trip
  automatisch automatically

B

  backen (u, a, ä,) bake
das Bad, ⸚er bath
sich baden bathe
  bald soon; bald ... bald
  now ... now
der Bankier, -s banker
der Bankierssohn, ⸚e banker's
  son
der Bankraub bank robbing
  bar cash
der Barsch bass
das Baseball-Resultat, -e base-
  ball result
  bauen build
der Bauer, -n farmer, peasant

der Baum, ⸚e tree
der Baumstamm, ⸚e tree trunk
  beachten pay attention to
der Beamte, -n official
  beantworten answer
  bearbeiten work up, revise
  bedauern be sorry, regret
  bedecken cover
die Bedeutung, -en meaning
  bedeutungsvoll meaning-
  ful
  bedienen run, take care of
  bedrohlich threatening
das Beefsteak beefsteak

beeinflussen influence

die Beerdigung, -en funeral

sich befinden* be
befindlich (to be) found

begegnen (ist) [*dat.*] meet;
happen

die Begegnung, -en meeting,
encounter

beginnen (a, o) start, begin

begleiten accompany

die Begleiterin, -nen companion [*female*]

begraben* bury

behandeln treat, handle

behaupten claim

bei at, with, among, near,
by, at the house of; bei
sich to himself

bei-bringen*: einem etwas
beibringen teach some-
one something

beide both

beinahe almost

das Beispiel, -e example

bei-stehen* [*dat.*] help,
assist

der Beitrag, -e contribution

bei-wohnen [*dat.*] attend

bekannt known

bekannt-geben* make
known

bekommen* receive, get

beladen* load

sich belaufen* (auf) amount to

benachbart neighboring

benebeln befog

das Benzin gasoline

beobachten observe

die Beobachtung, -en observa-
tion

bereit ready

bereiten prepare

bereits already

der Berg, -e mountain

der Berghang, -e slope

das Bergwasser, - mountain
water

der Bericht, -e report
berichten report

die Berichtigung, -en correction

der Berliner man from Berlin

der Beruf, -e profession

die Berufswahl, -en choice of
profession

berühmt famous

beschädigen damage

sich beschäftigen be busy

die Beschäftigung, -en occupation

beschießen* shoot at, bom-
bard

beschließen* decide

besehen* look at

besessen possessed; wie
besessen as if possessed

besetzen occupy

besitzen* possess

der Besitzer, - owner

das Besitztum, -er property

besonder special; beson-
ders especially

besser better

best- best

bestätigen confirm

bestehen* exist, consist; pass
[*an examination*]

bestellen order

bestimmt definite, certain

besuchen visit; go to [*a
theater*]

der Betracht consideration; in
Betracht ziehen* take
into consideration

beträchtlich considerably

betreten* step upon, enter

betrügen (o, o) deceive,
cheat

das Bett, -en bed

beunruhigen disturb

die Beunruhigung worry

der Bevölkerungsmittelpunkt
center of population

bevor [*conj.*] before

bewegen move
bewußt conscious, aware;
 bewußtlos unconscious
bezahlen pay (for)
die Bezahlung, -en payment,
 wages
der Bezirk, -e precinct, postal
 zone
bezweifeln doubt
biegen (o, ist o) bend,
 round [*a corner*]
das Bier, -e beer
bieten (o, o) offer
das Bild, -er picture
die Bildung formation; educa-
 tion
billig cheap
binden (a, u) bind, tie
der Biologe, -n biologist
bis until, up to, by
bißchen bit, little
bitte please; you're welcome
bitten (a, e) (um) ask (for)
bitter bitter
blaß pale
bleiben (ie, ist ie) remain,
 stay
das Bleiben stay
der Bleistift, -e pencil
blenden blind, dazzle
blicken look, glance
blitzen flash; lightning flash
bloß mere
die Blume, -n flower
bluten bleed
der Boden, -̈ ground, floor

das Boot, -e boat
das Bootshaus, -̈er boathouse
die Börse, -n stock exchange
böse bad, evil; angry
der Brand, -̈e conflagration,
 fire
brauchen need
braun brown; braun-
 gebrannt tanned
brausen rush
brausend uproarious
brechen (a, o, i) break
breit broad
brennen (brannte, ge-
 brannt) burn
der Brennstoff fuel
das Brett, -er board
der Brief, -e letter
der Briefträger, - postman
bringen (brachte, ge-
 bracht) bring, take
der Bruder, -̈ brother
das Buch, -̈er book
die Büchersendung, -en shipment of books
die Buchhandlung, -en bookstore
die Bühne, -n stage
bunt colorful, variegated
der Bürger, - citizen
das Büro, -s office
das Büromädchen, - office
 girl
der Bursch, -en boy, fellow
die Butter butter

C

das Café, -s cafe, restaurant
der Cent cent
die Chemie chemistry
die Chemikerin, -nen chemist
 [*female*]

die Chinesenstadt Chinatown
die Chinesin, -nen Chinese
 [*female*]
der Chirurg, -en surgeon
das Chloroform chloroform

D

da [*adv.*] there, then; [*conj.*] since; dabei thereby, present, along, in the process

das Dach, ⁼er roof

dadurch through the fact

daher therefore

dahin there

dahin-fahren* (ist) drive to, drive along

damals at that time

die Dame, -n lady, woman

das Dämmerlicht dusk

der Dampf, ⁼e steam, vapor

danach about it; afterwards

der Däne, -n Dane [*male*]

danken [*dat.*] thank; dankend gratefully, with thanks

dann then

darauf on it, to that; afterwards

darum for that reason

der Darwinismus Darwinism

das Dasein existence

daß [*conj.*] that

dauerhaft lasting, durable

dauern last, take [*time*]

dazu in addition

die Decke, -n cover

decken cover

der Demokrat, -en democrat

denken (dachte, gedacht) think (of)

denn [*adv.*] then, anyway; [*conj.*] because, for

derartig in such a way

derjenige that (one)

derselbe (dieselbe, dasselbe) the same

deshalb therefore, for that reason

deutlich clear, plain

deutsch [*adj.*] German

das Deutsch (the) German (language)

der Deutsche, -n German [*male*]

(das)Deutschland Germany

dicht thick, close

dichten write poetry

die Dichtkunst poetry

dick thick

der Dieb, -e thief

dienen [*dat.*] serve

der Dienst, -e service

dies this, these

dieser this one, the latter

der Dieselmotor, -en diesel (motor)

das Ding, -e thing

DM (Deutsche Mark) German mark

doch yet, however, but, nevertheless, after all; oh yes [*after negatives*]

die Dogmatik dogmatics

der Doktor, -en doctor, Dr.

der Dollar, -s dollar

donnern thunder

das Dorf, ⁼er village

der Dorn, -en thorn

dort there

dorthin (to) there

der Dramaturg, -en theatrical director

der Drang urge, drive

sich drängen press, crowd, shove; drängend driving

draußen outside

dringen (a, ist u) push, urge

dritt third

dröhnend resounding

drüben over there

der Druck, ⁼e pressure

drücken press

dumm stupid

die Dummheit, -en stupidity

dunkel dark

die **Dunkelheit, -en** dark, darkness
dünn thin
durch through, by (means of)
durchaus absolutely
durch-brechen* (ist) break through

dürfen (durfte, gedurft/dürfen, darf) be permitted to, may
durstig thirsty
der **Düsenjäger, -** jet fighter plane
das **Dynamit** dynamite

E

eben just, just then
ebenfalls likewise, also
ebenso just as, equally
die **Ecke, -n** corner
ehe before
der **Ehestand** marriage
die **Ehre, -n** honor
das **Ei, -er** egg
eifrig eager, zealous, busy
eigen [*adj.*] own
eigentlich true, essential; actually, really; anyway
die **Eile** hurry, haste
eilen (ist) hurry
einander each other, one another
der **Eindruck, ⁼e** impression
einfach simple
ein-fahren* (ist) drive in, enter
ein-fallen* (ist) [*dat.*] occur to
sich **ein-finden*** show up, appear
der **Einfluß, ⁼sse** influence
der **Eingang, ⁼e** entrance; arrival, receipt
ein-graben* dig in
ein-holen catch up with
einig agreed, at one
einige a few, several, some
ein-laden* invite
einmal once, sometime; **auf einmal** suddenly; **noch einmal** once more, again
einsam lonesome, lonely

ein-schlafen* (ist) fall asleep
sich **ein-schreiben*** register
die **Einschreibung, -en** registration
das **Eintauschen** trade in, exchange
eintönig monotonous
ein-treffen* (ist) arrive, come in
ein-treten* (ist) enter
das **Eintreten** entering, entry
der **Eintritt** admission, entry
die **Eintrittskarte, -n** ticket
einwickeln wrap
der **Einzelne** individual
einzig- single, only
das **Eis** ice
eitel vain
die **Eitelkeit** vanity
elegant elegant
elektronisch electronic
die **Eltern** parents
empfangen* receive
die **Empfangsstation, -en** receiving station
das **Ende, -n** end
endlich at last, finally
endlos infinite, endless
die **Endstation, -en** terminal
die **Energie, -n** energy
eng narrow
das **Englisch(e)** (the) English (language)
enorm enormous
entdecken discover
die **Entdeckung, -en** discovery

entfernen remove, take away
entfernt distant, removed
entgegen towards, against
entgegen-fahren*(ist) [dat.]
  drive towards
entgegen-sehen*[dat.]await,
  look forward to
entgegen-strecken [dat.]
  reach out toward
entgegnen [auf + dat.] answer, reply
enthalten* contain
der Enthusiast, -en enthusiast
entkommen* (ist) [dat.]
  escape
entlang along
entlassen* dismiss
entlasten unburden
entlaufen* (ist) escape
sich entschließen* decide
der Entschluß, ¨sse decision
entschuldigen excuse
sich entschuldigen be sorry
entstehen* (ist) arise
enttäuschen disappoint
die Enttäuschung, -en dis-
  appointment
entweder... oder either... or
entwickeln develop
erblicken see
die Erbsensuppe, -n pea soup
das Erdbeben earthquake
die Erde earth, ground
das Ereignis, -se event
erfahren* learn, experience
die Erfahrung, -en experience
erfinden* invent
der Erfinder, - inventor
der Erfolg, -e success
erfolgen (ist) take place
erforschen investigate
erfüllen fulfill, complete
die Erfüllung, -en fulfillment
ergeben* devoted, "sin-
  cerely" [in complementary
  closing of a letter]
sich ergeben* surrender

ergreifen* take up
erhalten* receive, obtain
sich erheben* rise
erinnern remind
sich erinnern [an + acc.] remember
die Erinnerung, -en memory,
  reminder; in Erinnerung
  haben* have in mind, remember
sich erkälten catch cold
die Erkältung, -en cold
erkennen* recognize
die Erkennungsmarke, -n iden-
  tification tag, dog tag
erklären explain, declare
die Erklärung, -en explanation
sich erkundigen inquire
erlauben permit
erleben experience
das Erlebnis, -se experience
erledigen take care of, do
erliegen* (ist) [dat.] suc-
  cumb to
erleuchten illuminate
ermöglichen enable, make
  possible
ernähren feed, nourish
ernst serious
eröffnen open
erreichen reach, attain
errichten erect
der Ersatzteil, -e spare parts
erscheinen* (ist) appear
erschießen* kill, shoot
erschöpfen exhaust
die Erschöpfung exhaustion
erschrecken (-schrak, ist
  -schrocken) be frightened
ersetzen replace, substitute
ersparen save
erst first; not until; only;
  erst recht kein certainly
  not a
erstaunt astonished
erstens firstly

ersticken (ist) choke
erwarten await, expect
das Erwarten expectation
sich erwehren [*gen.*] suppress, keep from, get rid of
erzählen relate, tell
die Erzählung, -en tale, story
erzeugen manufacture, produce
eßbar edible
essen (a, e, i) eat
das Essen meal

der Eßsaal, -säle dining hall
die Ethik ethics
etwas something, somewhat
das Exemplar, -e copy
der Existentialismus existentialism
die Exkursion, -en excursion
das Experiment, -e experiment
die Explosion, -en explosion
exterminieren exterminate
das Extrageld extra money

F

die Fabel, -n fable, tale
fähig able, capable, (of)
fahren (u, a, ä) [*trans.,or intrans. with* ist] drive, travel
das Fahren driving
der Fahrer, - driver [*male*]
die Fahrerin, -nen driver [*female*]
der Fahrschein, -e railway ticket
die Fahrt, -en trip, journey, ride
das Fahrzeug, -e vehicle
der Fall, ⁻e case; auf alle Fälle, auf jeden Fall in any case
fallen (ie, ist a, ä) fall, drop
fällen fell, cut down
falsch false
falten fold
die Familie, -n family
fangen (i, a, ä) catch
die Farbe, -n color
fassen take; grab
fast almost
die Feder, -n pen, feather
fehlen be lacking, be missing
der Fehler, - error
der Feiertag, -e holiday
der Feind, -e foe, enemy
feindlich hostile
feindselig hostilely

das Feld, -er field
das Feldlazarett, -e field hospital
der Fels, -en rock
das Fenster, - window
die Fensterscheibe, -n window pane
die Ferien [*pl.*] vacation, holidays
fern far, distant
der Fernsehapparat, -e television (set)
fernsehen (a, e, ie,) look at television
fertig ready, finished
fest firm, steady
fest-halten* hold fast; keep
fest-stellen establish, determine
das Fett, -e fat
das Feuer, - fire
die Feuerwache, -n fire station
die Feuerwehr, -en fire department
die Feuerwehrleute firemen
fieberhaft feverish
das Filet, -s filet
der Film, -e film
finden (a, u) find
der Finger, - finger
finster dark

die **Finsternis** darkness
die **Firma, Firmen** firm
der **Fisch, -e** fish
    fischen fish
das **Flachland** flat country, plains
die **Flamme, -n** flame
die **Fledermaus, ⁼e** bat
der **Fleiß** industry, eagerness
    fleißig industrious, diligent
    fliegen (o, ist o) fly
das **Fliegen** flying
der **Flieger, -** flyer
    fliehen (o, ist o) flee
der **Flug, ⁼e** flight
der **Flügel, -** wing
der **Flughafen, ⁼** airport
der **Flugplatz, ⁼e** airport
die **Flugrichtung, -en** direction of flight
das **Flugzeug, -e** airplane
der **Fluß, ⁼sse** river
    flüstern whisper
die **Folge, -n** consequence, result
    folgen (ist) [*dat.*] follow
die **Form, -en** form
    fort away
    fort-fahren* (ist) continue, drive on
    fort-rasen (ist) rush on, rush forth
die **Frage, -n** question
    fragen ask
der **Franzose, -n** Frenchman
die **Frau, -en** woman; wife; Mrs.
das **Fräulein, -** young lady, Miss
    frei free
    frei-geben* open up, yield
    frei-gebig generous
die **Freigebigkeit** generosity
die **Freiheit, -en** freedom

    freilich of course, to be sure
    fremd strange
die **Freude, -n** pleasure, joy
    freuen please, make (someone) glad
sich **freuen [auf + *acc.*]** look forward to
der **Freund, -e** friend [*male*]
die **Freundin, -nen** friend [*female*]
    freundlich friendly, kind
die **Freundschaft, -en** friendship
der **Friede, (-ns), -n** peace
    frieren (o, o) freeze
    frisch fresh
    froh happy, merry
    fröhlich happy, merry
die **Frucht, ⁼e** fruit
    früh early
    früher earlier; formerly
der **Frühling** spring
der **Frühlingstag, -e** spring day
    frühzeitig too early, premature
    fühlen feel
    führen lead
der **Führer, -** leader, driver
der **Führerschein, -e** driver's license
    füllen fill
    funken transmit (radio)
    funktionieren function
    für for
    was für what kind of
    furchtbar terrible
sich **fürchten (vor)** fear, be afraid
    fürchterlich terrible
das **Fußballspiel, -e** football game
    füttern feed [*animals*]

G

gähnen yawn

der Gang, ⸚e passageway

ganz entire, whole; **ganz und gar** quite completely

das Ganze the whole

gar at all

die Garage, -n garage

der Garten, ⸚ garden

die Gasse, -n street, lane

das Gebäude, - building

geben (a, e, i) give; **es gibt** there is, are

das Gebiet, -e field

das Gebirge, - mountains

geboren born

gebrauchen use

der Gedanke, (-ns), -n thought

das Gedicht, -e poem

gedruckt printed

geduldig patient

geehrt honored; **sehr geehrter Herr!** Dear Sir:

die Gefahr, -en danger

gefallen* [*dat.*] please, like

der Gefallen, - favor

gefaltet folded

gefangen caught

gefangen-nehmen* take prisoner

das Gefühl, -e feeling

gegen against; toward; around

die Gegend, -en area, region

gegenüber opposite

der Gegenwind, -e head wind

geheimnisvoll mysterious

gehen (ging, ist gegangen) go, walk

gehören [*dat.*] belong (to)

der Geist, -er spirit, ghost; intellect

gelangen (ist) reach

gelb yellow

das Geld, -er money

das Geldstück, -e coin

gelegen situated

die Gelegenheit, -en opportunity, occasion

gelingen (a, ist u) succeed

genau exact, close, precise

geneigt disposed, inclined

genießen (-o, -o) enjoy

genug enough

genügen be enough, suffice

der Genuß, ⸚sse enjoyment

die Geologie geology

gerade just, just now, just then; directly; even; straight

geraten* (ist) get, turn out

gereift matured

gern(e) gladly; [*with any verb*] like to

das Gerücht, -e rumor

das Geschäft, -e business; office

der Geschäftsbrief, -e business letter

geschehen (a, ist e, ie) happen

das Geschenk, -e gift, present

die Geschichte, -n story, history

das Geschirr, -e dishes

geschlichen sneaked

der Geschmack, ⸚er taste

das Geschwätz chatter

die Geschwindigkeit, -en speed

der Geschwindigkeitsmesser, - speedometer

der Geschwindigkeitsrekord, -e speed record

der Geselle, -n companion, comrade

die Gesellschaft, -en company, party, society

das Gesetz, -e law

das Gesicht, -er face
das Gespräch, -e conversation;
  ins Gespräch kommen*
  get into a conversation
der Gesprächston, ¨e conversational tone
die Gestalt, -en form, shape,
  figure
  gestehen (-stand, -standen)
  confess
  gestern yesterday
  gestrandet stranded
  gesund healthy
  gewaltig powerful
  gewandt sophisticated
das Gewehr, -e rifle
  gewinnen (a, o) win, gain,
  obtain
  gewiß certain
das Gewissen conscience
  gewissermaßen to a certain extent
das Gewitter, - thunderstorm
sich gewöhnen [an + acc.] get
  used (to)
die Gewohnheit, -en habit
  gewöhnlich usual
das Gewölbe, - arch
  gierig greedy
der Gipfel, - top, peak
  glänzen sparkle
das Glas, ¨er glass
das Glasfenster, - glass window
der Glaube, (-ns), -n belief
  glauben [dat.] believe, think
  gleich [adj.] same, equal;
  [adv.] immediately, directly
  gleichen (i, i) [dat.] resemble
das Gleichgewicht balance
  gleiten (-itt, ist -itten) glide

das Glück luck, happiness
  glücklich lucky, happy
  glühen glow
  golden golden
der Goldgräber, - gold digger
  gondeln (ist) shove off
der Gott, ¨er God; (um) Gotteswillen! For heaven's
  sake!
das Grab, ¨er grave
  graben (u, a, ä) dig
der Grad, -e degree
das Grammophon, -e record
  player
die Grammophonplatte, -n
  record
  grau gray
das Grauen terror
  greifen (i, i) grasp, reach
die Grenze, -n border
der Grieche, -n Greek [male]
(das) Griechenland Greece
die Griechin, -nen Greek [fe-
  male]
der Griff, -e handle
die Grille, -n cricket
  groß large; big; great
  großartig magnificent
die Großstadt, ¨e metropolis
  grün green
der Grund, ¨e bottom, reason,
  cause; im Grunde basically, fundamentally
  gründlich thoroughly
der Grundstoff, -e material, basic element
das Grundstück, -e lot
die Gruppe, -n group
  gut good, well
  gutherzig kind
  gut-machen make good,
  recoup

H

das **Haar, -e** hair
haben* have
der **Hafen, ⸚** harbor
hageln hail
halb half
der **Hals, ⸚e** neck
der **Halt, -e** stop; **Halt machen**
stop; **halten (ie, a, ä)**
stop; **halten für** consider;
ich kann mich nicht hal-
ten (vor) I can't keep
(from)
die **Hand, ⸚e** hand
handeln trade; **es handelt**
sich um it is a question
(matter) of
die **Handgranate, -n** hand gre-
nade
das **Handköfferchen, -** overnight bag
die **Handtasche, -n** suitcase
hängen (i, a, ä) hang
hart hard
hassen hate
das **Haupt, ⸚er** head
das **Haus, ⸚er** house; **nach Hau-**
se homeward; **zu Hause**
at home
die **Haustür, -en** outside door
die **Hauswirtin, -nen** landlady
heben (o, o) lift, raise
heftig violent, vigorous
der **Heide, -n** heathen
heil well, whole
heilen heal
heilig holy, sacred
heim home
die **Heimat, -en** homeland, native land or city
heimlich secret
heim-suchen punish
heiraten marry
heiß hot

heißen (ie, ei) be called;
es hieß it was said
helfen (a, o, i) [*dat.*] help
die **Helferin, -nen** nurse's aide
hell bright
her hither [*toward the spea-*
ker]
sich **herablassen*** condescend
heran-kommen* (ist) approach
herauf-steigen* (ist) climb
up, arise
heraus-finden* find out
heraus-kommen* (ist) get
out (of)
heraus-nehmen* take out
heraus-springen* (ist)
jump out
heraus-treten* (ist) come
out of
herbei-eilen (ist) hurry to
the scene
der **Herbst, -e** fall, autumn
herein! Come in! Enter!
herein-lassen* let in,
admit
herein-rollen (ist) roll in
herein-tragen* bring in
her-fahren* (ist) travel
der **Herr, -n, -en** gentleman;
Mr., master
herrlich wonderful
herrschen rule, prevail
herüber-kommen* (ist)
come over
sich **herüber-lehnen** lean
toward
herum-fahren* (ist) drive
around
herum-fragen inquire; ask
around
herum-reißen* jerk, pull
around
herum-sitzen* sit around

herunter-gehen* (ist) go down

herunter-kommen* (ist) come down, descend

das Herz, -ens, -en heart; einem ans Herz wachsen* grow dear to someone

die Herzlichkeit, -en cordiality; mit eifriger Herzlichkeit with exaggerated cordiality

der Herzschlag, ⁻e heart attack

heulen howl, scream

das Heulen howling

heute today

hier here

hierher here

hierzulande in this country

die Hilfe, -n help

hilflos helpless

die Hilflosigkeit, -en helplessness

der Himmel, - heaven

hin there [away from the speaker]; hin und her back and forth

hinauf-springen* (ist) spring up

hinaus-schieben* shove out

hinaus-sehen* look out

hindern hinder

sich hin-legen go to bed, lie down

hin-sehen look

hin-stellen place before

hinten behind

hintergehen* cheat

die Hintertür, -en back door

hinüber-lehnen lean over

hinüber-nicken nod towards

hinunter-fahren*(ist) drive down

hinunter-gehen* (ist) go down, descend

die Hitze heat

hoch high

die Hochachtung esteem

das Hochgebirge, - high mountain range

hoffen hope

hoffentlich (I) hope

die Hoffnung, -en hope

höflich polite

hoh-, höh- [see hoch]

die Höhe, -n height

höhnisch scornfully

holen go and get, fetch

die Hölle, -n hell

das Holz, ⁻er wood

die Holzindustrie, -n lumbering

hören hear

die Hosentasche, -n pants pocket

das Hotel, -s hotel

hübsch pretty

hüllen envelop, hide

der Humor sense of humor

der Hund, -e dog

der Hunger hunger; Hunger haben*, be hungry

hungern starve; mich hungert I'm hungry

die Hupe, -n horn

das Hupen honking

husten cough

die Hypothese, -n hypothesis

I

der Idealismus idealism

immer always; immer kleiner smaller and smaller; immer noch still

immerwährend continual

importiert imported

in in, into

der Indianer, - Indian

die Inflation, -en inflation

infolge as a result of

inmitten   in the midst of
innen   within
die Innenstadt, ⸚e   old part of city, in area once enclosed by walls
der Insasse, -n   occupant
interessant   interesting
das Interesse, -n   interest
sich interessieren (für)   be interested (in)
international   international

inzwischen   meanwhile
ionisieren   ionize
irgend   any;   irgendein   any(one)
irgendwo   anywhere, somewhere
sich irren   be mistaken
irrsinnig   crazy, mad
der Irrtum, ⸚er   error
der Italiener, -   Italian [*male*]
die Italienerin, -nen   Italian [*female*]

J

ja   yes; well; certainly
die Jagd, -en   chase, hunt
das Jahr, -e   year
je   ever
jed-   each, every
jedoch   however
jemals   ever
jemand   some one
jen-   that, those
jener   that one, the former
jetzt   now

das Joch, -e   yoke
der Journalist, -en   journalist
der Jude, -n   Jew
die Jugend   youth
die Jugendfreundin, -nen   girl friend; childhood sweetheart
jung   young
der Junge, -n   boy
der Jüngling, -e   youth

K

der Kaffee   coffee
(das) Kalifornien   California
kalt   cold
die Kälte   cold
der Kamin, -e   fireplace
der Kampf, ⸚e   fight
kämpfen   fight
das Kapitel, -   chapter
der Karabiner, -   carbine
die Karte, -n   card(s)
der Kauf, ⸚e   purchase
kaufen   buy
der Kaufmann, -leute   merchant
kaum   hardly
die Kehle, -n   throat
kein   no, none
keineswegs   by no means

die Kellnerin, -nen   waitress
kennen (kannte, gekannt)   to know, be aquainted with
kennen-lernen   meet
das Kind, -er   child
das Kino, -s   movies
die Klage, -n   complaint
die Klappe, -n   flap;   in die Klappe gehen*   'hit the hay'
der Klapperkasten, ⸚   rattletrap
das Klappern   clatter
klappernd   rattling
klar   clear
die Klasse, -n   class
das Klassenzimmer, -   classroom
klein   small

die **Kleinigkeit,-en** trifle, detail
kleinlaut meekly
klingen (a, u) sound
die **Klugheit** good sense
der **Knabe, -n** boy
die **Knabenschule, -n** boys' school
das **Knie, -e** knee
der **Knopf, ⁼e** button
der **Knoten, -** knot
der **Knüppel, -** stick, club
kochen cook, boil
das **Kochen** boiling, cooking
komisch funny
das **Komma** comma
kommen (a, ist o) come; **auf etwas ankommen** depend on
der **Kommunismus** communism
komponieren compose
der **König, -e** king
können (konnte, gekonnt/ können, kann) be able to, can
der **Kopf, ⁼e** head
kopfschüttelnd shaking one's head
der **Körper, -** body
kosten cost
die **Kraft, ⁼e** strength, force

kräftig strong
krank sick
der **Kranke, -n** sick man, patient
das **Krankenhaus, ⁼er** hospital
die **Krankenpflegerin, -nen** nurse
die **Krankheit, -en** sickness, illness
der **Kreis, -e** circle
kreischen shriek
kriechen (o, ist o) crawl
der **Krieg, -e** war
kriegerisch warlike
die **Krise, -n** crisis
die **Kritik, -en** criticism
kritisieren criticize
die **Küche, -n** kitchen
die **Küchentür,-en** kitchen door
die **Kuh, ⁼e** cow
kühl cool
kümmern concern
die **Kunst, ⁼e** art
der **Künstler, -** artist
der **Kurs, -e** quotation, rate of exchange
die **Kurve, -n** curve
kurz short
das **Kurzwellensystem, -e** short-wave system
küssen kiss

L

lächeln smile
lachen laugh
das **Lachen** laughter
das **Lachkabinett, -e** fun house
laden (u, a, ä) load
der **Laden, ⁼** store
die **Lampe, -n** lamp
das **Land, ⁼er** land, country
die **Landarbeit, -en** farm work
landen land
das **Landen** landing
die **Landstraße, -n** highway
lang long

lange a long time, long
langsam slow
längst for a long time, long since
der **Lärm** noise
lärmen to make noise
lassen (ie, a, ä) let, leave, permit
sich **lassen** can be [done, etc.]
die **Last, -en** load, burden
der **Lastkraftwagen, -** truck
der **Lastwagen, -** truck
laufen (ie, ist au, äu) run
laut loud

der **Laut, -e** sound
läuten ring
das **Läuten** ringing
leben live
das **Leben** life
der **Lebensraum, ⁼e** living space
der **Lebensumstand, ⁼e** situation, circumstance
die **Lebenszeit, -en** span of life
lebhaft lively
leblos lifeless
die **Lederjacke, -n** leather jacket
leer empty
legen lay, put, place
lehren teach
der **Lehrer, -** teacher
der **Lehrling, -e** apprentice
leicht easy, light
leichtfüßig with light steps
leid tun* [*dat.*] be sorry
leiden (litt, -litten) suffer
die **Leidenschaft, -en** passion
leidenschaftlich passionate
leider unfortunately
leihen (ie, ie) lend
leise soft, quiet
leisten accomplish
sich **leisten** afford
die **Leistung, -en** achievement
lenken steer
lernen learn
lesen (a, e, ie) read
letzt- latest, last
die **Leutchen** [*pl.*] 'dear little people'

die **Leute** [*pl.*] people
das **Licht, -er** light
die **Lichtreklame, -n** advertisements
das **Lichtspieltheater, -** movie
lieb dear; **lieb haben*** to like, love
die **Liebe** love
lieben love
die **Liebenswürdigkeit, -en** kindness
lieber [*see* **gern**]
Liebster dearest
liegen (a, e) lie
die **Linie, -n** line
die **Linke, -n** left hand
die **Lippe, -n** lip
die **Liste, -n** list
die **Literatur** literature
das **Logis** lodgings
der **Lohn, ⁼e** pay
das **Lohngeld, -er** payroll
das **Lokal, -e** place [*bar, dançe hall*]
los loose; **Was ist los?** What's the matter?
löschen extinguish
los-lassen* let go
los-werden* (ist) get rid of
die **Lösung, -en** solution
die **Luft, ⁼e** air
der **Luftangriff, -e** air-raid
die **Lust, ⁼e** desire; **Lust haben* zu etwas** to feel like
lustig merry

M

machen make, do
das **Mädchen, -** girl
mager skimpy
die **Mahlzeit, -en** meal
das **Mal, -e** time, instance; **zum vierten Mal** 'for the fourth time'

malen paint
man one, 'they,' 'you,' 'people'
manch- many (a)
der **Mann, ⁼er** man
das **Männlein, -** little man
marinieren marinate

der Mars Mars
   marschieren march
die Maschine, -n machine
die Masse, -n mass
der Materialismus materialism
die Materialverschwendung waste of material
die Mathematik mathematics
die Mauer, -n wall
das Meer, -e sea
   mehr more, (any) longer
   mehrere several
   mehrfach often
die Meile, -n mile
   mein my
   meinen think, mean, opine
   meinetwegen 'for all I care'
die Meinung, -en opinion; meiner Meinung nach in my opinion
   meist most
   meistens usually
   melden announce, report
die Meldung, -en report, announcement
die Menge, -n crowd
der Mensch, -en person, human being
die Menschheit humanity
   menschlich human
   merken notice
   merkurieren mercurate
   merkwürdig strange, remarkable
   messen (a, e, i) measure, take temperature
die Methode, -n method
der Mikrofilm, -e microfilm
der Milchwagen, - milk wagon
   mindestens at least
   minus minus, less
die Minute, -n minute
   mir me [*dat.*]
sich mischen mix

   mißmutig peevishly
   mit with; [*adv.*] along
   mit-bringen* bring along
   mit-gehen* go along, come along
   mit-kommen* (ist) come along
der Mitmensch, -en fellow man
   mit-nehmen* take along
die Mitte, -n middle
   mit-teilen inform, notify
der Mittelpunkt, -e center
   mittels by means of
der Mittwoch Wednesday
das Modell, -e model
   mögen (mochte, gemocht/ mögen, mag) like
   möglich possible
die Möglichkeit, -en possibility
der Monat, -e month
der Mond, -e moon
der Montag, -e Monday
der Morgen, - morning
   morgen tomorrow
   morgens in the morning
der Morgenhimmel, - morning sky
der Morgennebel, - morning fog
der Motor, -en motor
das Motorboot, -e motor boat
   müde tired
die Mühe, -n trouble
der Münchner, - man from Munich
die Münchnerin, -nen woman from Munich
   multiplizieren multiply
der Mund, ⁻er mouth
die Musik music
die Muskel, -n muscle
   müssen (mußte, gemußt/ müssen, muß) must, have to
die Mutter, ⁻ mother

N

nach after, toward, to; according to
der Nachbar, -n neighbor
die Nachbarin, -nen neighbor
  [*female*]
die Nachbarschaft, -en neigh-
  borhood
nachdem [*conj. only*] after
nach-denken* consider,
  think over
nach-fragen ask, inquire
nach Hause home
nachher afterwards
die Nachlässigkeit negligence
der Nachmittag, -e afternoon
die Nachricht, -en news, report
nach-sehen* [*dat.*] watch
nach-setzen (ist) [*dat.*] set
  out after
nächst next
die Nacht, ⁼e night; nachts at
  night
nah near
sich nähern [*dat.*]   approach,
  come close to
näher-treten* (ist)   step
  closer
der Name, -ns, -n name
nämlich namely, you know
der Narr, -en fool
natürlich of course

der Nebel, - fog
neben beside, next to
nebenan next door
necken tease
nehmen(nahm, -nommen,
  nimmt) take
der Neid envy
nennen (nannte, genannt)
  call
nett nice
neu new; aufs Neue anew
neugierig curious
neulich recently
nicht not
nichts nothing
nicken nod
nie never
nieder-rauschen (ist) gush
  down
nieder-setzen set down
niemand nobody
noch still, yet, in addition
nördlich northern
der Nordwesten the northwest
nordwestlich northwesterly
nötig necessary
notwendig necessary
die Nummer, -n number, figure
nun now; well
nur only, just
nützlich useful

O

ob if, whether
oben above, upstairs
obgleich although
das Objekt, -e object
offen open, frank
der Offizier, -e officer
öffnen open
oft often
ohne without
das Ohr, -en ear

der Onkel, - uncle
opfern sacrifice
der Orangensaft orange juice
die Ordnung, -en order
der Orient Orient, Middle East
der Ort, -e place, locality
der Osten East
oxydieren oxydize
der Ozean, -e ocean

P

ein **paar** a couple, a few
das **Paket, -e** package
das **Papier, -e** paper
der **Park, -s** park
der **Parkplatz, ⁼e** parking place
die **Partie, -n** game
    passieren (ist) happen
der **Pastor, -en** pastor
der **Pathologe, -n** pathologist
der **Patient, -en** patient
das **Pech** bad luck ('pitch')
    per by
    pfeifen (pfiff, -pfiffen)
    whistle
    pflegen take care of, nurse
    pflegen (zu) be accustomed
    to, be used to
die **Pflicht, -en** duty
    pflücken pick [*flowers*]
der **Pharmakologe, -n** pharma-
    cologist
der **Philologe, -n** philologist
der **Philosoph, -en** philosopher
die **Phonetik** phonetics
die **Physik** physics
der **Physiker, -** physicist
der **Physiologe, -n** physiologist
die **Physiologie** physiology
die **Pille, -n** pill
der **Plan, ⁼e** plan
    planen plan

die **Platte,-n** phonograph record
    platz-nehmen* have a seat
das **Plätzchen, -** spot, place
    plaudern chat
    plötzlich suddenly
die **Poesie** poetry
die **Poetik** poetics
    polieren polish
die **Politik** politics, policy
    politisch political
die **Polizei** police
der **Polizeibeamte, -n** police
    official
der **Polizeiwagen, -** police car
der **Polizist, -en** policeman
das **Porto** postage
der **Portugiese, -n** Portuguese
    [*male*]
die **Post** post office, mail
    prahlerisch boastingly
der **Präsident, -en** president
der **Preis, -e** price
    privat private
das **Problem, -e** problem
der **Professor, -en** professor
das **Programm, -e** program
    prüfen test
der **Psychiater, -** psychiatrist
die **Psychiatrie** psychiatry
der **Puls, -e** pulse
der **Punkt, -e** point

R

das **Rad, ⁼er** wheel
das **Radio, -s** radio
    ragen jut
die **Rakete, -n** rocket
der **Raketenführer, -** rocket
    pilot
    rasch quick(ly)
    rasen (ist) race, race along
der **Rasen, -** grass, lawn
die **Rasselbande,-n** noisy gang
der **Rat** counsel, advice

    raten (ie, a, ä) advise
    rauben rob
der **Rauch** smoke
    rauchen smoke
der **Raum, ⁼e** room, space
    rauschen rustle
der **Realismus** realism
die **Realität** reality
der **Realist, -en** realist
    rechnen figure
die **Rechnung, -en** bill; **auf**

seine Rechnung kom-
men* get one's money's
worth

recht right (hand); correct,
rightly

rechtfertigen justify

die Rechtfertigung justification

rechts on the right

rechtzeitig promptly, on
time

reden speak, talk

die Rede, -n speech, talk

der Regen rain

regnen rain

reich rich

reichen pass, tender

der Reichtum, ¨er wealth, for-
tune

reif mature

der Reifen tire

die Reifenpanne, -e flat tire

rein pure

reisen (ist) travel

reißen (riß, -rissen) tear

reiten (ritt, -ritten) ride

reizend charming

die Rennbahn, -en race track

rennen (rannte, ist ge-
rannt) run

der Rennfahrer, - racing driver

die Reparatur, -en repair

die Reparaturwerkstätte, -n
repair shop

reparieren repair

das Resultat, -e result

retten save

der Rettungsgürtel, - life belt

der Rhythmus, -men rhythm

richtig correct

die Richtung, -en direction

riechen (o, o) smell

die Riesenexplosion, -en big
explosion

riesig gigantic

der Rinnstein, -e curb, gutter

der Ritt, -e ride

rollen roll

die Rose, -n rose

rot red

rötlich reddish

rücken move

der Rücken, - back

die Rückgabe, -n return

die Rückkehr return

die Rückreise, -n return trip

das Ruderboot, -e rowboat

rudern row [*a boat*]

rufen (ie, u) call

die Ruhe quiet, rest, composure

ruhelos restless

ruhen rest

ruhevoll restful

ruhig restful, quiet

sich rühmen [*gen.*] boast of

die Ruine, -n ruins

rund round

der Russe, -n Russian [*male*]

S

der Saal, Säle hall, room

die Sache, -n thing, matter

sagen say, tell

das Sägewerk, -e sawmill

sammeln collect

der Samstag, -e Saturday

saugen (o, o) suck

schade: das ist schade
that's too bad

schaden do damage, hurt

der Schaden, ¨ harm, injury;
Schaden nehmen* to
suffer injury

die Schallplatte, -n phonograph record

der Schalter, - ticket window

scharf sharp

der Schatten, - shadow

das Schaufenster, - show window
die Schauspielerin, -nen actress
der Scheck, -s check
die Scheibe, -n disc
sich scheiden lassen* get a divorce
der Schein, -e appearance
scheinen (ie, ie) shine, seem
der Scheinwerfer, - searchlight
schenken give [*as a present*]
scherzen joke
die Schicht, -en layer
schicken send
das Schicksal, -e fate
schieben (o, o) push, shove
schießen (o, o) shoot
das Schiff -e ship
der Schlaf sleep
schlafen (ie, a, ä) sleep
das Schlafen sleeping
schläfern [*impersonal*] be sleepy
der Schlag, ¨e blow
schlagen (u, a, ä) strike, hit, beat [*a record, an opponent*]
der Schlager, - hit tune
schlank slender
schlecht bad
schleichen (i, ist i) sneak
schlicht plain, smooth, simple
schließen (o, o) close, shut
schließlich finally; after all
die Schlucht, -en gorge
schmecken taste
der Schmerz, -en pain
schmerzen hurt
die Schmiere, -n lubrication
die Schnecke, -n snail
der Schnee snow
schneien [*impersonal*] snow
schnell fast
die Schnelligkeit speed

der Schnitt, -e cut
schon already
schön pretty, beautiful
schrecklich terrible
schreiben (ie, ie) write
das Schreiben writing, letter
der Schreibtisch, -e desk
schreien (ie, ie) scream, cry
der Schritt, -e step
der Schulbeginn beginning of school
die Schuld, -en blame, guilt
schuldig guilty
die Schule, -n school
das Schulgeld, -er tuition, fee
die Schulter, -n shoulder
schütteln shake
schwach weak
die Schwäche, -n weakness
schwarz black
der Schwede, -n Swede [*male*]
schweigen (ie, ie) be silent
das Schweigen silence
schweigsam in silence, quiet
schwer heavy, serious
schwerfällig heavy
schwermütig melancholy, sad
die Schwester, -n sister
die Schwierigkeit, -en difficulty
schwimmen (a, ist o) swim
das Schwimmen swimming
schwören (u *or* o, o) swear
der See, -n lake
die Seele, -n soul
die Seelenheilkunde psychiatry
der Seemann Seeleute sailor(s)
segeln (ist) sail
der Segen, - blessing
sehen (a, e, ie) see
die Sehnsucht, ¨e longing, yearning
sehr very
sein (war, ist gewesen, ist) be

sein his
seit since, for [*time*]
seitdem since
die Seite, -n side, page
die Seitenwand, ⸚e side (wall)
selber self [*see 13.1,2*]
selbst self
das Selbst self
selten seldom, rare
der Senator, -en senator
senden (sandte, gesandt) send
die Sendung, -en shipment
sentimental sentimental
sich setzen sit, place
(das) Sibirien Siberia
sicher sure(ly)
die Sicherheit safety
sichtbar visible
siegen be victorious
silbern silver
singen (a, u) sing
sinken (a, ist u) sink
sinnvoll sensible
die Sirene, -n siren
der Sitz, -e seat
sitzen (saß, gesessen) sit
so thus, in this way
sobald as soon as
so ein such a one, one like that
sofort immediately
der Sohn, ⸚e son
solch such
der Soldat, -en soldier
sollen (sollte, gesollt) be said to; ought to
der Sommer, - summer
die Sommerferien [*pl.*] summer vacation
die Sommerschule, -n summer school
die Sommerluft, ⸚e summer air
sondern but
die Sonne, -n sun
der Sonnenaufgang, ⸚e sunrise
der Sonnenschein sunshine

der Sonntag, -e Sunday
sonnverbrannt sunburned
sonst otherwise
die Sorge, -n care, sorrow
der Sozialismus socialism
sich spalten split
der Spaß, ⸚e fun, joke
spät late
sperren close, block
der Spiegel, - mirror
das Spiegelkabinett, -e hall of mirrors
sich spiegeln reflect
das Spiel, -e play, game
der Spielapparat, -e record player, juke box
spielen play
das Spielzeug, -e toy
der Sportrock, ⸚e sport jacket
der Sportwagen, - sports car
der Spott sarcasm, scorn
die Sprache, -n speech, language ; zur Sprache bringen* discuss
sprechen (a, o, i) talk, speak
die Sprenganlage, -n sprinkler
springen (a, ist u) jump
der Staat, -en state
der Stab, ⸚e rod
die Stadt, ⸚e city
das Städtchen, - small town
der Stahlhelm, -e steel helmet
die Stahltrosse, -n steel cable
stammeln stammer
stark strong
starren stare
statt instead of
statt-finden* take place
der Staub dust
stecken stick, put, place
stehen (stand, gestanden) stand; be (printed, listed, exhibited)
stehen-bleiben* (ist) stop, stand
stehlen (a, o, ie) steal

steigen (ie, ist ie) climb, rise
steigern increase
der Stein, -e stone
die Stelle, -n place
stellen set, place, put
die Stellung, -en position, job
sterben (a, ist o, i) die
sterblich mortal
der Steuerberater, - tax consultant
das Steuerrad, ̈er steering wheel
still quiet
die Stille quiet, peace
die Stimme, -n voice
die Stirn, -en forehead
stolz proud
das Stopplicht, -er tail light
der Strafzettel, - ticket
die Straße, -n street
der Straßenbahnwagen, - streetcar

die Straßenecke, -n corner
der Straßengraben, ̈ ditch
die Straßenlampe, -n street light
die Straßenreinigungsmaschine, -n street sweeper
streifen (ist) roam
streng strict, stern
der Strom, ̈e stream, current
das Stück, -e piece
der Student, -en student
studieren study
der Stuhl, ̈e chair
die Stunde, -n hour, class
stürzen (ist) fall headlong
subtrahieren subtract
suchen seek, look for
summen hum
der Sumpf, ̈e swamp
der Syphon, -s syphon
das System, -e system

T

die Tafel, -n blackboard
der Tag, -e day
täglich daily
das Tal, ̈er valley
der Tank, -s tank
die Tanne, -n fir tree
der Tannenwald, ̈er fir forest
der Tanz, ̈e dance
tanzen dance
tapfer brave(ly)
die Tasche, -n pocket
der Taschendieb, -e pickpocket
die Tasse, -n cup
der Täter, - culprit
die Tatsache, -n fact
tatsächlich in fact, actually
täuschen deceive
teilen divide
teil-nehmen* participate
telefonieren telephone

terminieren terminate
teuer expensive
der Teufel, - devil
der Teufelsberg Mt. Diabolo
das Thema, -men topic, theme
der Theosoph, -en theosophist
tief deep
die Tiefe, -n depth
der Tisch, -e table
der Titel, - title
die Tochter, ̈ daughter
der Tod, -e death
der Ton, ̈e tone, sound
der Tourist, -en tourist
tragen (u, a, ä) carry, wear
tragisch tragic
die Träne, -n tear
die Trauer mourning
der Traum, ̈e dream
träumen dream
traurig sad

treffen (a, o, i) hit, meet
treiben (ie, ie) drive
die Treppe, -n stairs
treten (a, ist e, i) step, walk
der Trieb, -e urge, drive
trocken dry
trösten comfort
trotz in spite of
trotzdem nevertheless

der Tscheche, -n Czech
die Tschechoslowakei Czecho-
slovakia
tüchtig capable, excellent
tun (tat, getan) do
die Tür, -en door
der Türke, -n Turk [*male*]
die Türkei Turkey
die Türkin, -nen Turk [*female*]

U

übel bad, evil, offensive;
einem übel nehmen* to
take offense
über over, concerning, about
überall everywhere
überfallen* attack
überhaupt at all, in general
überholen overtake, pass
die Überraschung, -en surprise
überreden convince
überschwemmen overflow,
inundate
übersetzen translate
übersteigen* exceed
übrig-bleiben* (ist) be left
(to do)
das Ufer, - shore, bank
die Uhr, -en clock, o'clock
um around, at, for, in order
to; um etwas kommen*
lose something
sich um-drehen turn about
umgeben* surround
die Umgebung, -en surroundings, environs
sich um-kleiden change clothes
der Umsatz turnover
sich um-schauen look around
umso [*plus comparative*] all
the more
der Umstand, ⁼e circumstance
die Unabhängigkeit indepen-
dence

unaufhörlich unceasing
unbehindert unhindered
unbekannt unknown
unbequem uncomfortable
unbesorgt unconcerned
undeutlich unclear
undurchdringlich impene-
trable
unerfahren inexperienced
unermüdlich indefatigably
unfähig incapable
der Unfall, ⁼e accident
unfreundlich unfriendly
ungeduldig impatient
ungefähr approximately,
about
ungeheuer huge
ungewiß uncertain
ungewohnt unusual
das Unglück, -e misfortune,
disaster
unheilbar incurable
das Unheil disaster
die Universität, -en university
unmöglich impossible
unser our
der Unsinn nonsense
unten below
unter under, beneath
unterbrechen* interrupt
unterdrücken suppress
der Untergang, ⁼e downfall
unter-gehen* (ist) set (of
sun)

sich **unterhalten*** entertain oneself, converse
die **Unterhaltung, -en** conversation
unter-kommen* (ist) find a place (lodgings, position)
unterlaufen* (ist) occur
sich **unterscheiden*** be different
untersuchen examine

die **Untertasse, -n** saucer
unvorhergesehen unforeseen
unwillkommen unwelcome
unzählig countless
der **Urlaub** leave, furlough
die **Ursache, -n** cause
der **Ursprung, ⁼e** origin

V

der **Vater, ⁼** father
die **Verabredung, -en** date
sich **verabschieden** say goodbye, leave
die **Veranda, -en** porch, veranda
verändern alter, change
die **Veränderung, -en** change
verbergen (a, o, i) hide, conceal
verbessern improve
verbieten (o, o) forbid
verbinden* combine, bandage
die **Verbindung, -en** contact; **in Verbindung kommen*** get in touch
verbrennen* burn
verbringen* spend [time]
verdächtig suspicious
verderben (a, ist o, i) spoil, perish
verdienen earn, deserve
verdunsten (ist) evaporate
vereinigen unite, combine
Vereinigte Staaten United States
verfolgen persecute
die **Vergangenheit** past
der **Vergaser, -** carburetor
vergehen* pass, go away
vergessen (a, e, i) forget
vergleichen* compare
das **Vergnügen, -** pleasure, fun

vergolden gild
verhaften arrest
sich **verheiraten** get married
verhindern hinder
verkaufen sell
der **Verkehr** traffic
verlangen demand, ask for
verlassen* leave, abandon
sich **verlassen auf** rely on
verleben spend, pass time
verlegen embarrassed
verlieren (o, o) lose
die **Verlobte, -n** fiancée
der **Verlust, -e** loss
vermeiden (ie, ie) avoid
vermögen* be able
verneinen deny, say no
vernichten destroy
die **Vernunft** reason
vernünftig rational
verpacken pack
verringern decrease
die **Versammlung, -en** meeting
verschaffen get, obtain
verschieben* adjust, postpone
verschieden different, various
verschönern beautify
die **Verschönerung, -en** adornment
verschwenden waste
die **Verschwendung** waste

verschwinden (a, ist u) disappear

versichern insure

die Versicherung, -en insurance

die Versprechung, -en promise

der Verstand understanding, mind

verstecken hide

verstehen* understand

versteinert petrified

versuchen try, attempt; versucht sein* be tempted

das Versuchstier, -e 'guinea pig'

verteidigen defend

verteilen distribute

vertrocknen dry (up)

der Verunglückte, -n victim

verursachen cause

vervollkommnen make perfect

verwandeln change, transform; wie verwandelt as if transformed

der Verwandte, -n relative

die Verwandtschaft, -en relationship

die Verwirklichung realization

verwirren confuse

die Verwirrung confusion

verwundert surprised

verzehren consume

verzeihen (ie, ie) forgive

sich verziehen* disperse

viel much

viele many

vielleicht maybe, perhaps

das Vogelgesicht, -er birdlike face

die Völkerkunde anthropology

voll full

die Vollkommenheit perfection

von of, from, by

vor before, ago

vorbei over, past, by

vorbei-brausen (ist) zoom past

vorbei-fahren* (ist) drive past

vorbei-gehen* (ist) go by

vorbei-gleiten* (ist) glide by

vorbei-rasen (ist) race by

die Vorbereitung, -en preparation

der Vordergarten, ⸚ front lawn

vor-fahren* (ist) drive up

vor-flüstern whisper

vorig previous, last

vor-kommen* appear, happen

vorläufig for the time being

der Vormittag, -e forenoon

vorne in front

vor-nehmen* undertake

auf Vorposten on outpost duty

der Vorpostenkampf, ⸚e outpost fighting

der Vorschlag, ⸚e suggestion

vorsichtig careful

vor Sonnenaufgang before sunrise

vor-stellen introduce, present

sich vor-stellen imagine

vorüber past, over

der Vorteil, -e advantage

vorüber-brausen (ist) zoom by

vorüber-fahren* (ist) drive past

vorüber-gehen* (ist) go by

vorwärts forward; nach vorwärts ahead

vorzüglich especial, excellent; mit vorzüglicher Hochachtung respectfully yours

der Vulkan, -e volcano

W

wachsen (u, ist a, ä) grow
das Wachsfigurenkabinett, -e
  waxworks
die Waffe, -n weapon
der Wagemut daring
  wagen dare
der Wagen, - car
die Wahl, -en election, choice
  wählen choose
der Wahlkampf, ⸚e election
  campaign
  wahr true
  während [*prep*.] during;
  [*conj*.] while
die Wahrhaftigkeit truthful-
  ness
  wahrhaft truthful
die Wahrheit, -en truth
der Wald, ⸚er forest, woods
der Waldbrand, ⸚e forest fire
die Wand, ⸚e wall
  wandern (ist) stroll, wander
  wann? when?
  warm warm
  warnen warn
die Warnung, -en warning
  warten (auf) wait (for)
  warum why
  was what, which
die Wäsche, -n laundry, linens
  waschen (u, a, ä) wash
  was für (ein) what kind of
das Wasser water
der Wassergraben, ⸚ drainage,
  ditch
die Wasserrechnung, -en water bill
der Wasserstrom, ⸚e stream of
  water
der Wecker, - alarm clock
  weder... noch neither... nor
  weg away
der Weg, -e way, road
  wegen on account of

das Weggehen leaving
  weg-laufen* (ist) run away
  weg-springen* (ist) jump
  away
  weg-werfen* throw away
  weh tun* hurt
  weil because
die Weile, -n while
der Wein, -e wine
die Weise, -n way
  weiß white
  weit far
  weither further
  weiter-fahren* (ist) drive on
  weiter-gehen* (ist) pass on
sich weiter-schleppen move
  slowly onward
  welch- which, who, that
die Welle, -n wave
die Welt, -en world
der Weltkrieg, -e world war
die Weltliteratur world literature
der Weltraum, ⸚e outer space
die Weltstadt, ⸚e metropolis
sich wenden (wandte, gewandt)
  turn
  wenig few, little
  weniger less
  wenigstens at least
  wenn when(ever), if
  wer who; whoever, he who
  werden (u, ist o, i) become,
  be
  werfen (a, o, i) throw
das Werk, -e work
der Werkführer, - foreman
die Werkstätte, -n shop, studio
das Werkzeug, -e tool
  wert worth
  weshalb why, for what reason
  wessen? whose?
der Westen west

das **Wetter,** - weather
wickeln wrap
wider against
widersprechen* [*dat.*] contradict
widerstehen* [*dat.*] resist
widmen devote
wie how, as, like
wieder again
wieder-erkennen* recognize
wiederholen repeat
(auf) Wiederhören goodbye [*in telephoning*]
wieder-kommen*(ist) come back
wieder-sehen* see again
das **Wiedersehen** reunion, meeting again
wieso? why? how? in what way?
wieviel- how many, how much
wild wild
der **Wille, -ns, -n** will
die **Windrichtung, -en** wind direction
der **Winkel,** - angle
winken wave
der **Winter,** - winter
die **Winternothilfe** winter relief
wirken to have an effect
wirklich real, really
die **Wirklichkeit, -en** reality
wischen wipe
wissen (wußte, gewußt, weiß) know
die **Wissenschaft, -en** science

der **Wissenschaftler,** - scientist
der **Witz, -e** joke
wo where
die **Woche, -n** week
das **Wochenende, -n** week-end
wodurch? by (or through) what means?
woher where... from
wohin where... to
wohl well, indeed, in fact, probably
das **Wohlgefühl** feeling of well-being
der **Wohlstand** prosperity
wohnen live, dwell
die **Wohnung, -en** dwelling, apartment
das **Wohnzimmer,-** living room
die **Wolke, -n** cloud
das **Wolkenmeer** sea of clouds
wollen (wollte, gewollt/ wollen, will) want to
woran? on what? by what? of what? through what?
worauf? on what? for what? to what?
das **Wort, ⸚er** word
wozu? what for? why?
das **Wunder,** - wonder, miracle
sich **wundern** be surprised, wonder
wundervoll splendid, wonderful
der **Wunsch, ⸚e** wish
wünschen wish
die **Wüste, -n** desert
wütend raging

Z

zahlen pay
die **Zahlung, -en** payment
der **Zahn, ⸚e** tooth
zehnpfündig ten pounds
zeigen show
die **Zeit, -en** time

die **Zeitung, -en** newspaper
der **Zeitungsjunge, -n** newsboy
die **Zeitverschwendung** waste of time
der **Zentimeter,** - centimeter

zerbrechen* break
zerfallen* collapse, fall apart
zerlegen dissect
zerspringen* burst
zerstören destroy
der Zettel, - slip of paper
das Zeug, -e material
ziehen (zog, -zogen) pull, draw
das Ziel, -e goal, target
ziemlich rather
die Zigarette, -n cigarette
die Zigarre, -n cigar
das Zimmer, - room
zittern tremble, shake
die Zivilisation, -en civilization
zögern hesitate
zu to, at, too
zuerst (at) first
zu-flüstern [dat.] whisper
die Zufuhr, -en supplies
der Zug, -e train
zu-gehen* (auf jemand) go up (to somebody)
zu-hören [dat.] listen
der Zuhörer, - listener
zu-kommen* (auf jemand) come up (to somebody)
die Zukunft future
zunächst at first, for the time being
zu-nehmen* increase
die Zunge, -n tongue
zurück back, behind
zurück-führen lead back

zurück-geben* return
zurück-gehen* go back
zurück-kehren (ist) return
zurück-kommen* return
zurück-legen cover (ground)
zurück-rennen* run back
zurück-schnellen (ist) snap back
zurück-sinken* sink back
zusammen together
zusammen-brechen* collapse
zusammen-fallen* collapse
zusammen-führen lead back together
sich zusammen-schließen* close
zusammen-sitzen* sit together
der Zusammenstoß, -e collision, impact
zusammen-stoßen* collide
zu-schauen [dat.] watch, look on
zuvor [adv.] before
zu-wenden turn to
zu-winken [dat.] wave to
zu-ziehen* draw together
zwar to be sure
der Zweck, -e purpose
zwecks for the purpose of
der Zweifel, - doubt
zweifelhaft doubtful
zweifelnd doubtingly
zweimal twice
zwingen (a, u) force, compel
zwischen between
der Zylinderdruck compression

English—German Vocabulary

A

abandon verlassen
about über [acc.]
accept an-nehmen
accident der Unfall
get acquainted kennen-lernen
across über
act tun (als ob)
actor der Schauspieler
actress die Schauspielerin
address die Adresse, die Anschrift
adjust verschieben
advise raten
after all doch
afterwards nachher, später
again wieder, noch einmal
ago vor [+ dat.]
airplane das Flugzeug
all all [adj. or pron.]; ganz [adv.]
all sorts of allerlei

be allowed to dürfen
alone allein
already schon
alter verändern
angry ärgerlich
be (or get) angry sich ärgern
answer antworten [+ dat.]
anyone jeder, irgend jemand
apartment die Wohnung
approach sich nähern [+ dat.]
area die Gegend
arise entstehen
army die Armee, das Heer
arrange, revise bearbeiten
arrive an-kommen
artillery die Artillerie
artist der Künstler
as well auch
ask fragen, bitten (um), eine
Frage stellen

assist bei-stehen [+ *dat.*]; helfen
at um, bei, an
attack der Angriff

attain erreichen
attend bei-wohnen [+ *dat.*]
awful(ly) furchtbar

B

bad schlecht
bank das Ufer; die Bank
basic element *or* **material** der Grundstoff
be sein
beat schlagen
become werden
bed das Bett
begin beginnen, an-fangen
behave sich benehmen
believe glauben [+ *dat.*]
belong to gehören [+ *dat.*]

book das Buch
border die Grenze
boy der Junge, der Knabe
bread das Brot
break out aus-brechen
bright hell
bring bringen
brother der Bruder
burn brennen
bus der Omnibus
business das Geschäft
buy kaufen

C

café das Café
call rufen, nennen
called, to be heißen
call up an-rufen
call for ab-holen
car der Wagen, das Auto
carburetor der Vergasser
careful sorgfältig
carry tragen
case der Fall; **in any case** auf jeden Fall
catch up with ein-holen
cause verursachen
cease auf-hören
center das Zentrum
certainly gewiß, freilich, sicher
change ändern, verändern
change [*n.*] die Veränderung
change clothes sich um-kleiden
chapter das Kapitel
be characterized by sich dadurch aus-zeichnen
chemistry die Chemie
child das Kind

circumstance der Umstand
city die Stadt
claim behaupten
clean rein
clear klar
clever klug
climb besteigen, steigen
close schließen, zu-machen
cold [*n.*] die Kälte
come kommen
come back zurück-kommen
comfortable bequem
condescend sich herab-lassen
condition der Umstand
take into consideration in Betracht ziehen
become conspicuous auf-fallen
contradict widersprechen [*dat.*]
conversation das Gespräch
conversational tone der Gesprächston
converse sich unterhalten
copy das Exemplar
could have... hätte...können

country das Land; **in the country** auf dem Lande; **to the country** auf das Land
cover bedecken

cow die Kuh
crowd die Menge
culprit der Täter
cut off ab-schneiden

D

dance tanzen
daughter die Tochter
day der Tag
decide sich entschließen, entscheiden, beschließen
decline ab-lehnen
depart ab-fahren
departure die Abfahrt
deserve verdienen
desk der Schreibtisch
die sterben
different ander-
differently anders
difficulty die Schwierigkeit
dig graben

dining room der Eßsaal, das Eßzimmer
disappear verschwinden
discover entdecken
discovery die Entdeckung
do tun, machen
doctor der Arzt
dollar der Dollar
door die Tür
draw near sich nähern [+ *dat.*]
drive fahren
driver der Fahrer
during während
dwell wohnen

E

eagerness der Fleiß, der Eifer
early früh
earn verdienen
easy leicht
eat essen
eating das Essen
have an effect wirken
either [*not neg.*] auch
either...or entweder...oder
employee der Angestellte
enjoy genießen
enough genug
entire ganz
entrance der Eingang
Europe (das) Europa

ever je
every jed-
examine untersuchen
example das Beispiel
excellent ausgezeichnet
exchange der Austausch
exclude aus-schließen
exhale aus-atmen
exhibition die Ausstellung
expect erwarten
experience das Erlebnis, die Erfahrung
explain erklären
express oneself sich aus-drücken
extremely äußerst-, aufs äußerste

F

face das Gesicht
fact die Tatsache
familiar bekannt
family die Familie

famous berühmt
fast schnell
fetch holen
fight kämpfen

figure die Gestalt
film der Film
find finden
fire das Feuer, der Brand
first erst-, zunächst
fish angeln
fly fliegen
fog der Nebel
follow folgen [+ *dat.*]
for für, um, zu, auf, seit
force die Kraft
foreign ausländisch, fremd

foreman der Werkführer
forest der Wald
forget vergessen
forgive verzeihen, entschuldigen
former derjenige, jener
forsaken verlassen
fourth der Vierte
franc der Frank
free frei, offen
friend der Freund
from von, aus
future die Zukunft

G

gain gewinnen
garage die Garage
German [*adj.*] deutsch
get [*intrans.*] geraten
get [*trans.*] bekommen
get to erreichen
get used to sich gewöhnen an
  [*acc.*]

ghost der Geist
glide gleiten
go gehen
grasp greifen
great groß, großartig
green grün
group die Gruppe

H

half halb
happen geschehen, passieren,
  begegnen
happiness das Glück
happy glücklich
hat der Hut
have haben, lassen
have to müssen
he er
heal heilen
hear hören
heart das Herz
heavy schwer, stark
help helfen [+ *dat.*]
her ihr
hide verstecken

here hier, da
highway die Landstraße
super-highway die Autobahn
hit schlagen
home, at zu Hause
home(ward) nach Hause
hope die Hoffnung
hospital das Krankenhaus
hot heiß, warm
house das Haus
how wie
however aber
howl heulen
huge groß, ungeheuer
husband der Mann

I

imagine sich vor-stellen
improve verbessern
increase vermehren, zu-nehmen
industry der Fleiß
inflation die Inflation

influence beeinflussen
inform melden, mit-teilen
inquire fragen, nach-fragen, sich
  erkundigen
inside in [*dat.*], innerhalb [*gen.*]

intend wollen
interest interessieren
interesting interessant

invite ein-laden
it es

J

jacket die Jacke
job die Arbeitsstellung, die Stellung
join sich an-schließen

joke der Witz
jump springen
just nur, eben, gerade

K

keep busy sich beschäftigen
king der König

know kennen, wissen

L

lake der See
last dauern
last vorig-, letzt-
late spät
later später, nachher
latter der letztere, dieser
laugh lachen
laziness die Faulheit
learn lernen
leave (depart) ab-fahren
leave lassen
lend leihen
letter der Brief
life das Leben
like to gern [+ *verb.*]

license (driver's) der Führerschein
little klein, wenig
live wohnen [*dwell*], leben
living room das Wohnzimmer
load laden, beladen
long lang
look at an-sehen, sehen *auf* +
  [*acc.*]
look for suchen nach
lose verlieren
a lot of viel
love lieben
lovely schön

M

get mad sich ärgern
machine die Maschine
make a mistake, be mistaken
  sich irren
make up one's mind sich entschließen
mark die Mark
me mich [*acc.*], mir [*dat.*]
meaning die Bedeutung
meet begegnen, treffen
metropolis die Großstadt
middle die Mitte
milk die Milch
million die Million
mistake der Irrtum, der Fehler

model das Modell
moment der Augenblick, der
  Moment
Monday der Montag
money das Geld
month der Monat
moon der Mond
more mehr
motor der Motor
mountain der Berg
mourning die Trauer
movie das Kino
much viel
must müssen

N

necessary nötig
negligence die Nachlässigkeit
neighbor der Nachbar
never nie, niemals
nevertheless doch
new new
newspaper die Zeitung
next nächst-
night die Nacht

nod nicken
none keiner
northwest der Nordwesten
not at all gar nicht, überhaupt
  nicht
nothing nichts
now jetzt, nun
nurse die Krankenschwester

O

occur (take place) vor-kommen,
  statt-finden
occur to ein-fallen [*dat.*]
o'clock (die) Uhr
office das Büro
office girl das Büromädchen
official der Beamte
often oft
old alt
on account of wegen
once einmal

at once auf einmal, sofort,
  (plötzlich)
opportunity die Gelegenheit
in order to um... zu
other ander-
ought to sollte
out (of) aus
outer space der Weltraum
overtake überholen
own besitzen

P

package das Paket
page die Seite
parents die Eltern
park der Park
participate (in) teil-nehmen (an)
patience die Geduld
payment die Bezahlung
peasant der Bauer
people die Leute
per (share) pro Aktie, die Aktie
persecute verfolgen
physician der Arzt
picture das Bild
piece das Stück
pill die Pille
pilot der Flieger, der Raketenführer
place der Platz
at your place bei Ihnen

place stellen
plan der Plan
plane das Flugzeug
play spielen
policeman der Polizist, der Polizeibeamte
polite höflich
population die Bevölkerung
postman der Briefträger
power die Kraft
prefer lieber [+ *verb*]
be present bei-wohnen [+ *dat.*]
pretty schön
previous vorig
probably wohl, wahrscheinlich
profession der Beruf
proud of stolz [auf + *acc.*]
purchase kaufen
put stellen, setzen, legen

Q

question die Frage	**quiet** die Ruhe
quick schnell	**quite** ganz

R

race by vorbei-rasen	**repeat** wiederholen
rain regnen	**reply** antworten
rattletrap der Klapperkasten	**report** [*n.*] der Bericht
read lesen	**report** berichten
reason der Grund, die Vernunft	**return** zurück-kommen
recognize erkennen	**rich** reich
recollection die Erinnerung	**ride** reiten
refuse ab-lehnen	**rocket** die Rakete
relative der/die Verwandte	**run** laufen, rennen
remember sich erinnern an [*acc.*]	**run** [*a motor*] bedienen
	rush rasen, eilen
remind erinnern	**Russian** der Russe
repair reparieren	

S

sail segeln	**short-wave system** das Kurzwellensystem
Saturday der Samstag, der Sonnabend	**should have...** hätte...sollen
sawmill das Sägewerk	**sick man** der Kranke
say sagen	**sickness** die Krankheit
boys' school die Knabenschule	**side** die Seite
sea die See	**sight** die Ansicht
see sehen	**be silent** schweigen
seem scheinen, aus-sehen	**simple** einfach
self das Selbst	**sing** singen
sell verkaufen	**siren** die Sirene
send senden, schicken	**sit** sitzen
sense der Sinn	**sixteenth** der Sechzehnte
service [*a motor*] bedienen	**sky** der Himmel
several mehrer-	**sleep** schlafen
severe streng, schwer	**slip** der Zettel
shake schütteln	**slow** langsam
shall werden	**smile** lächeln
share die Aktie	**smoke** der Rauch
she sie	**soldier** der Soldat
short kurz	**something** etwas

soon bald
sound der Laut
speak reden, sprechen
speedometer der Geschwindigkeitsmesser
speed record der Geschwindigkeitsrekord
in spite of trotz [gen.]
spoil verderben
sport car der Sportwagen
stammer stammeln
stand fast fest-stehen
stare starren
stay bleiben
stop [intrans.] stehen-bleiben,
  an-halten

story die Geschichte
street die Straße
streetcar der Straßenbahnwagen
study lernen
stupid dumm
subject das Thema
succeed gelingen [dat.]
such (a) solch-, so (ein)
suddenly plötzlich, auf einmal
supper das Abendessen
suppose [see wohl, Lesson 4]
be supposed to sollen
surprise die Überraschung
be surprised sich wundern
surround umgeben
swim schwimmen

T

take nehmen, bringen
take part (in) teil-nehmen (an)
take place statt-finden
talk das Gespräch, die Rede
tall groß
task die Aufgabe
teacher der Lehrer
tear reißen
telegraph telegraphieren
tell sagen, erzählen
terribly furchtbar
terror das Grauen
than als
thank danken [+ dat.]
the der, die, das
then dann
think denken
thirty dreißig
this dies-
as though (as, if) als ob
thousand tausend

threatening bedrohlich
through durch
throw werfen
railway ticket der Fahrschein
title der Titel
tomorrow morgen
too auch
too [+ adj. or adv.] zu [+ adj. or
  adv.]
top der Gipfel
topic das Thema
get in touch with sich in Verbindung mit jemand setzen
town die Stadt
traffic der Verkehr
train der Zug
travel fahren, reisen
trouble die Schwierigkeit, die
  Mühe
try versuchen
turn off ab-drehen, aus-drehen

U

understand verstehen
use gebrauchen

usual gewöhnlich

V

valuable wertvoll
various verschieden

visit besuchen
voice die Stimme

W

wait warten
wake up auf-wachen
walk laufen, gehen
take a walk spazieren gehen
want wollen, wünschen
warning die Warnung
wash waschen
way; in the way auf die Weise
we wir
weather das Wetter
week die Woche
well gut
what was
when als

when? wann
when(ever) wenn
whisper flüstern
whoever wer
whole ganz
why warum
win gewinnen
window das Fenster
wonderful herrlich
woods der Wald
work arbeiten
worker der Arbeiter
write schreiben
write poetry dichten

Y

year das Jahr
yearly jährlich
you du, Sie, ihr

young jung
your dein, euer, Ihr

INDEX

Index

References are to the Grammar portions of lessons (unless otherwise stated); *e.g.*, 10.2,1 refers to Lesson 10, section 2, subsection 1 of the Grammar discussion. References to the Grammatical Appendix are preceded by the word "Appendix," *e.g.*, Appendix 1.1.